Cultivating Spiritual and Biblical Discernment

Steve Griffith

Cultivating Spiritual and Biblical Discernment
© Copyright 2022 by Steve Griffith

Allard Press

Except where otherwise indicated, Scripture quotations are taken from the New American Standard Bible, copyright 1960, 1962, 1963, 1968, 1971, 1972, 1973, 1975, 1977, 1995 by The Lockman Foundation. Used by permission.

> Available from Amazon.com and other online stores

Acknowledgements

The author would like to acknowledge and thank long-time Christians and Bible teachers Len Sykes, Jobe Martin, Dennis Henkel, Clare Hakeman, and Jack Tschetter for reading the drafts of *Cultivating Spiritual and Biblical Discernment*. Their insights, wisdom, feedback, and suggestions helped to shape and refine the substance of this book.

Table of Contents

Introduction xi

I.   Knowing the Enemy
    01. Discernment's Foes: the World, the Flesh, and the Devil 3
    02. Spirit Beings—and a Closer Look at the Devil 7
    03. The Devil's Principal Agents: Demons 10
    04. Doctrines of Demons 14

II.   Surveying the Enemy's Handiwork
    05. The Roots of Paganism, Humanism, and the Occult 19
    06. The World's False Belief Systems 22
    07. The World's False Religions 25
    08. Occult Beliefs and Practices 31
    09. The New Age/New Spirituality Movement 36

III.   Becoming Proficient with the Sword of the Spirit
    10. The Bible: Man's Sole Repository of Divine Truth 45
    11. The Power of the Bible 51
    12. Major Themes of the Bible 55
    13. Handling God's Word Accurately 59
    14. Studying God's Word Effectively 70
    15. Conditions Which Derail Sound Doctrine 75

IV.   Understanding the Church Age and the Church
    16. Differentiating the Bible's Three Kingdoms of God/Heaven 81
    17. Why It Matters 84
    18. Matthew's Inter-Advent "Kingdom of Heaven" Parables 86
    19. The Parable of the Wheat and Tares 90
    20. The Parable of the Sower 93

V.   Examining the Beliefs, Errors, Deceptions, and Corrections in Church History
    21. What the Scriptures Teach about Deception in the Church 103
    22. Christian Doctrine at the End of Paul's Ministry 109
    23. The Seven Churches of Revelation 2 & 3 111
    24. The Summer-Fall-Winter-Spring Pattern of Church History 116
    25. Downward Trends During the First Twelve Hundred Years 118
    26. The False Church in 1200 A.D. 121
    27. Upward Trends During the Past Eight Hundred Years 127

	28. Covenant Theology vs. Dispensational Theology	131
	29. The De Facto Second Protestant Reformation	138
	30. Present-Day Christianity	140
	31. Today's Apostolic Counterpart: Biblical Christianity	147
VI.	Sharpening Your Discernment	
	32. Salvation Approaches in the Evangelical Church Today	153
	33. Major Doctrinal Errors in Evangelicalism	168
	34. Origins Errors in Evangelicalism	178
	35. Evangelical Movements that Differ from Biblical Christianity	183
	36. Evangelical Movements that Differ—Part II	188
	37. Deceptive Practices in the Evangelical Church	197
	38. Testing the Spirits	203
VII.	Discerning the Times	
	39. Harbingers of the End-Times Deluding Influence	217
	40. Is Summer Near?	228
	41. The Church is Sound Asleep	236

A Final Word 239

Appendices 239

    A. Verses Which Attest to a Millennial Kingdom
    B. Christ's Revelation of a Pre-Tribulation Rapture
    C. The Question of Evil in the World
    D. Perpetual Reminders of Man's Rebellions Against God
    E. Assorted Occult Symbols
    F. Other Occult Practices
    G. Discernment Websites
    H. Additional Discernment Resources

Footnotes 270

About the Author 277

Introduction

*But the Spirit explicitly says that in the latter times **some will fall away from the faith, paying attention to deceitful spirits and doctrines of demons** (I Tim. 4:1).*

*Beloved, **do not believe every spirit, but test the spirits to see whether they are from God**, because many false prophets have gone out into the world (I John 4:1).*

*In pointing out these things to the brethren, you will be a good servant of Christ Jesus, **constantly nourished on the words of the faith and the sound doctrine** which you have been following (I Tim. 4:6).*

*Be diligent to present yourself approved to God as a workman who does not need to be ashamed, **accurately handling the word of truth** (II Tim. 2:15).*

*The brethren immediately sent Paul and Silas away by night to Berea, and when they arrived, they went into the synagogue of the Jews. Now these were more noble minded than those in Thessalonica, for they received the word with great eagerness, **examining the Scriptures daily to see whether these things were so** (Acts 17:10-11).*

In approximately 62 A.D., the Apostle Paul sent a letter of counsel to his young protégé, Timothy. In it he reveals the reality and result of spiritual deception: some would fall away from the faith and would in turn pay attention to deceitful spirits (I Tim. 4:1). Because of this, the apostle John (in the second passage above) points out the crucial need for ***spiritual discernment*** in the church—and the necessity for Christians to "test the spirits" in order to determine the origin of what is being taught: is it from God or a different source. In the third passage above, the apostle Paul spells out the need for Christians to be nourished by the words of sound doctrine. Paul thus (in the fourth passage) exhorts Timothy—and all who teach the Bible today—to handle the Word accurately to ensure that no one is misled. Finally, the Holy Spirit (through Dr. Luke) informs Christians to measure all teaching against the sure truth of the Scriptures (Acts 17:10-11). To do so requires ***Biblical discernment***—the ability to think Biblically and to distinguish between truth and error. Indeed, I Thessalonians 5:21 affirms the responsibility of every Christian to cultivate both types of discernment—spiritual and Biblical: *"Examine everything carefully; hold fast to that which is good."*

What, then, can we propose about these two types of discernment? **First, *spiritual discernment* involves the testing of spirits to determine the *source* behind a particular message: is it from the Holy Spirit or a deceiving spirit?** At its most basic level, spiritual discernment asks the following question: is the writer, speaker or messenger a Hindu, a Buddhist, a Shinto, a Muslim, a secular humanist, an atheist, an agnostic, a Spiritist, a Catholic, an Orthodox, a liberal Protestant, or an Evangelical (a born-again Christian)? If the writer, speaker or messenger is not a born-again Christian, then the source of the message will likely be worldly (I Cor. 2:12; Eph.

2:2), fleshly (I Cor. 3:3; II Cor. 1:12), or demonic (I John 4:3; I Tim. 4:1). Spiritual discernment must also be used when determining the source behind spiritual "experiences." Are these "experiences" from a deceiving spirit or the Holy Spirit. These potentially dangerous activities will be examined more fully in Chapter 38. **In addition,** *spiritual discernment* **assesses the** *substance* **of a message: does it come with the spirit of truth or the spirit of error** (I John 4:6)? Is the message one of deceit and craftiness or one of trustworthiness and guilelessness?

Only believers in Jesus Christ have the capacity for spiritual discernment; unbelievers do not. Paul makes this truth clear in I Corinthians 2:12-14: *"Now we have received, not the spirit of the world, but the Spirit who is from God, so that we may know the things freely given to us by God. . . . But a natural man does not accept the things of the Spirit of God, for they are foolishness to him; and he cannot understand them, because they are spiritually appraised."* Moreover, while it is true that some believers have been given the spiritual gift of discerning or distinguishing spirits (I Cor. 12:10), all Christians are exhorted to cultivate a measure of spiritual discernment. How else is the Christian to stand firm against the wiles of the devil (I Peter 5:8)?

Second, if the writer, speaker or messenger indeed *is* a born-again Christian, then *Biblical discernment* involves the skill of determining how this person's message or teaching lines up with Scripture. Does it agree with or contradict Scripture? Is the teaching an accurate handling of God's Word? *Biblical discernment* also asks the following: does the writer, speaker or messenger adhere to Biblical Christianity (discussed in Chapter 31) or to some other form of Evangelicalism (discussed in Chapters 35 and 36)? It also asks: what are the salvation views of the messenger (Chapter 32), and what is the basic eschatology of the messenger—premillennial, amillennial, or postmillennial? Answers to these questions give the Christian a sense of the writer-speaker-messenger's theological underpinnings. To be sure, Biblical discernment develops increasingly as the believer grows in his knowledge of the Word and unreservedly chooses to take Scripture at face value. It is a heart which agrees with the prophet Isaiah who wrote: *"For My hand made all these things; thus, all these things came into being,"* declares the Lord. *"But to this one I will look, to him who is humble and contrite of spirit, and **who trembles at My word** [emphasis added]" (Isa. 66:2).*

Throughout the past 1900 years well-meaning born-again theologians have at times mishandled God's Word. In addition, unbelieving false teachers have periodically challenged the teachings of the first century apostles, and false prophets have at times attempted to derail the gospel of Jesus Christ entirely. Over time, because the spirits behind certain teachings were not tested, or Biblical discernment was lacking when examining such teachings, unsound doctrine and questionable practices eventually found their way into the Church (as we will see later in the book). Consequently, it is vitally important for present-day Christians to cultivate both types of discernment—spiritual discernment and Biblical discernment.

In order to accomplish this goal, *Cultivating Spiritual and Biblical Discernment* will help the believer to (1) identify discernment's foes; (2) recognize the nature of demonic deception; (3) explore the roots of paganism, humanism, and the occult; (4) become familiar with the world's false belief systems and false religions; (5) become more proficient in handling God's Word; (6) understand the uniqueness of the Church Age in God's overall plan for human history; (7) become familiar with the beliefs, errors, deceptions, and corrections in church history; (8) understand the composition of Christendom today; (9) understand the four major salvation views in Evangelicalism today; (10) survey the major errors and deceptions in Evangelicalism today; (11) understand Biblical Christianity (versus other forms of Evangelicalism); and (12) recognize the times in which we live.

By design, the book at times focuses the reader on salient points rather than exhaustive discussion. Indeed, several chapters in *Cultivating Spiritual and Biblical Discernment* could be turned into books themselves. In addition, most chapters have a Point of Discernment "text box" at chapter's end. These boxes typically either summarize the chapter or offer a key disclosure for the reader to absorb.

All outside sources of commentary have been footnoted. Wikipedia citations (e.g., "Per Wikipedia:") have been copied verbatim. Rather than using the more precise terms of "his/her" and "he/she" throughout the book, the generic use of the word "he" has been used most of the time. Finally, the terms "Evangelical" or "Evangelical Christian" in this book are synonymous with the terms "born-again" or "born-again Christian"—i.e., a person who has put his faith in Jesus Christ's finished work on Calvary's cross for his eternal salvation. A supernatural transaction from above (John 3:1-7) has taken place, and the person is indwelled with the Holy Spirit. The term "liberal" or "liberal Christian" is a spiritual (not political) term that describes a person who calls himself a Christian, but who has not been born again; no supernatural transaction has taken place. Instead, he attempts to come to Christ, for example, on the basis of ethical living or good works or infant baptism or church membership or partaking in the sacraments of his church. Because none of these things can save him, this person is a "Christian" in name only; he is not indwelled with the Holy Spirit. The distinction between Evangelicals and Liberals will be examined more fully in Chapter 19.

Part I

Knowing the Enemy

But the Spirit explicitly says that in the latter times some will fall away from the faith, **paying attention to deceitful spirits and doctrines of demons** *(I Tim. 4:1).*

> Part I of *Cultivating Spiritual and Biblical Discernment* alerts the Christian to the forces unleashed by the devil to deceive believers and to diminish the effectiveness of their witness. Not only has the unbelieving world paid attention to seducing spirits for millennia, but unsuspecting, gullible Christians, according to Scripture, have likewise paid attention to these spirits—causing some to fall away from the faith. At a minimum, this falling away includes a departure from sound doctrine into various forms of error; at its worst, the falling away actually incorporates shades of demonic doctrine and occult practices. To guard against these seductions, the born-again Christian must learn to recognize the deceptions used by these spirits. In short, he must know his enemy.

CHAPTER 1

Discernment's Enemies: the World, the Flesh, and the Devil

The Bible teaches that all humans, including Christians, face three adversaries who endeavor to conform individuals to the thinking of the age, seduce individuals into besetting sins, and blind individuals from the truths of God's Word—particularly its good news of eternal salvation through faith in Jesus Christ. These adversaries are the world, the flesh, and the devil. All three represent a threat to the believer's ability to discern spiritual matters biblically.

The World

See to it that no one takes you captive through philosophy and empty deception, according to the tradition of men, according to the elementary principles of the world (Col. 2:8).

What is the "world" and what does the term mean? One evangelical dictionary describes it as follows: "The New Testament word '*kosmos*' may denote mankind as a whole (John 3:16); society as alienated from God and under the sway of Satan (I John 5:19); and the complex ideas and ideals which govern men who belong to the world in this ethical sense (I John 2:15-17; James 4:4)."[1]

What else do we know about the world:

- The world is under the control of the evil one, Satan, its unseen leader (I John 5:19; Rev. 12:9).
- Satan uses the allures of the world to deceive men into thinking that material goods, pleasure, and status of the world can satisfy. In contrast, book of Ecclesiastes declares that everything the world has to offer is vanity and like "striving after the wind" (Eccl. 1:14).
- Men of the world love darkness (sin) rather than light (righteousness) (John 3:19-20)
- The world is under condemnation (I Cor. 11:32)
- The world hates Jesus Christ (John 15:18-19)
- Much of the world hates believers in Jesus Christ (John 15:19)

Because the world is ruled by Satan, the Apostle John challenges the believer to turn away from its seductions: *"Do not love the world, nor the things of the world. If anyone loves the world, the love of the Father is not in him"* (I John 2:15). In the next verse John adds: *"For all that is in the world—the lust of the flesh, the lust of the eyes, and the boastful pride of life—is not from the Father, but is from the world."* The lust of the flesh says, "I must experience this." The lust of the eyes says, "I have to have this." The boastful pride of life says, "I need to achieve this." In the end, the focus of all three is on self rather than on God and others.

Likewise, Paul exhorts believers not to be conformed to the world, but to be transformed by the renewing of their minds (Rom. 12:2). How does this transformation take place? It occurs when a believer sets his heart on seeking Christ first (Matt. 6:33), grows in his knowledge of the Word of God (Eph. 4:14-15), and learns to apply it consistently to his daily life (James 1:25). Even when being severely tested, Job declares: *"I have treasured the words of His mouth more than my necessary food" (Job 23:12)*. So, too, should you and I.

The Flesh

For I know that nothing good dwells in me, that is, in my flesh (Rom. 7:18a).

The "flesh" is the core nature—the soulish and behavioral "DNA" if you will—of unsaved men, also called the natural man (I Cor. 2:4). The flesh is that part of the saved man which sometimes does battle with the indwelling Holy Spirit (Rom. 7:14-23). To be sure, believers at times operate in the flesh rather than in the Spirit.

The apostle Paul reveals how the flesh manifests itself: *"Now the deeds of the flesh are evident, which are immorality, impurity, sensuality, idolatry, sorcery, enmities, strife, jealousy, outbursts of anger, disputes, dissensions, factions, envying, drunkenness, carousing, and things like these." (Gal. 5:19-21)*. The devil and his demons work to entice the flesh. Men, for example, seem particularly susceptible to sexual sin; women often are more susceptible to gossip. In spiritual matters, men can be prone to spiritual negligence (Gen. 3:6); woman seem more susceptible to spiritual deception (Gen. 3:1-6).

How does a believer overcome the flesh? It is through the power and enabling of the indwelling Holy Spirit: *"It is the Spirit who gives life; the flesh profits nothing; the words I [Christ] give you are spirit and are life" (John 6:63)*. Paul corroborates Christ's teaching when he states in Romans 8:6: *"The mind set on the flesh is death; but the mind set on the Spirit is life and peace."* Paul then adds: *"And if Christ is in you, though the body is dead because of sin, yet the spirit is alive because of righteousness. But if the Spirit of Him who raised Jesus from the dead dwells in you, then He who raised Christ Jesus from the dead will also give life to your mortal bodies through His Spirit who indwells you" (Rom. 8:10-11)*.

What does the reality of a Spirit-empowered life look like in a growing or maturing Christian? Paul describes it as a life which produces and displays spiritual "fruit": *"And the fruit of the Spirit is love, joy, peace, patience, kindness, goodness, faithfulness, gentleness, and self-control; against such things there is no law" (Gal. 5:22-23)*. The Christian thus has the capacity to live apart from the flesh—and in newness of life—through the power of the indwelling Holy Spirit. In turn, it is this Spirit-enabled newness of life which develops and sharpens a believer's spiritual discernment.

The Devil

Be of sober spirit, be on the alert. Your adversary, the devil, prowls around like a roaring lion, seeking someone to devour (I Pet. 5:8).

The devil (Satan) is a spirit being—specifically, a fallen angel. His fall into the sin of pride (Isa. 14:12-14) occurred sometime before his temptation of Eve. The word devil means "slanderer." The word Satan means "adversary." In many parts of Scripture a reader observes that the devil is the adversary of Jesus Christ, the holy angels, Israel, and believers in Jesus Christ.

The Bible uses several phrases to describe the devil's current position as ruler over the world in which we live. Satan is called the "god of this age" (II Cor. 4:4) and the "prince of this world" (John 12:31). Indeed, the world and all its major institutions come under the influence or control of the devil (I John 5:19; Rev. 12:9).

Satan is also called "the ruler of darkness" (Eph. 6:18). According to the Bible, he is the ruler over one-third of heaven's angels (Rev. 12:4). These angels—now called demons—sided with Satan in his rebellion against God, a rebellion which apparently took place even before the creation of man (and certainly before Satan's temptation of Eve). Scripture has other names for these fallen angels: seducing spirits, deceitful spirits, and familiar spirits. Thus, when Paul warns his protégé Timothy that some will pay attention to deceitful spirits, he indicates that many of these persons will be deceived by the demons and their doctrines (I Tim. 4:1).

Satan employs several cunning strategies as the prince of this world and the ruler of darkness: He blinds the minds of the unbelieving, so they might not see the light of the gospel of the glory of Christ (II Cor. 4:4); he deceives men (and even believers) with doctrines of demons (I Tim. 4:1); he tempts all men (including believers) to sin (I Pet. 5:8); he works to divide marriages, families, friends, people groups, nations, and churches (Matt. 12:25; Mark 3:24-25; Luke 11:17). States Bible teacher Len Sykes: "Satan uses lies to wed our greatest hopes to this fallen world—which in turn leads to shattered dreams, bitterness and a self-focused, worldly mindset."[2]

Not only does Satan seek to destroy individuals, but Satan has corporate purposes as well—particularly with regard to Israel and God's plan for Messiah. In the past, Satan has attempted to cut off the human line to Jesus Christ (and thus prevent Messiah from coming to the earth). On several occasions he tempted Christ to sin (and thus ruin a sinless atonement). On other occasions he has attempted to destroy the Jews, the most recent attempt being the World War II Jewish Holocaust engineered by Adolph Hitler. With of this background in mind, let the Christian understand the following reality: *"The whole world is under the control of the evil one" (I John 5:19)*.

Nevertheless, though the Christian has a fierce and deceptive adversary in the devil, the Christian also has effective defenses to withstand him. The Christian is eternally secure in Jesus Christ (John 10:29). Nothing can separate the Christian from Christ's love (Rom. 8:38-39)—including "principalities" (demonic forces) (Eph. 6:12; Rom. 8:38). The Christian is instantly cleansed of sin and restored to fellowship with Christ when he confesses his sin to the Lord (I John 1:8-9). In addition, the Christian can (and should) avail himself of "the full armor of God" in order to stand firm against the schemes of the devil (Eph. 6:10-18). And finally, let every Christian recognize that his ultimate weapon against the devil is the indwelling Christ: *"Greater is He [Jesus] who is in you than he [Satan] who is in the world" (I John 4:4)*.

Point of Discernment: The world wants to keep you in its mold. The flesh wants to do battle with your new nature. And the devil wants you to doubt the truth, accuracy, reliability, and power of the Bible. Without complete confidence in God's Word and the renewing of your mind through the truths of the Bible, the enemy will diminish your capacity to have spiritual discernment.

CHAPTER 2

The Existence of Spirit Beings—and a Closer Look at the Devil

Jesus said to them: ". . . . You are of your father the devil, and you want to do the desires of your father. He was a murderer from the beginning, and does not stand in the truth because there is no truth in him. Whenever he speaks a lie, he speaks from his own nature, for he is a liar and the father of lies" (John 8:42-44).

The Existence of Angels

The existence and reality of angels is established throughout the Bible. The Old Testament mentions angels more than a hundred times, and the New Testament mentions angels approximately one hundred sixty-five times.[1] Who are these beings? What are they like? What is their purpose? Who is Satan? Are there both "good" and "fallen" angels? What role do fallen angels play in the world today?

- **Their Nature**

First, angels are *created* beings (Ps. 148:2-5; Ezek. 28:13). Second, they are *spirit* beings (rather than flesh and blood beings like humans) (Heb. 1:14). Third, they do not procreate (Matt. 22:30); thus, there are a fixed number of angels in the universe. Fourth, they operate both in heaven (where they have access to God) and on earth. They can also move back and forth between heaven and earth (Luke 9:26; 16:22, et.al.). Fifth, they possess intelligence (I Pet. 1:12; II Cor. 11:3), emotions (Luke 2:13), and a will (II Tim. 2:26; Jude 6). Sixth, unlike humans, they do not die (Luke 20:34-36). Seventh, they are superior in strength to men (II Pet. 2:9-11). Eighth, there are an innumerable number of angels—"myriads and myriads" (Dan. 7:10; Rev. 5:11).

- **Their Origin**

Angels apparently were created before the preparation of the earth for human habitation (Job 38:4-11), likely "in the beginning" when God created the heavens and the earth (Gen. 1:1); and angels were created by God the Son, Jesus Christ (Col. 1:13-17). When created, all angels were holy angels.

- **Their Types**

It seems that at least two types of angels exist—cherubim and seraphim. Lucifer (Satan) is a cherub (Ezek. 28:14). It is likely that Michael is a cherub. It also appears that the cherubim and seraphim have different functions. The former seem to function as the guardians of the holiness of God; the latter apparently serve as attendants at the throne of God.[2]

- **Their Hierarchy/Rank**

Angels have a hierarchy of some sort (Eph. 3:10). At least one is an archangel (Michael, Jude 1:9). There appear to be other high-ranking angels as well, perhaps "chief princes" (Dan. 10:13) (e.g., Gabriel). In addition, lesser angels in rank apparently exist.[3]

- **Their Purpose**

In times past, the angel Gabriel brought important messages to certain individuals: to Daniel (Dan. 8:16; 9:21); to Zacharias (Luke 1:19); to Mary (Luke 1:26). Today, holy angels (1) minister to believers (Heb. 1:14; I Kings 19:5-7); (2) guard and protect believers (Ps. 91:11; Dan. 6:22; Acts 12:7-10); (3) carry the soul of a deceased believer into heaven (Luke 16:22); (4) minister to God in His heavenly temple (Isa. 6:1-3); and (5) surround God's throne in worship of Him (Heb. 1:6; Rev. 4 – 5). In the future, holy angels will dispense divinely-designated judgments (Matt. 13:39; Rev. 16).

- **Their Mode**

Normally, angels are invisible. Nevertheless, the Bible records several times when angels have become visible (e.g., Mark 16:5; John 20:12).

Demons (Fallen Angels)—and Their Leader, Satan

Upon his creation, the angel Lucifer (Isa. 14:12, KJV) is said to have had the *"seal of perfection, full of wisdom and perfect in beauty"* (Ezek. 28:12). Lucifer means "light bearer." Before his fall Lucifer apparently was God's greatest bearer of both physical and spiritual light ("full of wisdom"). He walked in the presence of God (Ezek 28:14) and was blameless in all his ways (Ezek. 28:15)—until his fall into sin (Isa. 14:13-14), when "unrighteousness" was found in him (Ezek. 28:15).

- **Satan's fall**

What was Lucifer's sin? Ezekiel 28:17 states: *"Your heart was lifted up because of your beauty; you corrupted your wisdom by reason of your splendor."* Isaiah 14:13-14 adds: *"But you have said in your heart, 'I will ascend to heaven; I will raise my throne above the stars of God, . . . I will ascend above the heights of the clouds; I will make myself like the Most High."* Lucifer, full of wisdom and perfect in beauty, succumbed to the sin of pride—and wanted to be like God. As a result, God removed him from his position of privilege and cast him out of heaven (Ezek. 28:16) to the earth (Isa. 14:15).

God also changes Lucifer's name to Satan. Revelation 12:3-4 indicates that Satan at some point (possibly soon after his fall) led a rebellion in heaven, persuading one-third of the angels to follow him instead of God. In numerous places the New Testament calls these fallen angels "demons." Revelation 9:11 discloses that Satan is king over these fallen angels.

- **Satan's Character**

Whereas Lucifer was once God's principal *light bearer*, now he is God's (and the believer's) principal *adversary*. [Note: before you and I were saved, we were God's *adversaries* (Matt. 12:30); now we are to be God's *light bearers* (Matt. 5:16).]

Scripture also uses other names for Satan, including the following: the devil (slanderer); the prince of the power of the air; the god of this age; the king of death; the prince of this world; the ruler of darkness; the dragon; the deceiver; Apollyon (destroyer); Beelzebub (prince of demons); Belial (vileness; ruthlessness); the wicked one; the tempter; the accuser of the brethren; an angel of light; a liar; a murderer, the enemy; and a roaring lion.[4]

Point of discernment: Though invisible, holy angels serve God in different capacities in heaven and on earth. Satan, on the other hand, is a fallen angel and the ruler over all fallen angels. In addition, Satan is the Christian's arch enemy—an enemy who is a liar, deceiver, divider, destroyer, accuser, slanderer, tempter, and murderer.

CHAPTER 3

The Devil's Principal Agents of Deception: Demons

In the synagogue there was a man possessed by the spirit of an unclean demon, and he cried out with a loud voice, "Let us alone! What business do we have with each other, Jesus of Nazareth? Have you come to destroy us? I know who You are—the Holy One of God!" But Jesus rebuked him, saying "Be quiet and come out of him?" And when the demon had thrown him down in the midst of the people, he came out of him without doing any harm (Luke 4:33-35).

The Existence of Demons

Demons are fallen angels. Scripture describes them as being seducing spirits, deceitful spirits, or familiar spirits. To be sure, all demons seduce and deceive. "Familiar spirits," however, go a step beyond and actually communicate with persons who choose to explore the spirit world. Today's false belief systems and false religions testify to the shrewdness of demonic deception.

- **Their Structure**

As do the holy angels, the demons have a hierarchy. Ephesians 6:11 identifies the believer's enemies as Satan and his demons, and Ephesians 6:12 gives us a sense of their structure: *"For our struggle is not against flesh and blood, but against the rulers, against the powers, against the world forces of wickedness in the heavenly places."*

- **Their Purpose**

Demons work diligently today . . .

- To tempt humans to sin (John 13:2; Eph. 4:27; Eph. 6:11-13; I Tim. 3:7; II Tim. 2:26; I Pet. 5:8)
- To oppress (Acts 10:38)
- To destroy (John 10:10)
- To turn evil into good, and good into evil (Isa. 5:20)
- To deceive the whole world into rebelling against God (Rev. 12:9)
- To blind unbelievers from the truth of the Gospel (Luke 8:12; II Cor. 4:4)
- To divide families and friends (Matt. 12:25)
- To bring wrong thinking into the minds of believers (II Cor. 10:5)
- To divide the church (Luke 11:17)
- To get believers to doubt the promises and goodness of God (Gen. 3:1-6)

- To distract and derail believers (Rom. 13:12; Heb. 12:1)
- To rob believers of joy (Ps. 30:5b; Heb. 12:2b)
- To deceive believers and unbelievers with demonic doctrines (I Tim. 4:1; II Cor. 11:14-15)

- **Their Mode**

Like the holy angels, demons are invisible

- **Their Ability to Take Up Residence in a Human**

In a number of places Scripture reveals that demons can possess or take up residence in persons (Matt. 8:28-32; Matt. 9:34; Matt. 12:24; Mark 1:34; Mark 1:39; Mark 16:9; Luke 8:27; Acts 16:16-18). Indeed, it can be proposed that what psychiatrists today describe as "multiple personality disorder" is actually the possession of a person by several or many demons.

- **Their Ability to Speak Through a Human**

Scripture reveals that demons (1) can influence non-believers to speak forth words which oppose God (Mark 1:34; Luke 4:41; Acts 16:16-18) and (2) can even influence believers to speak forth words which oppose God's will, plan, or purpose (Matt. 16:22-23).

- **Their Approach**

Demons, like their leader Satan, disguise themselves as "angels of light" (II Cor. 11:14). Hence, Christians are exhorted to be sober-minded and ever-vigilant (I Pet. 5:8) in order to spot false teachers and deceptive messages (II Pet. 2:1-3).

Recognizing the "Voice" of Seducing Spirits

By being watchful, Christians can develop an ear for the "voice" (i.e., the message) of a seducing spirit. For example, the following familiar refrains in contemporary Western culture represent demonic seductions (which saturate the culture and appeal to the flesh)—all designed to deceive, tempt, divide, harm, or destroy:

- "Look out for number one"
- "If it feels good, do it"
- "Everybody's doing it"
- "Nobody will know"
- "Go for the gusto"
- "Eat, drink and be merry—for tomorrow you will die"
- "What happens in Las Vegas, stays in Las Vegas"
- "You're a woman trapped inside a man's body"

How a Seducing Spirit Might Operate in the Unbelieving World

When targeting a teenage unbeliever with sexual sin, a seducing spirit might work something like this—perhaps through the mind of an already deceived, more experienced teenager:

Older teenager: "What do you think God has to say about pre-marital sex?"

Younger teenager: "Well, I'm not so sure what God has to say, but my conscience tells me it's probably not a good idea."

Older teenager: "Nonsense, God created you to have sex, and it's the most beautiful, rewarding activity you'll ever experience."

Younger teenager: "I hadn't looked at it that way before. Yes, I know God has created me to have sex. For sure, I have a sex drive!"

Older teenager: "Look, talk to your friends about it. They'll tell you how great it is. Besides, everybody's doing it. You don't want to miss out on the fun."

Younger teenager: "Yeah, I guess if everybody's doing it, then it's probably be okay."

Soon the younger teenager succumbs to the temptation. The seducing spirit notches another victory—and for a time the young teen can't shake his guilty conscience.

How the Fruits of Demonic Deception Can Enter the Church

When targeting a Christian theologian, for example, a deceitful spirit might work something like this—perhaps through a more contrarian believer or a nominal Christian or even an unbeliever:

Deceitful spirit (through a nominal Christian to Augustine of Hippo): "Do you really think the Bible teaches that Christ will one day reign over the entire earth for a thousand years?"

Augustine: "Well, that's what the Bible teaches and what all the early church leaders have taught for more than three hundred years.

Deceitful spirit: "But maybe they've been wrong all this time; maybe Christ's already reigning over the earth—but from *heaven*. And maybe some of the 'kingdom' verses should be taken figuratively, not literally."

Augustine: "Perhaps, but I don't think so. I do know, however, that Origen has started to take some parts of the Scripture more figuratively."

Deceitful spirit: "And well he should. The 'kingdom' which the Bible talks about is being spread by the church here on earth. In fact, the growing Christian church is the kingdom of God, and Jesus is reigning over it right now from heaven. And the thousand years doesn't have to be taken literally."

Augustine: "In some ways such a view makes sense. In that same vein, I think a more metaphorical interpretation of the book of Revelation could also make more sense. After all, how could the world's armies, with spears and swords, kill one-fourth of the population? That's impossible. I've often wondered if the book of Revelation is but a metaphor of Christ overcoming evil."

Because of a deception similar to this (or simply because of his refusal to take Scripture at face value), Augustine systemized amillennialism and caused the church in the early fifth century to cast off its historic teaching of premillennialism in favor of amillennialism—a view which persists in much of the church to this day.

The Primary Method of Demonic Deception: "Indeed, has God said?"

The account of Eve's deception reveals Satan's primary method of deception. Speaking through a serpent, Satan engages an unsuspecting Eve in the following way: *Now the serpent was more crafty than any beast of the field which the LORD God had made. And he said to the woman,* **"Indeed, has God said,** *'You shall not eat from any tree of the garden'?" (Gen. 3:1).*

The account of Satan's deception of Eve continues:

> *The woman said to the serpent, "From the fruit of the trees of the garden we may eat; but from the fruit of the tree which is in the middle of the garden, God has said, 'You shall not eat from it or touch it, or you will die.'" The serpent said to the woman, "You surely will not die! For God knows that in the day you eat from it your eyes will be opened, and you will be like God, knowing good and evil."*
>
> *When the woman saw that the tree was good for food, and that it was a delight to the eyes, and that the tree was desirable to make one wise, she took from its fruit and ate; and she gave also to her husband with her, and he ate. Then the eyes of both of them were opened, and they knew that they were naked; and they sewed fig leaves together and made themselves loin coverings (Gen. 3:2-7).*

Previously, God had given Adam specific instructions: *"From any tree of the garden you may eat freely; but from the tree of the knowledge of good and evil you shall not eat, for in the day that you eat from it you will surely die" (Gen. 2:16-17).* Satan—fully knowing God's instructions to Adam—probes Eve to see how well acquainted she is with God's will for the human couple: *"Indeed, has God said that you shall not eat from any tree of the garden?" (Gen. 3:1).* When Eve tells the serpent that the couple can eat from any tree except the one in the middle of the garden—and that the punishment for eating from the forbidden tree is death—Satan quickly employs his other strategies: he challenges the veracity of God's Word (*"You surely will not die!"*); lies about God (*"For God knows that [when you eat from the forbidden tree] you will be like God"*); and offers an alluring alternative to God's Word (*"you will be like God, knowing good and evil"*). Though Satan's alluring alternative promises to be beneficial to Eve, it leads to the couple's destruction (Gen. 3:7).

Today, demons use the same tactics as their leader. First, they probe a person's familiarity with or understanding of God's Word. Second, they either challenge or impugn the reliability and meaning of God's Word. Third, they lie about God. Fourth, they offer an alluring alternative which promises to satisfy, but which always brings confusion or destruction in the end.

Point of discernment: Whether it be a challenge to morality, ethics, or apostolic doctrine, Satan and his demons will look for opportunities (I Peter 5:8) to lure a believer into deception with the serpent's Genesis 3 query, **"Indeed, has God said . . . ?"** Do not be enticed. Moreover, because of this device (Satan's deceptive challenge of God's Word), it is imperative a Christian grow in his knowledge of the Word and, indeed, let it dwell richly on his heart (Eph. 3:16; Heb. 5:12-14).

CHAPTER 4

Doctrines of Demons

Demons have doctrines. Satan thrust his first two doctrines upon mankind in the Garden of Eden when he tempted Eve with: "You will surely not die" and "You will be like God." Both of these doctrines—through the belief in reincarnation and belief in the inherent divinity of man—have tens of millions of adherents today.

Some doctrines of demons are more general in nature. For example, many of us have heard the following:

- There are many paths to God
- We are all part of the divine
- All religions are from God
- Spiritual truth can be gleaned from any of the world's religions
- Secret knowledge exists and is found outside of the Bible
- All truth is relative
- There is no such thing as evil
- There are no moral absolutes
- There is no such thing as sin
- Good deeds make you acceptable to God
- The Bible is man-made literature
- Man has evolved over millions of years to where he is today
- Man is evolving toward Godhood
- Mankind is on the cusp of entering a new dimension

All of these statements are lies. Humans are not divine; they are sinners in desperate need of reconciliation with a Holy God. Nothing created is part of the divine, nor is it to be worshiped. God is eternal and transcendent, outside of His creation. There is only *one* way to God: salvation through faith in Jesus Christ. The Bible has come to mankind from God through handpicked men; it is "God breathed."

Demons also have more specific doctrines, which in turn are designed to impugn God's Word, to devalue and diminish Jesus Christ, and to malign apostolic teaching. Virtually all **evangelicals** would agree with the following beliefs about the nature of the God:

- God is one God in three distinct persons
- The triune God is the Father, the Son, and the Holy Spirit
- God the Father is the first person of the Trinity
- God the Son is the second person of the Trinity

- God the Holy Spirit is the third person of the Trinity
- God is eternal: He has always existed and always will exist
- The Triune God created the universe and all that exists in it
- God is both transcendent and personal
- God is omnipotent, omniscient, and omnipresent
- God is perfect in His love, holiness, and justice
- Jesus Christ—God the Son—became flesh and dwelt among us
- Jesus Christ was conceived by the Holy Spirit and born of a virgin
- Christ's miracles attest to His divinity
- Jesus Christ—the sinless God-man—died for mankind's sins
- Jesus Christ was raised from the dead and today sits at the right hand of God the Father

Demonic doctrine, however, attempts to destroy these beliefs with the following deceptions:
- God is not "triune" in nature
- God is an impersonal, "watchmaker" God
- God is not a "transcendent God" outside of the universe
- The universe itself is God
- The natural world is God
- God is in everything and everyone
- God is the author of evil
- Because He allows evil, God cannot be a loving God
- God is an angry and vengeful God
- There are many gods
- Jesus was just a man, not God
- Jesus was merely a prophet, like many before him
- Jesus was not virgin born
- Jesus was not sinless
- Jesus was not the atonement for mankind's sins
- Jesus was not raised from the dead
- Jesus did not come in the flesh, but in spirit only
- Christ's miracles were not real

> **Point of discernment**: God's Word challenges every believer to become adept at discerning the doctrines of seducing spirits (John 4:1)—to develop an "eye and ear" for falsehood. Demonic doctrine always attacks, impugns, twists, or distorts the truth of God's Word. Have you taken up the challenge?

Part II

Surveying the Enemy's Handiwork

You are of your father, the devil. . . . He [the devil] was a murderer from the beginning and does not stand in the truth, because there is no truth in him. Whenever he speaks a lie, he speaks from his own nature, for he is a liar and the father of lies (John 8:44).

Part II of *Cultivating Spiritual and Biblical Discernment* (1) traces the origin of Satan's now worldwide attacks on God's truths and (2) the resultant plethora of false religions, belief systems, and practices. For the purpose of developing spiritual discernment, it is imperative for the believer to acquire a feel for Satan's deceptions by examining his counterfeit teachings. By acquiring this feel, the believer will be able to grasp more clearly the contrasts between the truths found in the Bible and the lies contained in Satan's false belief systems and false religions.

CHAPTER 5

The Roots of Paganism, Humanism, and the Occult

According to the Biblical record, the worldwide Genesis Flood and the story of Noah's ark took place approximately 4,500 years ago. When the flood subsided, God gave Noah the following instructions: *"Go out of the ark, you and your wife and your sons and your sons' wives, and bring out with you every living thing of all flesh that is with you, birds and animals and every creeping thing so that they may breed abundantly on the earth. Moreover, be fruitful and multiply on the earth" (Gen. 8:17).* For emphasis, God repeated the instructions two more times, first in Genesis 9:1 (*"Be fruitful and multiply, and fill the earth"*) and then in Genesis 9:7 (*"Be fruitful and multiply; populate the earth abundantly and multiply in it"*). Thus, God's instructions to Noah and his sons were explicit: be fruitful, multiply, and fill the earth.

Man's Post-Flood Rebellion

When the Bible picks up the story approximately a hundred years later, the fledgling family (birthing a fourth generation and now perhaps 10,000 in number, given pre-Flood lifespans and birth rates) has already rebelled against God:

> *Now the whole earth used the same language and the same words. And it came about as they journeyed east that they found a plain in the land of Shinar [present-day Iraq] and settled there.*
>
> *And they said to one another, "Come, let us make bricks and burn them thoroughly." And they used brick for stone, and they used tar for mortar. And they said, "Come, let us build for ourselves a city, and a tower whose top will reach into heaven, and let us make for ourselves a name, lest we be scattered abroad over the face of the whole earth." (Gen. 11:1-4)*

Rather than spreading out over the earth as God had instructed, the post-Flood human family has chosen to remain together in order to build a single grand city. Worse, their hearts have turned away from God toward self: *"Come, let us build for ourselves a city . . . and let us make a name for ourselves."* Their philosophy has become "man is to be exalted and glorified, not God. Man can make it on his own; man can be self-sufficient and self-determining. Man doesn't need a relationship with God; man need not follow the counsel and instruction of God." The seeds of humanism have taken root.

In addition, the post-Flood human family has not only turned away from God to self, but some in the human family have turned away from God to Satan: *"Let us build a tower whose top will reach into heaven."* Immediately after the flood, Noah built an altar on which to offer animal sacrifices (as prescribed by God) for atonement of personal sin. Noah's offspring, however, now want to build a tower (not prescribed by God) to "reach into heaven." Hence, the Bible reveals that post-Flood man is either attempting to come to God on his own terms (by works and ritual) rather than on God's terms (by faith and substitutionary atonement)—or simply casting off God altogether in favor of devil worship. To be sure, much of the human family has once again been seduced by Satan. [Note: Archaeologists working in the Babel region have unearthed towers similar to the one built by the post-Flood family[1]; all of them contain pagan symbols and evidence of what today we would call occult worship practices.[2]] Thus, instead of worshiping the Creator, a significant portion of post-Flood man is now worshiping the creation: the sun, the moon, the stars, the wind, the rain, the earth, fire, lightning, crops, flowers, trees, birds, animals, man, and—most tragic of all—the invisible world of Satan and his demons.

At Babel three forms of counterfeit worship emerged: **humanism** (man exalting man); **paganism** (man worshiping various animate or inanimate parts of the visible creation); and **occultism** (man investigating and even paying homage to the invisible creation, the world of fallen angels). All three of these post-Flood rebellions exist today.

God's Response to Man's Post-Flood Rebellion

God did not countenance man's rebellion for long:

> *And the Lord came down to see the city and the tower which the sons of men had built. And the Lord said, "Behold, they are one people, and they all have the same language. And this is what they began to do, and now nothing which they purpose to do will be impossible for them. Come, let Us go down and there confuse their language, that they may not understand one another's speech."*
>
> *So the Lord scattered them abroad from there over the face of the whole earth; and they stopped building the city. Therefore, its name was called Babel, because there the Lord confused the language of the whole earth; and from there the Lord scattered them abroad over the face of the whole earth.* (Gen. 11:5-9)

God judged mankind's rebellion at Babel in three specific ways: first, He confused man's language (He instantly brought forth the different languages seen on earth today); second, He scattered the post-Flood family into different parts of the earth (Gen. 10:31-32; Acts 17:26); and third, through the genetic makeup existing in every human, He brought forth the different "races" (the different human tribes or people groups) now seen on earth. [Note: in truth there is just *one* race: the human race (Acts 17:26).]

When God supernaturally removed the then seventy families to their different geographic locations (Gen. 11:8-9; Acts 17:26), their humanism, paganism, and occultism went with them. Though secular anthropologists and sociologists have long puzzled over the similarities of the "towers" built be ancient civilizations in various parts of the earth—e.g., the Egyptian, Mayan, and Incan pyramids—the answer for the discerning Christian rests in Satan's deception of man during the years leading up to God's judgment at Babel. This deception in turn was carried along with each of the seventy families when God dispersed them throughout the earth. Subsequently, some of these families built "towers into the sky" as shrines to their pagan deities or their "mystery" spirits (demons), little knowing that their "worship" was being orchestrated by the prince of darkness—Satan.

Finally, it should be noted that in the centuries following God's judgment of man at Babel, Satan began to bring forth the various false religions seen on earth today—e.g., Buddhism (c. 1500 B.C.), Hinduism (c. 1400 B.C.), Confucianism (c. 1200 B.C.), and Shintoism (c. 1500 B.C.). All four of these religions—and, indeed, all other religions on earth (except Judaism and Christianity) were spawned by Satan. Today, Satan has filled the earth with a plethora of counterfeit religions. As a result, much of mankind has been deceived into believing that there are many ways to reach or worship "God." Worse, some have even been deceived into believing that man himself is divine.

Point of Discernment: God brought this form of judgment on the post-Flood family so that it would be difficult for mankind ever again to unite *en masse* against Him for the purpose of exalting man and Satan. During the end-times Tribulation period, however, man will attempt once again to do just that. Indeed, the Antichrist and the False Prophet will champion the same message expressed at Babel: "Come, let us build for ourselves a world empire ('Babylon the Great'), let us make a name for ourselves (as 'global citizens'), and let us make towers that reach into 'heaven' so that we can be like gods." With the Western-world's political elites now clamoring for a one-world government to solve the world's problems, it is imperative for Christians to understand the times in which we live and the means by which Western world leaders hope to bring about their utopia. Five arrangements are subtly being touted: (1) a universal political system: "democracy" or "democratic socialism"; (2) a universal economic system: free markets and world trade; (3) a universal sociological philosophy: unity in diversity; (4) a universal religion: the New Age/New Spirituality movement (with its teaching of the inherent divinity of man); and (5) a universal language: English.

CHAPTER 6

The World's False Belief Systems

Let no man deceive himself. If any man among you thinks that he is wise in this age, he must become foolish so that he may become wise. For the wisdom of this world is foolishness before God (I Cor. 3:18-19).

And even if our gospel is veiled, it is veiled to those who are perishing, in whose case the god of this world has blinded the minds of the unbelieving so that they might not see the light of the gospel of the glory of Christ, who is the image of God (II Cor. 4:3-4).

Perhaps without even realizing it, each person on earth has put his or her faith in *something* or *someone*. Each person has a "faith system" (or belief system) of some sort. A small core (perhaps ten to fifteen percent of the earth's population) have put their faith in Jesus Christ. The overwhelming majority, however, have put their faith in something or someone else.

For those persons who have put their faith (consciously or unconsciously) in something else, numerous belief systems exist. Some persons put their faith in self: "*I* can do it; if it's not by *me*, it's not to be." Others put their faith in mankind ("humanism"): man has the capacity to solve the world's problems through science, technology, education, and global dialogue. Still others put their faith in the occult or the New Age: "I'm evolving into a higher level of attainment or enlightenment; I will be reincarnated; and I someday will be a god or goddess."

Accordingly, this chapter will survey a number of the world's false belief systems in order to glean their deceptions. Virtually all of these belief systems are either man-centered (living independently from God) or works-centered (to find favor with God). None of them recognize personal sin or incorporate the grace of God. [The next chapter will survey the world's major false religions.]

Man's False Belief Systems

Directly (through deception) or indirectly (working through the flesh), Satan has authored each of the man's false belief systems. Moreover, the Apostle Paul teaches that Satan, the god of this world, blinds the minds of the unbelieving (II Cor. 4:3-4). In addition, Jesus states that those who refuse to come to Him remain in darkness (John 12:46). What kind of belief systems do such persons embrace? Let us examine the major ones.

- Atheism – disbelief in the existence of any God or gods. *[The Bible, on the other hand, states that only a fool says there is no God (Ps. 10:4; 14:1; 53:1).]*

- Agnosticism – an intellectual doctrine or attitude which affirms the uncertainty of all claims to ultimate knowledge. Also, the belief that truth about certain metaphysical or religious claims—such as whether God or the supernatural exist—are unknown and perhaps unknowable. *[In contrast, the Bible teaches that God has made Himself evident to all men through His creation and the human conscience; therefore, all unbelievers, including agnostics, are without excuse before God (Rom. 1:19-21).]*

- Deism – the belief that God has created the universe but remains apart from it and permits his creation to be administered through natural laws.

- Polytheism – a belief in or worship of many gods.

- Humanism – an outlook or system which attaches prime importance to human rather than divine or supernatural matters. Humanist beliefs stress the potential value and goodness of human beings, emphasize common human needs, and seek solely humanistic ways of solving human problems.

- Naturalism – the belief that only natural laws and forces (as opposed to supernatural or spiritual laws and forces as well) operate in the world.

- Nihilism – the rejection of all religious and moral principles, often in the belief that life is meaningless.

- Existentialism – a belief system that emphasizes the existence of the individual person as a free and responsible agent determining his own development through acts of the will. *[In contrast, Jesus teaches that "apart from Me, you can do nothing" (John 15:5).]*

- Hedonism – a belief system that pleasure (in the sense of satisfaction of desires) is the highest good and the proper aim of human life. *[The book of Ecclesiastes states that the pursuit of pleasure (hedonism) is both ephemeral and in vain. In contrast, Jesus says that true satisfaction comes from seeking His kingdom and His righteousness (Matt. 6:33; Luke 16:11).]*

- Animism – the belief in a supernatural power that organizes and animates the material universe. Also, the view that non-human entities—such as animals, plants, and inanimate objects—possess a spiritual essence. *[The Bible, on the other hand, teaches that only man is created in the image of God—and therefore man alone has the capacity to know and to commune with God. Animals, plants, and inanimate objects have no such capacity.]*

- Pantheism – the belief that the Universe (or Nature as the totality of everything) is identical with divinity, or that everything composes an all-encompassing, immanent God. *[The Bible teaches that God transcends the universe and is eternal (has always existed and will always exist)—and that He created the universe and the natural world in it.]*

- Panentheism – a belief system which posits that the divine—whether a single God, a number of gods, or a form of "cosmic animating force"—interpenetrates every part of the universe. In other words, God is in everyone and everything. *[The Bible teaches that God the Holy Spirit indwells only one part of His creation—born-again believers in Jesus Christ.]*

Point of discernment: The Bible teaches that every human is born with a conscience—a knowledge of good and evil (Gen. 3:1-7,22; Ps. 51:5) and a knowledge of God: *"For the wrath of God is revealed from heaven against all ungodliness and unrighteousness of men who suppress the truth in unrighteousness, because that which is known about God is evident within them; for God made it evident to them. For since the creation of the world His invisible attributes, His eternal power, and His divine nature have been clearly seen, being understood through what has been made, so that they are without excuse. For even though they knew God, they did not honor Him as God or give thanks, but they became futile in their speculations, and their foolish heart was darkened (Rom. 1:18-21)."* Hence, because man is born with a conscience and a knowledge of God, all of the belief systems listed above are either deceptions from the devil or the futile speculations of men. Furthermore, based on the testimony of Romans 1:18-21, it no doubt grieves the heart of God when persons turn to and embrace such beliefs.

CHAPTER 7

The World's False Religions

For the word of the cross is foolishness to those who are perishing, but to us who are being saved it is the power of God. For since in the wisdom of God the world through its wisdom did not come to know God, God was well-pleased through the foolishness of the message preached to save those who believe (I Cor. 1:18, 21).

Not only is Satan the source of all the world's false belief systems, he is also the author of all the world's false religions. (Only Judaism and Biblical Christianity come from the one true God.) Thus, in order to comprehend their counterfeit nature, let us review and assess the major false religions:

Islam (1.5 billion adherents)

Per Wikipedia: Islam is a monotheistic religion based upon the Qur'an, a religious text considered by its adherents to be the verbatim word of God (Allah).[a] For the vast majority of adherents, Islam is also based on the teachings and normative example (called the *Sunnah*, composed of accounts called *hadith*) of Mohammad (c.570-632 A.D.)—considered by most of them to be the last prophet of God. An adherent of Islam is called a Muslim (sometimes spelled "Moslem").

Muslims believe that God is one and incomparable—and that the purpose of existence is to worship God. Muslims also believe that Islam is the complete and universal version of a primordial faith that was revealed many times before through prophets including Adam, Noah, Abraham, Moses, and Jesus.[b] ... As for the Qur'an, Muslims consider it to be both the unaltered and final revelation of God.

Religious concepts and practices include (1) the five pillars of Islam, which are basic concepts and obligatory acts of worship, and (2) the following of Islamic law, which touches virtually every aspect of life and society, providing guidance on multifarious topics from banking and welfare, to family life and the environment.[c]

[a Islam finds its authority in extra-Biblical revelation (the Qur'an), which to Islamic adherents supersedes the Bible. Notice, too, that its dictation to Mohammad as "the verbatim word of Allah" is in keeping with the demonic/occultic practice of "automatic dictation," described in the Appendix F.]

[b In Islam, Jesus is only a prophet, not God in the flesh.]

[c Islam is works-based—the keeping of Islamic law.]

Hinduism (1.1 billion adherents) ॐ

Per Wikipedia: Although Hinduism contains a broad range of philosophies, it is a family of linked religious cultures bound by shared concepts, recognizable rituals, cosmology, shared textual resources, pilgrimage to sacred sites and the questioning of authority. It includes Shaivism, Vaishnavism and Shaktism among others, each with an interwoven diversity of beliefs and practices.

Hinduism has been called the "oldest religion" in the world, and some practitioners and scholars refer to it as *Sanatana Dharma*, "the eternal law" or "the eternal way" beyond human origins.[a] Scholars regard Hinduism as a fusion or synthesis of various Indian cultures and traditions, with diverse roots and no founder. This "Hindu synthesis" started to develop between 500 B.C. and 300 A.D, after the Vedic times.[b]

Hinduism prescribes the eternal duties, such as honesty, refraining from injuring living beings, patience, forbearance, self-restraint, compassion, among others.[c] Prominent themes in Hindu beliefs include (but are not restricted to), the four *Purusathas*, the proper goals or aims of human life, namely (1) Dharma (ethics & duties), Artha (prosperity & work), Kama (emotions & sexuality) and Moksha (liberation & freedom); (2) *karma* (action, intent and consequences); (3) *samsara* (cycle of rebirth)[d]; and (4) the various Yogas (paths or practices to attain moksha).

Hindu practices include rituals such as puja (worship) and recitations, meditation, family-oriented rites of passage, annual festivals, and occasional pilgrimages.[e] Some Hindus leave their social world and material possessions, then engage in lifelong Sannyasa (ascetic practices) to achieve moksha.

Hindu texts are classified into Shruti ("heard") and Smriti ("remembered"). These texts discuss theology, philosophy, mythology, Vedic yajna, Yoga and agamic rituals, and temple building, among other topics. Major scriptures include the Vedas and Upanishads, the Bhagavad Gita, and the Agamas.[f]

[a Hinduism excludes the Bible entirely from its beliefs and instead finds its authority in various writings of humans—but "beyond human origins" (and, logically, demonically inspired).]

[b Notice that Hinduism consists of a fusion or synthesis of Indian cultures and "traditions"—i.e., the traditions of men rather than God-breathed revelation from the one true God.]

[c Hinduism has no conception that the human heart is "more deceitful than all else and is desperately sick" (Jer. 17:9) in its prescription of "eternal duties" to follow.]

[d Hinduism teaches reincarnation, not resurrection.]

[e Hinduism is works-based.]

[f Notice again that Hinduism excludes the Bible.]

Another source adds the following insights into Hinduism:

The Hindu pantheon has a plethora of gods and goddesses,[g] but what distinguishes it from the other major world religions is its henotheistic approach of looking at a faith, that otherwise would have been out-and-out polytheistic in nature. Hinduism believes in the presence of a single, ultimate, omnipresent reality (*Brahman*) that manifests itself from time to time in the form of several gods and goddesses that the Hindus essentially worship. That's why one of the basic teachings of Hinduism tells us that no matter which deity one worships, he/she is eventually worshiping the *Brahman*.[h] And what's more, there is a huge variety of deities in the Hindu pantheon—they not only worship a large number of immortal gods and goddesses in human forms, but they also worship an array of natural phenomena (more often than not, personified), plants, animals, and even mortal human beings (as Gurus and saints). So, we have, at the core of the Hindu pantheon, the Holy Trinity, formed by *Brahma* (the Creator), *Vishnu* (the Sustainer), and *Mahesha/Shiva* (the Destroyer).[i] They are followed by other major deities such as the elephant-headed God, *Ganesha*; the monkey-God, *Hanuman*; the Goddess of wealth, *Lakshmi*; the Goddess of wisdom, *Saraswati*; the Goddess of power, *Parvati*; etc.[1]

[g Hinduism has a plethora of gods and goddesses.]

[h Hinduism's "Brahman"—the Ultimate, Omnipotent Reality—is a Satanic counterfeit of the God of the Bible.]

[i Notice Hinduism's counterfeit "holy" trinity.]

Chinese folk religions (800 million adherents)

Per Wikipedia: Chinese folk religion is the religious tradition of the Han Chinese, in which government officials and common people in China share religious practices and beliefs, including veneration of forces of nature and ancestors, exorcism of harmful forces, and a belief in the rational order of nature which can be influenced by human beings and their rulers.

The gods of spirits (*shen*, can be nature deities, city deities, or tutelary deities of other human groups, national deities, cultural heroes and demigods, ancestors and progenitors, and deities of the kinship.[a] Stories regarding some of these gods are codified into the body of Chinese mythology.[b] By the eleventh century (Song period) these practices had been blended with Buddhist ideas of karma (retribution) and rebirth[c], and Taoist teachings about hierarchies of gods, to form the popular religious system which has lasted in many ways until the present day.

Various orders of ritual ministers operate in folk religion but outside of codified Taoism. Confucianism advocates the worship of gods and ancestors through proper rites, which have ethical importance. Confucian liturgy, led by Confucian ritual masters, is used on occasions in folk temples.[d] Taoism in its various currents, either comprehended or not within the Chinese folk religion, has some of its origins in Wuism. Chinese religion mirrors the social landscape, and takes on different shades for different people.

Despite their great diversity, all the expressions of Chinese folk religions have a common core [which can be summarized into] (1) *Tian*, Heaven, the source of moral meaning, the utmost god and the universe itself; (2) *qi*, the breath or substance of the universe; (3) *jingzu*, the veneration of ancestors[e]; (4) *bao ying*, moral reciprocity; (5) *ming yun*, the personal destiny or burgeoning; and (6) *yuan fen*, "fateful coincidence," good and bad chances and potential relationships. Yin and yang is the polarity that describes the order of the universe, held in balance by the interaction of principles of growth (shen) and principles of waning (gui), with act (yang) usually preferred over receptiveness (yin).[f]

[a The Chinese folk religions believe in the existence of many gods (polytheism), not the one true God of the universe.]

[b The source of religious authority in Chinese folk religion consists of stories about certain of these deities eventually codified into a body of mythology.]

[c Notice the belief in reincarnation.]

[d The Chinese folk religions are based on ritual and works, not grace and faith.]

[e Notice the veneration of ancestors rather than veneration of the one true God.]

[f In contrast, the Bible teaches that Jesus Christ created all things and holds all things together (Col. 1:15-17).]

Buddhism (500 million adherents)

Per Wikipedia: Buddhism is a nontheistic religion or philosophy that encompasses a variety of traditions, beliefs and spiritual practices largely based on teachings attributed to Gautama Buddha, commonly known as Buddha ("the awakened one"). According to Buddhist tradition, the Buddha lived and taught in the eastern part of the Indian subcontinent sometime between the 6th and 4th centuries B.C. He is recognized by Buddhists as an awakened or enlightened teacher who shared his insights to help sentient beings and their sufferings through the elimination of ignorance and craving. . . .

In Theravada Buddhism, the ultimate goal is the attainment of the sublime state of Nirvana, achieved by practicing the Noble Eightfold Path (also known as the Middle Way),[a] thus escaping what is seen as a cycle of suffering and rebirth.[b] Mahayana Buddhism instead aspires to Buddhahood via the bodhisattva path,[c] a state where one remains in this cycle to help other beings reach awakening. Tibetan Buddhism aspires to Buddhahood or rainbow body.

Buddhist schools vary on the exact nature of the path to liberation, the importance and canonicity of various teachings and scriptures,[d] and especially their respective practices. One consistent belief held by all Buddhist schools is the lack of a creator deity.[e] The foundations of Buddhist tradition and practice are the Three Jewels: the Buddha, the Dharma (the teachings), and the Sangha (the community). Taking "refuge in the triple gem" has traditionally been a declaration and commitment to the Buddhist path, and in general distinguishes a Buddhist from a non-Buddhist. Other practices may include following ethical precepts; support of the monastic community; renouncing conventional living and becoming a monastic; the development of mindfulness and practice of meditation; cultivation of higher wisdom and discernment; study of scriptures; devotional practices; ceremonies; and in the Mahayana tradition, invocation of buddhas and bodhisattvas.

[ª Works are central to Buddhism.]

[ᵇ Notice the belief in reincarnation.]

[ᶜ Again, notice that works characterize Buddhism.]

[ᵈ All Buddhist teachings come from man (mostly through Buddha) or demons. Buddhism excludes the Bible from its teachings.]

[ᵉ Such a belief is a doctrine of demons.]

Taoism (100 million adherents)

Per Wikipedia: Taoism (sometimes Daoism) is a philosophical, ethical or religious tradition of Chinese origin, or faith of Chinese exemplification, that emphasizes living in harmony with the *Tao* (also romanticized as *Dao*). The term *Tao* means "way," "path," or "principle," and can also be found in Chinese philosophies and religions other than Taoism. In Taoism, however, *Tao* denotes something that is both the source of, and the force behind, everything that exists.ª Taoism is practiced as a religion in various Asian communities. Its theology is not theist (even though some communities do worship Laozi as the attributed founder of the religious doctrine), and has more affinities with pantheistic traditions given its philosophical emphasis on the formlessness of the Tao.

[ª In contrast, the Bible teaches that Jesus Christ created all things and holds all things together (Col. 1:15-17).]

Shintoism (100 million adherents)

Per Wikipedia: Shinto is the ethnic religion of the people of Japan. It is defined as an action-centered religion, focused on ritual practices to be carried out diligently,ª to establish a connection between present-day Japan and its ancient past. Shinto practices were first recorded and codified in the written historical records of the *Kojiki* and *Nihon Shoki* in the 8th century. Still, these earliest Japanese writings do not refer to a unified "Shinto religion," but rather to a collection of native beliefs and mythology.ᵇ Shinto today is a term that applies to the religion of public shrines devoted to the worship of a multitude of gods (*kami*),ᶜ suited to various purposes such as war memorials and harvest festivals, and applies as well to various sectarian organizations. Practitioners express their diverse beliefs through a standard language and practice, adopting a similar style in dress and ritual, dating from around the time of the Nara and Heian periods.

[ª Shintoism is based on ritual and works, not grace and faith.]

[ᵇ All Shinto teaching comes from man, and Shintoism excludes the Bible from its teaching.]

[ᶜ Shintoism is polytheistic.]

Point of discernment: None of the world's false religions use the Bible as the basis of their doctrine. As well, none of the false religions include any of the following: (1) the recognition that man is a sinner; (2) the accountability of sinful man to a holy God; (3) man's separation from God because of sin; (4) God's gracious provision of reconciliation with man through the atoning work of Jesus Christ on Calvary's cross in man's place; (5) the responsibility of man to turn to God's gracious provision (repentance) and to put his faith in that provision for salvation from sin and a right relationship with God.

CHAPTER 8

Occult Beliefs and Practices

When you enter the land which the LORD your God gives you, you shall not learn to imitate the detestable things of those nations. There shall not be found among you anyone who makes his son or his daughter pass through the fire, one who uses divination, one who practices witchcraft, or one who interprets omens, or a sorcerer, or one who casts a spell, or a medium, or a spiritist, or one who calls up the dead. For whoever does these things is detestable to the LORD; and because of these detestable things the LORD your God will drive them out before you (Deut. 18:9-12).

What is the occult? Perhaps it is best summarized by the phrase, "knowledge of the hidden." Explains one source:

> In common English usage, "occult" refers to "knowledge of the paranormal," as opposed to "knowledge of the measurable," usually referred to as science. The term is sometimes taken to mean knowledge that "is meant only for certain people" or that "must be kept hidden." But for most practicing occultists it is simply the study of a deeper spiritual reality that extends beyond pure reason and the physical sciences. The terms "esoteric" and "arcane" can also be used to describe the occult, in addition to their meanings unrelated to the supernatural.[1]

This same source adds that "occultism has its basis in a religious way of thinking, the roots of which stretch back to antiquity...."[2]

Antiquity indeed! Thirty-five hundred years ago, the Living God, through His servant Moses, warns His people to avoid certain detestable practices—practices which still take place today in the occult. And *why* does God tell His people to avoid them? Because all of them are demonic in nature.

Occult Practices

What are the practices mentioned in the Deuteronomy passage above? [Definitions are taken from Webster and other dictionaries.]

1. Initiation ("anyone who makes his son or his daughter pass through the fire") – a rite of passage marking entrance or acceptance into a group or a society. *[The danger in this practice lies in the fact that the initiation takes the initiate away from truth and farther into spiritual darkness. The initiate might even be inviting demonic possession.]*

2. Divination – the practice of seeking knowledge of the future or the unknown by supernatural means; also, the attempt to gain insight into a question or situation by way of an occultic standardized process or ritual.

3. Witchcraft – the practice of, and belief in, magical skills and abilities that are able to be exercised by persons with the necessary esoteric secret knowledge. Witchcraft (though usually described as being distinct from the following) often shares common ground with related concepts such as sorcery, the paranormal, magic, superstition, necromancy, possession, shamanism, nature worship, and spiritualism.

4. Interpreting omens – an omen is a phenomenon which is believed to foretell the future, often signifying the advent of change. Practitioners believe that omens contain a divine message from their gods. These omens often include natural phenomena, such as an eclipse or freak births of animals and humans. *[All such activity is done in spiritual darkness, and none of it comprehends the one true God.]*

5. Sorcery – the use of rituals, symbols, actions, gestures and language that are believed to exploit supernatural forces; and the use of the magical powers obtained through evil spirits. *[The obvious danger in this practice is that the "supernatural forces" being "exploited" are demons; moreover, it is the demons who do the exploiting, not the practitioner.]*

6. Spell casting – a person who uses a set of words, spoken or unspoken, to invoke some magical effect. Binding a person with a spell by use of spoken word formulas is known as an incantation. *[Once again, the obvious danger of such a practice is the placing of the recipient under demonic oppression.]*

7. Mediumship – a person who mediates communication between spirits of the dead and living human beings. *[The medium is being deceived by a demon or demons who masquerade as "spirits" of the dead. The actual spirits of dead persons do not and cannot communicate with living persons.]*

8. Spiritism – the belief in the existence of nonphysical beings—or spirits—who inhabit a spirit world. In Spiritism, people often try to contact the spirits, which can include the "spirits" of people who have died. The contact is for various reasons: to learn about the future (hence, "spirit guides"), to influence the outcome of future events, and to gain knowledge.[3] *[Scripture forbids the practice of Spiritism because it opens up the individual to demonic oppression or possession.]*

9. Necromancy ("one who calls up the dead") – a form of magic involving communication with the deceased—by summoning their spirit (sometimes as an apparition)—for the purpose of foretelling future events, discovering hidden knowledge, or using the deceased as a weapon.[4] *[Any actual communication with the dead in reality is communication with a demon masquerading as a deceased person or loved-one.]*

All of these practices of thirty-five hundred years ago—each being both dangerous and demonic in nature—still take place throughout the world today in what is now called the "occult." Moreover, many present-day occult beliefs and practices have become more mainstream in the West through esoteric literature and the New Age movement.

Occult Beliefs

The following list represents a survey of current-day occult beliefs. All definitions are taken verbatim from Wikipedia.

Spiritualism – Spiritualism is a belief that spirits of the dead have both the ability and the inclination to communicate with the living. The afterlife, or "spirit world," is seen by spiritualists, not as a static place, but as one in which spirits continue to evolve. These two beliefs—that contact with spirits is possible and that spirits are more advanced than humans—leads spiritualists to a third belief: spirits are capable of providing useful knowledge about moral and ethical issues as well as about the nature of God. Thus, many spiritualists will speak of their "spirit guides"—specific spirits, often contacted, who are relied upon for spiritual guidance.

Mysticism – Mysticism is "a constellation of distinctive practices, discourses, texts, institutions, traditions, and experiences aimed at human transformation, variously defined in different traditions." The term "mysticism" has Ancient Greek origins with various historically determined meanings. Derived from the Greek word μυω, meaning "to conceal," mysticism referred to the biblical, liturgical, spiritual, and contemplative dimensions of early and medieval Christianity. [Note: mysticism, however, was not part of the first century's Apostolic Christianity.]

Gnosis – Gnosis is the common Greek noun for knowledge. In Christian, Islamic, or Jewish mysticism, in the mystery religions and in Gnosticism, the word *gnosis* generally signifies a spiritual knowledge or "religion of knowledge," in the sense of mystical enlightenment or "insight." Gnosis taught a deliverance of man from the constraints of earthly existence through insight into an essential relationship, as soul or spirit, with a supramundane (transcending the mundane) place of freedom.

Astrology – Astrology is the study of the movements and relative positions of celestial objects as a means for divining information about human affairs and terrestrial events. Contemporary Western astrology is often associated with systems of horoscopes that purport to explain aspects of a person's personality and predict significant events in their lives based on the positions of celestial objects; the majority of professional astrologers rely on such systems.

Paranormal activity – Paranormal events are phenomena described in popular culture, folklore and other non-scientific bodies of knowledge, whose existence within these contexts is described to lie beyond normal experience or scientific explanation. The most notable paranormal beliefs include those that pertain to ghosts, extraterrestrial life, unidentified flying objects, psychic abilities or extrasensory perception, and cryptids.

Parapsychology – Parapsychology is a pseudoscience concerned with the investigation of paranormal and psychic phenomena which includes telepathy, precognition, clairvoyance, psychokinesis, near-death experiences, reincarnation, apparitional experiences, and other paranormal claims.

Ascended Masters – Ascended Masters are believed to be spiritually enlightened beings who in past incarnations were ordinary humans, but who have undergone a series of spiritual transformations originally called *initiations*.

Totemism – Totemism is a belief in which either a human or a group of humans (e.g., a clan or tribe) is thought to have a spiritual connection or kinship with another physical being, such as an animal or plant, often called a "spirit-being" or "totem." The totem is thought to interact with a given kin group or an individual and to serve as their emblem or symbol.

Omens – An omen (also called *portent* or *presage*) is a phenomenon that is believed to foretell the future, often signifying the advent of change. People in the ancient times believed that omens lie with a divine message from their gods. These omens include natural phenomena such as an eclipse, the freak births of animals or humans, and the behavior of the sacrificial lamb on its way to the slaughter. Omen-believing peoples had specialists—the diviners—to interpret these omens.

Astral projection – Astral projection (or astral travel) is an interpretation of an out-of-body experience (OBE) that assumes the existence of an "astral body" separate from the physical body and capable of traveling outside it. Astral projection or travel denotes the astral body leaving the physical body to travel in an astral plane. The idea of astral travel is rooted in common worldwide religious accounts of the afterlife in which the consciousness' or soul's journey or "ascent" is described in such terms as "an... out-of-body experience, wherein the spiritual traveler leaves the physical body and travels in his/her subtle body (or dream body or astral body) into 'higher' realms."

Spirit portals – In simple terms a spirit portal is a doorway in the physical world that allows free access to and from the spirit world. The existence of a portal can rely on a vortex of energy to sustain it.

Kabbalah – Kabbalah (Hebrew: קַבָּלָה) is an esoteric method, discipline, and school of thought that originated in Judaism. A traditional Kabbalist in Judaism is called a *Mekubbal* (Hebrew: מְקוּבָּל). Kabbalah's definition varies according to the tradition and aims of those following it, from its religious origin as an integral part of Judaism to its later Christian, New Age, and Occultist syncretic adaptations. Kabbalah is a set of esoteric teachings meant to explain the relationship between an unchanging, eternal, and mysterious Ein Sof (infinity) and the mortal and finite universe (God's creation). . . . It forms the foundations of mystical religious interpretation. Kabbalah seeks to define the nature of the universe and the human being, the nature and purpose of existence, and various other ontological questions.

Kundalini energy – Kundalini (Sanskrit kuṇḍalinī, "coiled one"), in yogic theory, is a primal energy, or *shakti*, located at the base of the spine. Different spiritual traditions teach methods of "awakening" kundalini for the purpose of reaching spiritual enlightenment. Kundalini is described as lying "coiled" at the base of the spine, represented as either a goddess or sleeping serpent waiting to be awakened. In modern commentaries, Kundalini has been called an unconscious, instinctive or libidinal force, or "mother energy or intelligence of complete maturation". Kundalini awakening is said to result in deep meditation, enlightenment and bliss. This awakening involves the Kundalini physically moving up the central channel to reach within the Sahasrara Chakra at the top of the head. Many systems of yoga focus on the awakening of Kundalini through meditation, pranayama breathing, the practice of asana and chanting of mantras.

Other Occult Practices

See Appendix F.

> **Point of discernment**: All of these beliefs and practices are Satan-inspired, demonic, anti-God, anti-Christ, and anti-Christian. Demons—like their leader Satan—want to use these beliefs and practices to deceive, destroy, discourage, defeat, frighten, blind, and bind as many people as possible. Indeed, a large percentage of the world's population falls prey to some elements of this darkness. Tragically, several of these occult beliefs and practices—specifically, spirit portals, shaktipat, yoga, chanting, magic circles, and necromancy (see Appendix F)—have found their way into segments of the Evangelical church, as we will see in later chapters.

CHAPTER 9

The New Age/New Spirituality Movement

During the past half century, Satan has brought forth another powerful false belief system: the New Age/New Spirituality Movement.

The New Age (or New Spirituality) Movement

Per Wikipedia:

> The New Age is a term applied to a range of spiritual or religious beliefs and practices that developed in Western nations during the 1970s. Precise scholarly definitions of the movement differ in their emphasis, largely as a result of its highly eclectic structure. Although analytically often considered to be religious, those involved in it typically prefer the designation of "spiritual" and rarely use the term "New Age" themselves. Many scholars of the subject refer to it as the New Age movement, although others contest this term, believing that it gives a false sense of homogeneity to the phenomenon.
>
> As a form of Western esotericism, the New Age movement drew heavily upon a number of older esoteric traditions, in particular those that emerged from the occultist current that developed in the eighteenth century. Such prominent occult influences include the work of Emanuel Swedenborg and Franz Mesmer, as well as the ideas of Spiritualism, New Thought, and the Theosophical Society. A number of mid-twentieth century influences, such as the UFO cults of the 1950s, the Counterculture of the 1960s, and the Human Potential Movement, also exerted a strong influence on the early development of the New Age movement. Although the exact origins of the movement remain contested, it is agreed that it developed in the 1970s, at which time it was centered largely in the United Kingdom. It expanded and grew largely in the 1980s and 1990s, in particular within the United States.
>
> Despite its highly eclectic nature, a number of beliefs commonly found within the New Age movement have been identified. Theologically, the movement typically adopts a belief in a holistic form of divinity which imbues all of the universe, including human beings themselves. There is thus a strong emphasis on the spiritual authority of the self. This is accompanied by a common belief in a wide variety of semi-divine non-human entities, such as angels and masters, with whom humans can communicate, particularly through the form of channeling. Typically viewing human history as being divided into a series of distinct ages, a common New Age belief is that whereas once humanity lived in an age of great technological advancement and spiritual wisdom, it has entered a period of spiritual degeneracy, which will be remedied through the establishment of a coming Age of Aquarius, from which the movement gets its name. There is also a strong focus on healing, particularly using forms of alternative medicine, and

an emphasis on a "New Age science" which seeks to unite science and spirituality.[1]

According to one New Age website, the following list includes some of the common beliefs found among New Agers: [2]

- All humanity—indeed all life, everything in the universe—is spiritually interconnected, participating in the same energy. "God" is one name for this energy. *[The belief that "everything in the universe is spiritually connected," participating in the "same energy" is a lie of the devil. Moreover, the God of the Bible is not an "energy," but a Person—indeed, the Almighty God, creator of the universe and all that is in it.]*
- Spiritual beings (e.g., angels, ascended masters, elementals, ghosts, and/or space aliens) exist, and will guide us, if we open ourselves to their guidance. *[Ascended masters and ghosts are demons; "space aliens" are demons masquerading as "aliens."]*
- The human mind has deep levels and vast powers, which are capable even of overriding physical reality. "You create your own reality." *[Such a belief is utterly false. God can override physical reality, but man cannot.]*
- Nevertheless, this is subject to certain spiritual laws, such as the principle of cause and effect (karma). *[Notice that there is no mention that all genuine spiritual laws come from God and are recorded for mankind in the Bible]*
- The individual has a purpose here on earth, in the present surroundings, because there is a lesson to learn. The most important lesson is love. *[Actually, the most important lesson is to love the Lord your God with all your heart, mind, strength, and soul.]*
- Death is not the end. There is only life in different forms. What some refer to as an afterlife does not punish us but teaches us, perhaps through the mechanisms of reincarnation or near-death experiences. *[Reincarnation is a doctrine of Satan. The Bible teaches that "it is appointed for men to die once and after this comes judgement" (Heb. 9:27).]*
- Science and spirituality are ultimately harmonious. New discoveries in science (evolution, quantum mechanics), rightly understood, point to spiritual principles. *[Evolution is a doctrine of Satan. In contrast, the Bible teaches creation by a Creator God.]*
- It shares with many major world religions the idea that Intuition or "divine guidance" is a more appropriate guide than rationalism, skepticism, or the scientific method. Western science wrongly neglects such things as parapsychology, meditation, and holistic health. *[The implication here is that all religions are valid and come from a divine source. Any such teaching is Satanic doctrine and false. Furthermore, parapsychology is occultic and is forbidden in the Bible.]*
- There exists a mystical core within all religions, Eastern and Western. Dogma and religious identity are not so important. *[The notion of a "mystical core" within all religions comes from Satan. The core doctrines of Evangelical Christianity contain no mysticism or "mystical core" whatsoever. Furthermore, Christian "dogma" (teaching) is vitally important. Such core Christian*

beliefs about man's desperate need for a Savior and God's gracious provision of Jesus Christ as the reconciler are nowhere to be found in New Age beliefs.]

- The Bible is considered by some, but not all, to be a wise and holy book. Many important truths are found in the Bible, or are referred to only very obliquely. Some say that Jesus was an Essene, or that he traveled to India in his youth to study Eastern religions. Others say that Jesus was a later avatar of Buddha. *[Jesus was not an Essene, nor did he travel to India as a youth to study Eastern religions, nor was he an avatar of Buddha. Such contentions are demonic in origin. Furthermore, the Bible is <u>the</u> truth, not merely a book having "many important truths."]*

- Feminine forms of spirituality, including feminine images of the divine, such as the female Aeon Sophia in Gnosticism, are viewed as having been subordinated, masked, or obliterated by patriarchal movements that were widely practiced when sacred teachings were first committed to writing. A renaissance of the feminine is particularly appropriate at this time. *[Such thinking is a subtle effort of the devil to undermine the Bible and its patriarchal structure. It is also an effort of the devil to make a woman dissatisfied with her God-given role of coming alongside her husband to support and complete him, as well as her wonderful privilege of bringing new human life into existence.]*

- Ancient civilizations such as Atlantis may truly have existed, leaving behind certain relics and monuments (the Great Pyramid, Stonehenge) whose true nature has not been discovered by mainstream historians. *[Such a belief is nothing more than futile speculation (Rom. 1:21).]*

- There are no coincidences (see Synchronicity). Everything around you has spiritual meaning, and spiritual lessons to teach you. You are meant to be here, and are always exactly where you need to be to learn from what confronts you. *[Unfortunately, the "spiritual lessons" to be learned by New Agers have little or nothing to do with Biblical spiritual lessons.]*

- The mind has hidden powers and abilities, which have a spiritual significance. Dreams and psychic experiences are ways in which our souls express themselves. *["Psychic experiences" have their source in demons—and are forbidden in the Bible.]*

- Meditation, yoga, t'ai chi, and other Eastern practices are valuable and worthwhile. *[In reality, these Eastern practices were all bred by Satan and are of no value to the Christian.]*

- The food you eat has an effect on your mind as well as your body. It is generally preferable to eat fresh organic vegetarian food. *[The Bible contains no mandate to eat vegetarian food only. See I Tim. 4:1-3]*

- Ultimately every interpersonal relationship has the potential to be a helpful experience in terms of our own growth.

- We learn about ourselves through our relationships with other people by observing what we need to work on ourselves and what strengths we bring to the other party in order to help them in their life.

- All our relationships are destined to be repeated until they are healed, if necessary over many lifetimes. *[Reincarnation is once again assumed. It is an anti-Biblical lie from the devil.]*

- As souls seeking wholeness, our goal is eventually to learn to love everyone we come in contact with. *[According to Scripture, our goal is to love God with all our heart, mind, strength and soul. In addition, we are to love others with the same love that Christ loves us (John 13:34).]*
- Naturally occurring irrational numbers such as Phi, Pi, and e might indicate a fundamental inability of nature to account for the extant universe and therefore imposes a limit to our corporeal understanding of god, or conversely, may be important clues to the attainment of said understanding. *[The extant universe was created by God (Gen. 1:1-3). Man has a knowledge of God by what is seen in the natural world (Rom. 1:20) and a knowledge of God written on his heart (Rom. 1:18-19,21.]*

Point of discernment: All of these New Age beliefs contradict Biblical Christianity and contain both subtle and frontal demonic deception. Furthermore, because the core New Age beliefs are drawn from the Eastern religions (particularly Hinduism), the New Age/New Spirituality Movement and its beliefs (including its belief in the inherent divinity of man, the "mystical core" of all religions, and the vast power of the mind) will likely form the basis of the Antichrist's "one-world religion."

CONTRASTS BETWEEN THE NEW AGE AND CHRISTIANITY

New Age/New Spirituality Beliefs

- All that exists is God [i.e., belief in monism: *all is one*; and belief in pantheism: *all is God*]
- All that exists in the natural realm is derived from a single source of energy
- Man himself is divine
- There is no such thing as sin; therefore, man has no need of salvation
- There are many ways to God
- All religions are simply different paths to ultimate reality
- The Bible is merely one holy book
- After death, a human is reincarnated
- At the end of life, man is judged on the basis of karma
- Transformation comes from a mystical experience
- In the coming Age of Aquarius, poverty will be eliminated

Biblical Christianity

- Nothing that has been created—animate or inanimate—is God
- All that exists in the natural realm was created by a transcendent, holy God—and living creatures reproduce "after their kind"
- Man is not divine, but a creature created by God in the image of God
- Because of Adam and Eve's original sin, man is born with a sin nature. Therefore, all humans need salvation (reconciliation with a holy God)
- There is only one way to God
- All religious paths other than faith in Jesus Christ lead to destruction
- Divinely inspired, the Bible is God's only revelation to man
- "It is appointed for man to live once, then comes judgment"
- Man is judged based on what he has believed about Jesus Christ
- Transformation comes through new birth and, subsequently, the renewal of one's mind by the living and active Word of God in conjunction with the indwelling Holy Spirit
- In the coming Millennial Kingdom, poverty will be eliminated

Part III

Becoming Proficient with the Sword of the Spirit

Be diligent to present yourself approved to God as a workman who does not need to be ashamed, accurately handling the word of truth (II Tim. 2:15).

For I did not shrink from declaring to you the whole purpose of God (Acts 20:27).

And you will know the truth, and the truth will make you free (John 8:32).

But to this one I will look: To him who is humble and contrite in spirit, and who trembles at My word" (Isa. 66:2)

Part III will enable the Christian to understand the God-breathed nature of the Bible; to see clearly the transforming power of the Bible; to become familiar with the major themes of the Bible; to learn the requisite principles for interpreting the Word of God accurately; and to become skilled in studying the Bible effectively.

CHAPTER 10

The Bible: Man's Sole Repository of Divine Truth

The Bible—and nothing else—is the believer's source of Divine authority, truth, wisdom and direction. God's plan of redemption through Jesus Christ as well as God's plans and purposes for human history are fully revealed in the Bible. Moreover, four main characteristics set the Bible apart from all other books and literature: it is **inspired**; it is **inerrant**; it is **authoritative**; and it is **sufficient**.

The Bible is Inspired (i.e., God-Breathed)

The Bible comes from God. Several passages of Scripture reveal its divine origin: II Timothy 3:16, II Peter 1:21, and I Corinthians 2:12-13.

In II Timothy 3:16 the Apostle Paul states that *"all Scripture is inspired by God and is profitable for teaching, for reproof, for correction, for training in righteousness; that the man of God may be adequate, equipped for every good work."* In II Peter 1:21 the Apostle Peter in turn reveals that *"no prophecy was ever made by an act of human will, but men moved by the Holy Spirit spoke from God."*

In these passages we notice the following: First, we see that *all* Scripture is inspired, not just most of it or parts of it. Second, we see that all Scripture is *inspired by God*, not by men (or acts of the human will). Third, we see that though Scripture is inspired by God, it is written down by men *moved by the Holy Spirit spoke from God*. Says one theologian, "This verse tells us how God used the human writers to produce the Bible. The Holy Spirit moved and bore them along. . . . To be sure, human authors wrote the texts, but the Bible originated as an action of God who breathed it out."[1] Fourth, we see that all Scripture is *profitable* for the believer's emotional and spiritual well-being and growth to maturity.

In I Corinthians 2:12-13 Paul states that *"we have received, not the spirit of the world, but the Spirit who is from God, that we might know the things freely given to us by God, which things we also speak, not in words taught by human wisdom, but in those taught by the Spirit."* Here Paul teaches that the very *words* of Scripture are God-breathed as well. This passage refutes the claim of some that the Bible could contain truthful thoughts from God that were nevertheless conveyed in erroneous words by men.[2]

The Bible is Inerrant

One contemporary pastor-teacher portrays a basic human reality—and its answer—when he states: "Apart from divine revelation, we can never attain certainty as to the meaning and the purpose of our existence. The Bible presents itself as that kind of 'Thus saith the Lord' revelation.' Listen to the distinction the Bible makes: 'When you received the word of God which you heard from us, you did not receive it as the word of men, but as it is in truth, the word of God'" (I Thess. 2:13).³ This same pastor-teacher then adds to his premise with the following comment about II Tim. 3:16 (*"All Scripture is inspired by God . . ."*):

> In this passage, the word 'inspiration' is translated from the Greek word *theopneutis*, which is a compound word literally meaning 'God-breathed.' The specific word, given to Paul by the Holy Spirit, begs the monumental question: Does God breathe error? Does God communicate error? There is only one correct answer. No. . . . The entire Bible commences with the words, 'In the beginning God created the heavens and the earth' (Gen. 1:1). Consider this: if God is capable enough to supernaturally create everything, is He not also capable to supernaturally communicate? He is infinitely capable, and did so without error. A god who breathes error is not worthy of our respect and worship. A god who breathes error must be crafty, deceptive, and untrustworthy. A god who breathes and communicates error has been created in our own sinful and finite image.⁴

He then concludes by putting forth the following definition of inerrancy: "The autographs—as originally given in Hebrew, Aramaic, and Greek—are wholly without error."⁵

Christ Himself viewed Scripture as inerrant: *"Then Jesus was led up by the Spirit into the wilderness to be tempted by the devil. And after He had fasted for forty days and forty nights, He then became hungry. And the tempter came and said to Him, 'If You are the Son of God, command that these stones become bread.' But He answered and said, 'It is written, "Man shall not live on bread alone, but on every word that proceeds out of the mouth of God"'" (Matt. 4:1-4)*. Jesus, here quoting from Deuteronomy 8:3, appeals to an inspired, inerrant Old Testament (*"out of the mouth of God"*).

In Matthew 5:18, Jesus shares the following truth with the multitudes: *"For truly I say to you, until heaven and earth pass away, not the smallest letter or stroke shall pass away from the Law [the Word], until all is accomplished."* According to Christ, every word and every *letter* is inerrant. Of His own inerrant words, Jesus states: *"Heaven and earth will pass away, but My words will not pass away" (Matt. 24:35)*.

The Bible is Authoritative

The word "authority" implies that someone has position and power over someone else. The someone else is to submit to this person's position and power—indeed, his authority. The Scriptures, of course, teach that the Living God has position and power—the final authority—over His creation and His creatures. Matthew 28:19 declares the following about Jesus Christ, the living Word (John 1:1-3): *"All **authority** has been given to Me in heaven and on earth [emphasis added]."* In light of God's authority over His creation, let us also look at the authority of the God's revealed Word, the Bible.

- **The Bible has Inherent Authority**

Because the Bible is God-breathed, it carries *inherent* authority. Says Theologian Lewis Sperry Chafer: "Recognizing the inspiration of the Bible as 'God-breathed' automatically assigns to the Scriptures the supreme authority that belongs to God alone. This authority proceeds from God immediately and without reduction or complications. The entire Bible is the Word of God and therefore has divine authority behind all that is written."[6]

- **The Bible's Authority is Attested to by Christ**

Says Chafer: "Though the Bible is fully authoritative because it is God-breathed, the evidence of its approval by Jesus Christ adds confirmation and recognition to the authority of the Bible. The four Gospels contain about 35 direct references and quotations by the Son of God to the Old Testament Scriptures. In this way Christ gave His own confirmation that the Old Testament is the Word of God."[7]

- **The Bible's Authority is Attested to by the Holy Spirit**

In John's Gospel, Jesus introduces to the disciples the impending role of the indwelling Holy Spirit: *"But when He, the Spirit of truth, comes, He will guide you into all truth; for He will not speak on His own initiative, whatever He hears, He will speak; and He will disclose to you what is to come" (John 16:13)*. What will the Holy Spirit use to guide the disciples (and us) into all truth? Whatever He hears from the Father—i.e., the Word of God. Thus, the indwelling Holy Spirit will illumine the hearts of believers as they read the Bible, the very Word of God.

Adds Chafer: "The Bible, being the Word of God, is suitable for perfect expression in every situation in which the Spirit functions. The Scriptures are 'the sword of the Spirit, which is the Word of God.' In a sense the phrase, 'the Spirit clearly says' (I Tim. 4:1), might with entire justification be applied to all the Word of God."[8]

The Bible is Sufficient

Finally, not only is the Bible inspired, inerrant, and authoritative, it is also *sufficient*. Christians need not turn to the wisdom of men for the solutions to the periodic relational and life difficulties which all humans face in a fallen world. These solutions can readily be found in the Word of God. To be sure, upon reading II Timothy 3:16, we see that *"all Scripture is . . . profitable for teaching, for reproof, for correction, for training in righteousness so that the man of God may be adequate, equipped for every good work."* Relational difficulties require wisdom, reproof, and correction. Who knows better the wisdom required in relational and life difficulties than the One who created us?

The all-sufficiency of Scripture is further delineated in Psalm 19:7-9: *"The law of the Lord is perfect, restoring the soul; the testimony of the Lord is sure, making wise the simple. The precepts of the Lord are right, rejoicing the heart; the commandment of the Lord is pure, enlightening the eyes. The fear of the Lord is clean, enduring forever; the judgments of the Lord are true; they are righteous altogether.* From this passage we learn that:

- The law of the Lord is perfect
- The testimony of the Lord is sure
- The precepts of the Lord are right
- The commandment of the Lord is pure
- The fear of the Lord is clean, and
- The judgments of the Lord are true

Notice the adjectives used to describe the Lord and His Word: perfect, sure, right, pure, clean, and true. All of these point to the fact that Scripture is all-sufficient.

One pastor-teacher presents the sufficiency of Scripture as follows:

> It is significant that one of the biblical names of Christ is Wonderful Counselor (Isa. 9:6). He is the highest and ultimate One to whom we may turn for counsel, and His Word is the well from which we may draw divine wisdom. What could be more wonderful than that? In fact, one of the most glorious aspects of Christ's perfect sufficiency is the wonderful counsel and great wisdom He supplies in our times of despair, confusion, fear, anxiety, and sorrow. He is the quintessential Counselor.[9]

This same theologian concludes with the following:

> Contrary to what many are teaching today, there is no need for additional revelations, visions, words of prophecy, or insights from modern psychology. In contrast to the theories of men, God's Word is true and absolutely comprehensive. Rather than seeking something more than God's glorious revelation, Christians need only to study and obey what they already have. Scripture is sufficient.[10]

Point of discernment: Interpretive error, reliance on human wisdom, or even an inadvertent succumbing to a demonic whisper can occur when a Christian ignores or resists any of the following characteristics of the Bible: its **inspiration**, its **inerrancy**, its **authority**, and its **sufficiency**.

Two other characteristics of the Bible are also noteworthy:

The Bible is Infallible

While the word "inerrant" posits that the Bible is free from error, the word "infallible" means that the Bible is incapable of error. "If something is infallible, it is never wrong and thus absolutely trustworthy[11].

States one commentator: "If God is infallible, then so will be His Word. The doctrine of Scripture's infallibility is based on the understanding of God's perfection and character. God's Word is "perfect, refreshing the soul" (Psalms 19:7), because God Himself is perfect."[12] He then adds: "It should be noted, however, that the doctrine of infallibility concerns only the original documents. Mistranslations, printing errors, and typos are obvious human mistakes and are easily spotted, most of the time. However, what the biblical writers originally wrote was completely free from error or omission, as the Spirit superintended their work. God is truthful and perfectly reliable (John 14:6; 17:3), and so is His Word (John 17:17)."[13]

The Bible is Perspicuous

"Perspicuity" means that the central message of the Bible is clear and understandable to the Christian reader/hearer. Deuteronomy 6:6-7 exhorts parents to teach the Scriptures to their children, thus indicating Scripture can be understood by children. The Apostle Paul encouraged Timothy to continue in the things he had learned from the Scriptures when the latter was a child (II Tim. 3:14-15). Psalms 119:130 offers the following: *The unfolding of Your words gives light; it gives understanding to the simple."* Accordingly, it is not necessary to have high intelligence to understand the Scriptures. The Bible's meaning is clear to all.[14]

Note: In future chapters the author will focus on the first four of these characteristics: the inspiration, inerrancy, authority, and sufficiency of the Bible. All Christians are encouraged to understand and embrace these bedrocks of Scripture.

"The truth, the whole truth, and nothing but the truth"

Not only is the Bible inspired, inerrant, authoritative, and sufficient, it is also **truth**. Unfortunately, unregenerate humans routinely swim in lies and half-truths, not realizing that the world, the flesh, and the devil have twisted their thinking and left them in darkness (John 3:19; 12:46). When speaking with the very author of truth, Pilate asks Jesus, "What is truth?" (John 18:38). This, of course, is a subconscious query of much of mankind today.

Scripture has much to say about truth. Jesus explains: *"I am the way, the **truth**, and the life"* (John 14:6). The psalmist states: *"The sum of Your word is **truth**, and every one of Your righteous ordinances is everlasting"* (Ps. 119:160). In John's Gospel, Jesus informs us that truth originates in and through God the Father: *"Your word is **truth**"* (John 17:17b). Jesus also informs us that the Helper—the Holy Spirit—is truth: *"I will ask the Father, and He will give you another Helper that He may be with you forever, that is the Spirit of **truth**, whom the world cannot receive, because it does not see Him or know Him, . . ."* (John 14:16-17). In short, God the Father, God the Son, and God the Spirit are truth and speak truth.

John's Gospel gives the believer further information about truth when Jesus states: *"But when He, the Spirit of **truth**, comes He will guide you into all **truth**"* (John 16:13). Furthermore, Jesus asks the Father to purify the believer in truth: *"Sanctify them in **truth**"* (John 17:17a). How does this good news manifest itself? Jesus explains: *"But an hour is coming, and is now, when the true worshipers will worship the Father in spirit and **truth**, for such people the Father seeks to be His worshipers"* (John 4:23).

To be sure, Jesus sets up a contrast between truth and error: *"We are from God; he who knows God listens to us; he who is not from God does not listen to us. By this we know the spirit of truth and the spirit of error"* (I John 4:6). The Bible presents itself as 100% truth (John's Gospel and letters [many verses])—and indeed offers 100% truth. God nevertheless graciously allows each believer to accept or reject this conclusion as he reads and digests the Word. For example, some Christians cannot accept the Bible's declaration that God prepared the earth for human habitation in six twenty-four-hour days [a topic to be discussed in Chapter 34]. Other believers cannot accept the Bible's assorted prophecies that Messiah will reign over the earth for a thousand years, and so on.

Satan's whisper to Eve—and to each person today—is always the same: "Indeed, has God said . . . ?" Do you, the reader, believe that the Bible is "the truth, the whole truth, and nothing but the truth?" For any Christian who desires to cultivate a high level of spiritual and biblical discernment, the answer to this question must be "yes."

CHAPTER 11

The Power of the Bible

The Bible is unlike any other book in the world:

It is living and active

The writer of Hebrews informs us that *"the Word of God is living and active and sharper than any two-edged sword, and piercing as far as the division of the soul and spirit, . . ." (Heb. 4:12a)*. Says one commentator: "The term *active* in Hebrews 4:12 means 'effective, powerful, producing or capable of producing an intended result.' The Word of God is vibrant, dynamic, energizing, and productive. It is not static or idle in the lives of genuine believers."[1] In addition, because the Bible is a God-breathed revelation, it *"is able to judge the thoughts and intentions of the heart" (Heb. 4:12b)*. A person's mind, heart, and motives are laid bare before the Word of God.

It convicts us of sin, righteousness, and judgment

Jesus Himself explains that the living and active Word of God, when heard or read, convicts the human heart of its sin condition: *"And He (the indwelling Holy Spirit), when He comes, will convict the world concerning sin, righteousness, and judgment" (John 16:8)*. The apostle Paul tells the Galatian Christians: *"The Scripture has shut up all men under sin, so that the promise by faith in Jesus Christ might be given to those who believe" (Gal. 3:22)*.

It reveals our lost condition—our separation from God

Paul leaves no doubt about the condition of unbelievers: *"And you were dead in your trespasses and sins, in which you formerly walked according to the course of this world, . . ." (Eph. 2:1-2a)*. A few sentences later he adds: *"Remember that you were at that time separate from Christ, excluded from the commonwealth of Israel, and strangers to the covenants and promises, having no hope and without God in this world" (Eph. 2:12)*. Notice the words "dead in your trespasses and sins," separate from Christ," and "having no hope and without God."

It points us to the Savior

Paul nevertheless tells us that the Old Testament law (which is impossible for any human to keep), became a *"tutor to lead us to Christ, that we may be justified by faith [in Christ]"* (Gal. 3:24). The Word of God shows us our need and drives the receptive heart to the Cross.

It is the power of God unto salvation

In his letter to the Romans, Paul reveals that the Word of God not only convicts of sin and points men to the Savior, but that its good news message of Jesus Christ is the power by which men are saved: *"For I am not ashamed of the gospel, for it is the power of God for salvation to everyone who believes, to the Jew first and also to the Gentile. For in it the righteousness of God is revealed"* (Rom. 1:16-17). Indeed, only the message of the gospel has the power to save. No other book—and no other message—can save. Paul adds that *"faith comes from hearing, and hearing by the word of Christ" (Rom. 10:17).* He also explains that *"the word of the Cross is foolishness to those who are perishing, but to us who are being saved it is the power of God" (I Cor. 1:18).*

We can see the inherent power of the gospel to save souls in Peter's testimony to the Jews on the day of Pentecost ten days after Christ's ascension: *"'Therefore, let all the house of Israel know for certain that God has made Him both Lord and Christ—this Jesus whom you crucified.' Now when they heard this, they were pierced to the heart, and said to Peter and the rest of the apostles, 'Brethren, what shall we do?' And Peter said to them, 'Repent, and let each one of you be baptized in the name of Jesus Christ for the forgiveness of your sins'"* (Acts 2:36-38). What was the response? *"So then, those who received his word were baptized; and there were added that day about three thousand souls" (Acts 3:41).*

It is the power of God unto sanctification

Toward the end of his letter to the Romans, Paul exhorts Christians not to be conformed to this world, but to be *transformed* by the renewing of his mind (Rom. 12:2). How is a person's mind renewed—and hence his life transformed? It occurs when the *living and active* Word of God, which is sharper than any two-edged sword (Heb. 4:12), dwells richly on a person's heart (Col. 3:16). The Psalmist informs us that the person whose delight is the Word of God—whose delight in fact is to meditate on it continually—will be like a tree firmly planted by streams of water, one which yields fruit in its season and whose leaf does not wither (Ps. 1:2-3). Like the tree firmly planted, this person will be stable and productive.

When a person treasures the Word of God, he increasingly eschews sin (Ps. 119:11) and experiences transformation. When a person treasures the Word of God (Job 23:12), he increasingly encounters Christ—and draws closer to Him (James 4:8). When a person draws closer to Christ, he soon realizes that "it is no longer I who live but Christ who lives in me" (Gal. 2:20). When he thus learns to live by faith in the Son of God (who lives in him), Christ manifests His life through him (Gal. 2:20), continues to do a good work in him (Phil. 2:13), and continues to transform him (Rom. 8:29).

It is a lamp unto our feet

When the Bible—the living and active Word—is read and grasped by the believer, it progressively delivers the believer out of spiritual darkness into light and life. Listen to Peter's heart response in the following interaction with Jesus: *"As a result of this, many of His disciples withdrew, and were not walking with Him anymore. Jesus therefore said to the twelve, 'You do not want to go away also, do you?' And Simon Peter answered Him, 'Lord, where shall we go? You have the words of eternal life'" (John 6:66-68).* Peter acknowledges that Jesus, the Living Word, has the words which lead to life. Jesus later tells Peter and the disciples: *"I am the light of the world; he who follows Me shall not walk in the darkness, but shall have the light of life" (John 8:12)*.

One of the Psalmists echoes Peter's sentiments: *"How sweet are Thy words to my taste! Yes, sweeter than honey to my mouth! From Thy precepts I get understanding, . . . Thy word is a lamp to my feet, and a light to my path" (Ps. 119:103-105)*. The Psalmist acknowledges that God's Word gives him understanding and that God's Word lights the path before him so that he doesn't stumble through life in spiritual darkness and foolish living. King David rejoices that the Living God *"leads me in the paths of righteousness" (Ps. 23:3)*.

Like the Psalmist above, Peter also proclaims this theme of the Word's power to deliver believers out of spiritual darkness into the light of God's truth: *"But you are a chosen race, a royal priesthood, a holy nation, a people for God's own possession, that you may proclaim the excellencies of Him who has called you out of darkness into His marvelous light" (I Pet. 2:9)*.

It assures us of a future and a hope

The Psalmist says, *"How blessed is he whose help is the God of Jacob, whose hope is the Lord his God" (Ps. 146:5)*. The prophet Jeremiah encourages God's people with the following promise: *"'For I know the plans that I have for you,' declares the Lord, 'plans of welfare and not for calamity, to give you a future and a hope'" (Jer. 29:11)*.

The Apostle Paul elaborates further on the blessedness of the Christian's future and hope: *"Therefore, we have been buried with Him through baptism into death [i.e., the crucifixion of the power of our old nature], so that as Christ was raised from the dead through the glory of the Father, we too might walk in newness of life" (Rom. 6:4)*. Because Christ lives in the born-again believer (Col. 1:27), the believer now has the capacity to walk in newness of life as he abides and grows in Christ. The believer no longer needs to be a slave to his old nature and to live life aimlessly. What better future and hope could a Christian have than the Lord of the universe living inside him, caring for him, and directing his steps (Prov. 16:9)?

Elsewhere, Paul discusses the believer's ultimate hope—indeed calling the future return of Christ for his own the "blessed hope": *"looking for the blessed hope and the appearing of the glory our great God and Savior, Jesus Christ" (Titus 2:13)*. Paul also points out the indescribable magnificence of the believer's future in heaven: *"But just as it is written, 'Things which eye has not seen and ear has not heard, and which have not entered the heart of man, all that God has prepared for those who love Him'" (I Cor. 2:9)*.

It predicts the future with 100% accuracy

All of the Old Testament prophecies regarding Christ's first coming were fulfilled literally and perfectly with 100% accuracy: He would come from the line of Abraham; he would come from the tribe of Judah; he would be from the house of David; he would be born of a virgin; he would be called Emmanuel; he would be announced by a forerunner; he would be born in Bethlehem; he would be worshiped by wise men and presented with gifts; he would be in Egypt for a season; his birthplace would suffer a massacre of infants; he would be called a Nazarene; he would be zealous for the Father;

he would be filled with God's Spirit; he would heal many; he would speak in parables; he would be rejected by his own people; he would make a triumphal entry into Jerusalem; he would be praised by little children; his miracles would not be believed; his friend would betray him for thirty pieces of silver; he would be a man of sorrows; he would be forsaken by his disciples; he would be scourged and spat upon; he would be crucified between two thieves; he would suffer the piercing of his hands and feet; his garments would be parted and gambled for; he would be surrounded and ridiculed by enemies; he would commend his spirit to the Father; his bones would not be broken; he would be buried with the rich; he would be raised from the dead; he would ascend; he would be seated at God's right hand.[2]

How could all of these prophecies be fulfilled with such precision—indeed, with *perfect* accuracy? Let us look to the words of Isaiah: *"Remember the former things long past, for I am God, and there is no other; I am God, and there is no one like Me, declaring the end from the beginning and from ancient times things which have not been done, saying, 'My purpose will be established, and I will accomplish My good pleasure'" (Isa. 46:9-10).* Only the Living God—who knows the beginning from the end of all things and who provides these prophecies to man through a God-breathed piece of literature, the Bible—could enable all of these prophecies (some written hundreds of year before the fact) to be fulfilled with 100% accuracy. Thus, because *all* Bible prophecy relating to the past has been fulfilled literally and perfectly, today's Christian can be certain that *all* Bible prophecy relating to the future will likewise be fulfilled literally and perfectly.

> **Point of discernment**: Any Christian who consciously or unconsciously minimizes the supernatural power of the Word of God has believed a lie of the enemy. The Bible is not only God's gift to man, but it unequivocally contains the power of God (1) to convict lives of sin, righteousness, and judgment and (2) to transform the lives of the repentant, teachable, tender-hearted, and trusting.

CHAPTER 12

Major Themes of the Bible

The Bible contains an assortment of themes, some woven throughout. Awareness of these themes can help a Christian tie together his overall understanding of Scripture.

For example, the Old Testament animal sacrifices for sin (mandated by God in Israel's tabernacle and temple worship) all point to and picture the eventual atoning sacrifice of Jesus Christ on Calvary's Cross for mankind's sins. An innocent animal was sacrificed as an acceptable substitute for the presenter's sins, just as Christ was the innocent and acceptable substitute (in the Father's eyes) for our sin nature and sins. Christ's atoning sacrifice thus allows the one who puts his faith in Christ to be reconciled to a Holy God. The New Testament continues this Old Testament theme when John the Baptist introduces Christ's earthly ministry with the exclamation: *"Behold, the Lamb of God who takes away the sin of the world!" (John 1:29)*. The theme of substitutionary atonement is consummated when Christ is crucified and confirmed when Christ is resurrected.

The theme of justification by faith is introduced in Genesis and then carried forth throughout the Old and New Testaments. It is said of Abram (Abraham) in Genesis 15:4-6: *"Then behold, the word of the Lord came to him [Abram], saying, 'This man will not be your heir; but one who shall come forth from your own body shall be your heir.'" And He took him outside and said, 'Now look toward the heavens, and count the stars, if you are able to count them.' And He said to him, 'So shall your descendants be.' Then he [Abram] believed in the Lord; and He reckoned it to him as righteousness."* In the New Testament the Apostle John continues the theme of justification by faith when he states: *"But as many as received Him, to them He gave the right to become the children of God, even those who believe in His name" (John 1:12)*. Jesus tells Nicodemus, the most ethical man in Israel, that keeping the law ("works righteousness") does not result in salvation. Instead, a person must *believe* in the work of God's provision—the Son of Man (Jesus): *"And as Moses lifted up the serpent in the wilderness, even so must the Son of Man be lifted up, that whosoever believes may in Him have eternal life. For God so loved the world that He gave His only begotten Son, that whosoever believes in Him should not perish, but have eternal life" (John 3:15-16)*. Paul likewise continues the O.T. theme of justification by faith (not works) in Romans 4:3 when he writes: *"For what does the Scripture say? 'And Abraham believed God, and it was reckoned to Him as righteousness.'"*

Almost unconsciously, a Christian will sharpen his overall level of biblical discernment when he familiarizes himself with the major Old and New Testament themes presented in the following pages.

MAJOR DOCTRINAL THEMES (O.T.)

- The Nature and Character of God
- God's Creation of the Heavens and the Earth
- The Fall of the Angel Lucifer (Satan)
- God's Preparation of the Earth for Human Habitation
- God's Creation Adam & Eve
- The Fall of Adam & Eve
- The Inherited Sin Nature of Man
- Man's Need for Salvation-Redemption
- Substitutionary Atonement
- Justification by Faith
- The Call of Abraham—and the Abrahamic Covenant
- God's Covenants with Israel
- The Nation and History of Israel—God's Chosen People
- The Revelation of God to His People Israel
- The Mosaic Law (and the Old Covenant)
- The Tabernacle/Temple, Sacrifices, and Priests
- The Paganism and Idolatry of Israel's Neighbors
- Israel's Cycles of Apostasy
- The Prophesied Advent of Messiah
- The Prophesied Future Kingdom and Reign of Messiah Over the Entire Earth
- Daniel's "Seventy Weeks" Prophecy (Dan. 9:24-27): the Broad Brush Israel's Post-Exilic History

MAJOR DOCTRINAL THEMES (N.T.)

- The Incarnation and Deity of Christ: God Becomes Flesh
- The Words and Works of Jesus Christ
- The Character of Jesus Christ—Including His Sinless Life
- The Crucifixion and Resurrection of Jesus Christ
- God's Redemptive Plan In and Through Jesus Christ
- God's Grace (and the New Covenant)
- Justification by Faith
- The Necessity of the New Birth
- The Enabling of Believers by the Indwelling Holy Spirit
- The Christian Life—and the Way of the Cross
- The True Church (the "Bride") Sown by Christ: A Living Organism of Jewish and Gentile Born-Again Believers
- The Priesthood of All Believers
- The World, the Flesh, and the Devil—and Spiritual Warfare
- The Temporary Setting Aside of Israel (Romans 9 – 11)
- The Rapture of the Church (the "Bride")
- The End-Times Tribulation Period
- The Second Coming of Christ to the Earth
- The Millennial Kingdom on Earth (Reigned Over by Christ from Jerusalem)—and the Exaltation of Israel
- The Ultimate Demise of Satan
- The Eternal Kingdom in Heaven

The Nation of Israel
Major Historical Periods in God's Dealings with Israel

Selected

 Covenanted With (the Abrahamic Covenant)

  Grown

   Enslaved

   Delivered

    Set Apart

    Tested

     Planted

      Seduced -- Restored / Seduced -- Restored

      Blessed (Saul – David – Solomon)

       Divided

        Captured & Scattered

        Chastened (for 483 years)

Set Aside Temporarily   *[during the Church Age]*

         Chastened (for 7 years)   [during the Tribulation period]

         Rescued & Saved   [at the Second Coming of Christ]

          Exalted (for 1000 years) [during the Millennial Kingdom]

CHAPTER 13

Handling God's Word Accurately

Be diligent to present yourself approved to God as a workman who does not need to be ashamed, accurately handling the word of truth (II Tim. 2:15)

When reading the Bible a Christian inevitably must ask the question: How should I interpret what I'm reading?

- Should I take the text at face value? i.e., should I interpret its words and figures of speech in their plain, normal sense? Furthermore, should I read all of Scripture in its plain, normal sense? If not, which parts?
- Should I treat some of the text allegorically? Should I spiritualize certain parts rather than taking them at face value? If so, which parts?
- Should I treat some of the text as legend or myth? If so, which parts?
- Should I assume that the supernatural events of the Bible never occurred—and that the Bible is primarily a book of moral precepts with little historical accuracy or relevance?

As evidenced by the questions above, the set of guidelines or principles one uses to interpret Scripture will have a significant bearing on his understanding of the Bible. In this chapter we'll examine the principles one should use when interpreting the Bible. Theologians use the word "hermeneutics" to describe any such set of guidelines or principles.

Most born-again theologians over the past several centuries have held to one basic hermeneutic: the Grammatical–Historical–Literal System. A well-known evangelical scholar summarizes this system as follows:

> One of the Reformation's chief accomplishments is the principle of the literal interpretation of Scripture. This concept has suffered from serious misunderstanding, having often been equated with naïve or wooden literalism. The actual principle, called *sensus literalis* states that the Bible must be interpreted according to the manner in which it is written. . . . The principle of literal interpretation was intended to put an end to a method that had become popular in the Middle Ages, the *quadriga*. This was a method of interpretation by which four distinct meanings were sought for each biblical text: the literal, moral, allegorical, and analogical. This led to excessive allegorization and obfuscation of the text. By contrast, sensus literalis was designed to seek the plain sense of Scripture and to focus on one meaning. . . . The principle of *sensus literalis* is closely related to the *gramatico-historical* method of interpretation. This method focuses on the historical setting in which Scripture was written and pays

> close attention to the grammatical structure of the biblical text. . . . In the Bible verbs are verbs and nouns are nouns. The normal structure of literature applies.[1]

In short, the Grammatical-Historical-Literal (G-H-L) system understands and interprets the Bible's words and figures of speech in their usual, ordinary, or normal sense.

Nevertheless, though most born-again theologians adhere to the G-H-L method in theory, some of them do not adhere to it in practice. Instead, the latter (including the scholar just cited) choose to interpret some passages of Scripture allegorically. These Christians thus apply a *dual* hermeneutic when interpreting Scripture: parts of the Bible are interpreted literally, other parts allegorically. For example, virtually all born-again theologians, pastors, and teachers contend that the Old Testament prophecies relating to Christ's first coming were fulfilled literally and perfectly. However, a significant percentage of these same born-again theologians, pastors, and teachers deny that the prophecies relating to Christ's second coming will be fulfilled literally and perfectly. Instead, they allegorize or spiritualize certain end-times prophecies rather than interpreting them in their usual, ordinary, normal sense.

The problem with this latter approach—the dual hermeneutic—is obvious: if one attempts to interpret parts of the Bible allegorically or spiritually, then the interpretation becomes subjective: it depends on the ideas or bias of the interpreter rather than the Author of Scripture. Hence, the Christian is best served when he interprets the Bible's words and figures of speech in their ordinary or normal sense *at all times*.

The Current Major Systems of Hermeneutics (among Evangelicals):

- Among some Evangelical Bible Colleges/Seminaries:

    1. **The Grammatical - Historical - Literal System (consistently applied)**

    This system understands words and figures of speech in their usual, ordinary, or normal sense *at all times*, including the creation account and Bible prophecy (e.g., Revelation 6:7-8: the one-fourth killed is a literal death-toll)

        a. G-H-L system consistently applied

        b. **a single hermeneutic** (one system employed)

            (the G-H-L method at all times, i.e., the usual, ordinary, normal meaning of words and figures at all times)

- Among other Evangelical Bible Colleges/Seminaries:

    2. **The Grammatical - Historical - Literal System (inconsistently applied)**

    This system understands words and figures of speech in their usual or normal sense—*with the exception (typically) of the creation account and Bible prophecy*. The latter are either *spiritualized* or treated *allegorically*—to varying degrees—rather than taken at face value (e.g., Revelation 6:7-8: the one-fourth killed is simply a metaphor of widespread judgment, not a literal death-toll)

        a. G-H-L system inconsistently consistently applied

        b. **a dual hermeneutic** (two systems employed)

            (the G–H–L method most of the time, i.e., the usual, ordinary, normal meaning of words and figures most of the time—and the allegorical or spiritualizing method at other times [e.g., 20% of the time]

Notable Evangelical Theologians/Pastors/Leaders
who apply the G-H-L system consistently

View of Scripture:
  Inerrant

Hermeneutic:
  Plain, Normal, Literal
  Consistently Applied (a single hermeneutic)
  "Consistent Literalism"

Anderson, Sir Robert
Benware, Paul
Blackstone, William E.
Chafer, Lewis Sperry
Darby, J. N.
Falwell, Jerry
Fruchtenbaum, Arnold
Hibbs, Jack
Hitchcock, Mark
Hunt, Dave
Ice, Thomas
Ironside, H.A.
Jeffress, Robert
Jeffrey, Grant
Jeremiah, David
LaHaye, Tim
Lindsey, Hal
Lotz, Anne Graham
MacArthur, John
Markell, Jan
Mather, Increase & Cotton
Pentecost, Dwight
Radmacher, Earl
Reagan, David
Ryrie, Charles
Scofield, C.I.
Smith, Chuck
Stanley, Charles
Stedman, Ray
Torrey, R.A.
Walvoord, John
Watts, Isaac

Notable Evangelical Theologians/Pastors/Leaders
who apply the G-H-L system inconsistently

View of Scripture:
  Inerrant

Hermeneutic:
  Plain, Normal, Literal
  Inconsistently Applied (a dual hermeneutic)
  "Inconsistent Literalism"

Allis, Oswald T.
Arnold, Matthew
Berkhof, Louis
Beza, Theodore
Boice, James Montogmery
Bruce, F.F.
Bunyan, John
Calvin, John
Edwards, Jonathan
Erdmans, Charles
Finney, Charles
Hanegraaff, Hank
Henry, Carl F.H.
Hodge, Charles
Horton, Michael
Keller, Tim
Kennedy, D. James
Ladd, George Eldon
Luther, Martin
Morris, Leon
Newton, Isaac
Packer, J.I.
Pink, A.W.
Piper, John
Simpson, A.B.
Sproul, R.C.
Stott, John
Strong, A.H.
Tyndale, William
Warfield, B.B.
Wesley, Charles
Wesley, John

Example of an Inconsistently-Applied G-H-L Hermeneutic

In Part IV of his book, *The Incomparable Christ*, esteemed Anglican theologian, John Stott (1921-2011), provides a seventy-page commentary on the book of Revelation. When analyzing Revelation 20:1-15, Stott makes the following statement: "Revelation is well known for its reference to a millennium, or one-thousand-year period. I am assuming that, as with other enumerations of the book, **we should not interpret this literally but as a very long though unspecified period, in fact the whole gospel age**" [*emphasis added*].[2] Thus, in one sentence, Stott informs his reader that Jesus Christ, in giving this revelation to the Apostle John, doesn't have in mind a literal thousand-year period—even though He states it six times in Revelation 20:2-7:

> *"And he laid hold of the dragon, the serpent of old, who is the devil and Satan, and bound him for a **thousand** years; and he threw him into the abyss, and shut it and sealed it over him, so that he could not deceive the nations any longer, until the **thousand** years were completed. After these things he must be released for a short time. Then I saw thrones, and they sat on them, and judgment was given to them. And I saw the souls of those who had been beheaded because of their testimony of Jesus and because of the word of God, and those who had not worshiped the beast of his image, and had not received the mark on their forehead and on their hand. And they came to life and reigned with Christ for a **thousand** years. The rest of the dead did not come to life until the **thousand** years were completed. This is the first resurrection. Blessed and holy is the one who has a part in the first resurrection. Over these the second death has no power, but they will be priests of God and of Christ and will reign with Him for a **thousand** years. And when the **thousand** years are completed, Satan will be released from his prison, and will go out to deceive the nations which are in the four corners of the earth, ..."*

Stott—an amillennialist who uses a dual G-H-L hermeneutic—here takes a Millennial passage and applies it to the Church Age (the "whole gospel age"). However, Stott's contention that the passage describes the Church Age has several interpretive problems. First, if Revelation 20:1-15 describe the "whole gospel age" and Satan is *bound* (vv. 2-3) during this "very long though unspecified period," then how come sin and deception have been (and currently are) so rampant during the Church Age? Has not Satan been behind much of the lying, deception, division, and destruction over the past two thousand years? Was not Satan behind Hitler's move to murder six million Jews during World War II? Surely, Stott's interpretation not only fails to line up with Scripture, but it also contradicts the tenor of known Church Age history. Second, have Christians during the past two thousand years been forced to receive a mark on their foreheads and right hands (v.4)? Certainly not. Once again, Stott's insistence that the passage relates to the Church Age is untenable. Third, have Christians who refused such a mark been raised from the dead (v.4)? Absolutely not. No resurrection (other than Christ's) has yet taken place. Again, Stott's "gospel age" view fails to correlate with Scripture. In addition, by assuming that "the gospel age" is the millennium, Stott subtracts from the earthly glory prophesied for Christ, when Jesus returns to rule over the earth with a rod of iron (Psa. 2:9; Rev. 2:27; 12:5; 19:15) as King of kings and Lord of lords (Rev. 17:14; 19:16),

These contradictions thus beg the following question: on what basis does Stott reject a literal interpretation of Revelation 20 in favor of amillennialism? Is it because Augustine chose to do so sixteen hundred years ago? Is it because it has been the official doctrine of the Roman Catholic Church for fifteen hundred years? Is it because it is the position held by the Anglican church—a doctrine inherited from the apostate Catholic Church? Whatever his reason, Stott both writes off Christ's straight-forward teaching about the length of the Millennial Kingdom and then allows his rejection of any future, literal reign of Christ over the earth to contradict other parts of the passage. It is a regrettable mishandling handling of God's Word.

To be sure, why couldn't Stott—or any other theologian who chooses to use an inconsistently-applied hermeneutic—also say of the **resurrection**: "we should not interpret the resurrection literally," or of the **virgin birth**: "we should not interpret the virgin birth literally," or of the universal **flood**: "we should not interpret this to mean a worldwide flood." As mentioned earlier, the problem with this interpretive approach—the dual hermeneutic—is obvious: if one attempts to interpret parts of the Bible in any other way than its plain normal sense, then the interpretation becomes *subjective*: it depends on the ideas or bias of the interpreter rather than the Author of Scripture.

Christ's simile in Matthew 12:38-40 is instructive: *"Then some of the scribes and Pharisees said to Him, 'Teacher, we want to see a sign from You.' But He answered and said to them, 'An evil and adulterous generation craves for a sign; and yet no sign will be given to it but the sign of Jonah the prophet; for just as Jonah was three days and three nights in the belly of the sea monster, so will the Son of Man be three days and three nights in the heart of the earth'."* In this simile Christ compares two actual, *literal* events. He does not compare an allegorical event with a literal one. And while many theologians allegorize the episode of Jonah and the whale, Jesus does not. Nor should we. In short, the Christian is far better served when he takes Scripture at face value—as Jesus Himself did with the Old Testament.

Note: The unfortunate interpretive errors caused by Evangelicalism's widespread use of a dual hermeneutic will be examined more closely in Chapters 33, 35, and 36.

Point of discernment: Use of a dual hermeneutic will inevitably lead to interpretive error, as the example above illustrates. If teachable, hungry-hearted Christians want to know the whole counsel of God, and Bible teachers truly want to handle God's Word accurately, then it is imperative they utilize a consistently-applied G-H-L hermeneutic throughout Scripture.

THE BEST OVERALL SYSTEM OF HERMENEUTICS

The "bedrock" for handling God's word accurately

1. **The Grammatical - Historical - Literal System (consistently applied)**

   This system understands words and figures of speech in their usual, ordinary, or normal sense *at all times*—including the creation account and Bible prophecy.

   (e.g., Revelation 6:7-8 pictures an actual death-toll)

   (e.g., Revelation 19:11-21; 20:4-6: Christ will return to the earth to reign for a 1,000 years)

   a. G – H – L *consistently* applied

   b. a single hermeneutic (one system employed; the plain, normal meaning of words and figures of speech at all times)

FOUR ADDITIONAL GUIDELINES OF INTERPRETATION

1. Interpret Scripture in light of the context

2. Interpret the less clear in light of the more clear

3. Scripture cannot contradict itself. Thus, if an interpretation of a passage of Scripture contradicts the clear teaching of another passage of Scripture on the same topic or contradicts known historical data, then the interpretation in incorrect. For example, the person who chooses to believe that the seven-year Tribulation period described in the book of Revelation took place in or around 70 A.D. also chooses to contradict the historical fact that one-half of mankind (Rev. 6:8; Rev. 9:13-18) was not killed during the 70 A.D timeframe. This person must either ignore the historical facts, redefine words (e.g., "mankind" means "Israel"), or allegorize the death tolls.

4. Be sure to "exegete" Scripture rather than "eisegete" it. Exegesis is a thorough study and analysis of a text or passage, from which a doctrine, theological view, or conclusion is formed or drawn. Eisegesis, on the other hand, reads a particular theological system or one's particular theological ideas into the text.

INTERPRETING THE END-TIMES PROPHECIES

Overarching Interpretive Principle:

If all of the prophecies relating to Christ's first coming were fulfilled *literally*—and they were—then a Christian can be certain that all of the prophecies relating to His second coming will likewise be fulfilled *literally*. There is no need or reason to spiritualize them or to treat them metaphorically or allegorically.

SCRIPTURE'S SOBERING WORD OF CAUTION

You shall not add to the word which I am commanding you, nor take away from it, that you may keep the commandments of the Lord your God which I command you (Deut. 4:2).

I testify to everyone who hears the words of the prophecy of this book: if anyone adds to them, God shall add to him the plagues which are written in this book; and if anyone takes away from the words of this prophecy, God shall take away his part from the tree of life and from the holy city, which are written in this book (Rev. 22:18-19).

According to the two exhortations above, the Christian is not to add to—or subtract from—the Word of God, the Bible.

Let it be stated again: the Bible alone is the believer's sole source of Divine authority, truth, wisdom and direction. All of God's purposes for human history and all of God's plans for the redemption of mankind through Jesus Christ have been revealed in the Bible. Nothing needs to be added to God's written Word, and no new "revelation from God" needs to be forthcoming. Claims to the contrary come from the flesh or the devil—and are false.

Any person who **adds** to the Bible is culpable before God and should not be heeded by a Christian. Examples of persons who have added to the Word of God are Joseph Smith (*the Book of Mormon*, *The Doctrine and Covenants*), and Mary Baker Eddy (*Science and Health with the Key to the Scriptures*). According to a Mormon website: "the books that are believed to be inspired scripture in addition to the Bible by Mormons are the Book of Mormon, the Doctrine and Covenants, and the Pearl of Great Price. Mormons also use an edition of the Bible that includes changes made by Joseph Smith."[1] An Evangelical apologist notes this about *Science and Health with Key to the Scriptures*: "It interprets the Bible in a radically different way. It is so different, in fact, that it absolutely rejects that substitutionary atonement of Jesus and states that it had not efficacious value (*S&H*, 25:6). It denies that Jesus is God, second person of the Trinity (*S&H*, 361:12-13). . . . To the Christian Scientist, Jesus is a Wayshower. He is someone who epitomized the true principle of the Christ Consciousness which [to Eddy] indwells us all. Therefore, Jesus did not really die on the cross. He was not God in flesh. He made no atonement in shedding His blood (*S&H*, 25:6)"[2]

Equally culpable are Christians who claim to be receiving new revelation from God and who claim to be prophesying in His name. To many of them, the Bible is "yesterday's manna . . . . It is no longer enough to feed my people."[3] According to these Christians, God is now giving them—and them alone—a fresh, new word: "There are going to be those in the end-time generation who will have Daniel-types of revelatory experiences."[4] However, no Christian should give heed to such persons. This deception of the flesh (and, in some cases, seducing spirits) will be discussed in Chapter 36.

Likewise, any person who **subtracts** from the Bible is culpable before God. Such a practice is more subtle, but just as problematic. Christians who subtract from the Bible either consciously reject certain parts of the Bible or simply ignore those parts of the Bible which they find objectionable. Some, for example, might simply say that the Book of Revelation is "unknowable." As a result, they refuse to study or teach the book—and, in effect, subtract from the Word of God. Similarly, Christians who spiritualize or allegorize certain parts of the Scripture also, in effect, subtract from the Word of God. Let this not be the case with you, the reader.

CHAPTER 14

Studying God's Word Effectively

Once a Christian has a trustworthy method of interpreting Scripture, the next step becomes learning how to read and study the Bible in greater depth. One widely-used system is called the **Inductive Bible Study Method.** As the word "inductive" suggests, the Christian looks to bring together the assorted data presented in a verse or verses so that he can come to an accurate understanding of a passage's intended meaning. It is the process of reasoning from the particular to the general, or from particular observations to a general conclusion.

The Inductive Bible Study Method employs three steps: (1) **Observation**; (2) **Interpretation**; and (3) **Application**. Each of these steps asks a simple question of a verse or passage of Scripture:

- Observation: **What does it say**?
- Interpretation: **What does it mean**?
- Application: **How does it apply to my life**?

Let it become your custom to utilize these three questions as you read through the Scriptures.

Finally, in addition to the three practical steps of inductive Bible Study, the believer has the indwelling Holy Spirit to illumine his heart and mind with the truths and life application of the Scripture he studies.

OBSERVATION

"What does it say?" What <u>information</u> is conveyed?
What <u>facts</u> are presented?

The reader should look for:
> key words
> repeated words
> key phrases
> genealogies
> comparisons
> contrasts
> quotations from the O.T. (if reading the N.T.)
> references to the O.T. (if reading the N.T.)
> types or foreshadows of Christ (if reading the O.T.)

The reader should ask **"Who, What, When, Where, Why, How, and How Much/Many"**:

> e.g., Who's the speaker?
> Who's the audience?
> Where's the location?
> What's the geography?
> What city or town?
> What nation?

What literary genre?	What figures of speech?
e.g., narrative	e.g., simile
exposition	metaphor
parable	hyperbole
poetry	paradox
song	euphemism
wisdom	personification
prophecy	
proverb	

Finally: if the passage is a <u>narrative</u>, put yourself in the scene. What do you see? What's going on?

INTERPRETATION

"What does it mean?"

What's the <u>context</u>? (Be sure to understand the context!)

What am I to **know** and **learn** ...

> about God/Christ/Holy Spirit?
> about man?
> about sin/sin nature / the human heart?
> about salvation (justification)?
> about sanctification?
> about judgment?
> about heaven? hell?
> about Satan?
> about Israel?
> about the Church?
> about the Christian life?
> about the end times?
> about marriage? children?
> about love?
> about forgiveness? etc., etc.

What's the **meaning** of <u>key words</u>, <u>expressions</u>, or <u>phrases</u>?

What's the **core meaning** of the passage?

What am I to learn about **God's will for my life**, **God's ways**, **God's purposes**?

- Look for **Principles to Live By** [literally hundreds in Scripture]
- Look for the **Character** of God the Father / God the Son
- Look for **Doctrinal truths** (e.g., the deity of Christ; the necessity of the new birth (John 3:1-7)

APPLICATION

"How does it apply to my life?"

For example, Proverbs 15:1 tells us that *"A gentle answer turns away wrath, but a harsh answer stirs up anger."*

When looking to apply this passage to his life, the Christian should

1. Find and state the spiritual **Principle to live by:** "Based on Proverbs 15:1, the Christian should return a gentle answer rather than a harsh answer when offended or confronted." Why? Because the offender usually expects a harsh answer and confrontation, a soft answer catches him off guard and typically diffuses the situation. The "wind" is taken out of the offender.

2. Then ask a rhetorical question of yourself based on the **Principle to live by** taught in the passage: "Am I continually attempting, through the enabling of the indwelling Christ, to return a gentle answer when offended or confronted? Or am I returning a harsh answer which is only going to stir up more anger?"

3. Finally, commit yourself to *applying* the Proverbs 15:1 principle in your daily life. Specifically, when confronted verbally (perhaps even unjustly), *put into practice* the principle of returning a soft answer rather than a harsh answer.

Note: It is the application of Scripture to our lives—*the living out of Scriptural principles in our daily lives*—which enables the Christian to be a fragrant aroma and a light to the hurting world. It is the Christian *living out* the expression, "What would Jesus do?"

The Hermeneutics "Triangle"

The Inductive Bible Study Process

Theme

Key Verse

Key Word/Words

Repeated Words

Figures of Speech

Literary Style or Styles

Author – Audience – Date

Historical – Political Context

Major Doctrinal Themes
(Old & New Testaments)

Overall System of Hermeneutics:
**The Grammatical – Historical – Literal System
(consistently applied)**
plain, normal interpretation of words and figures of speech

"Hermeneutics" = Principles of Biblical Interpretation

CHAPTER 15

Conditions Which Derail Sound Doctrine

Seven conditions exist in the Evangelical church today that can lead to the presence and teaching of unsound doctrine:

1. Having a Deficient View of God's Word

The Bible, as discussed in Chapter 10, is inspired, inerrant, authoritative, and sufficient. *Any teaching that denies or minimizes any of these truths about God's Word will eventually produce error and unsound doctrine.* This phenomenon will be observed in Chapters 35 and 36.

2. Handling God's Word Cavalierly or Poorly

An inaccurate or erroneous interpretation of God's Word can be caused by any of the following reasons:

- a refusal to interpret *all* of Scripture in its plain, normal sense

    This condition exists throughout Evangelical circles today and is a major reason for imprecise, inaccurate, erroneous, or poor teaching.

- unbelief

    A particular teacher, for example, may not believe that an unseen spiritual battle is actually taking place, or he simply may not believe that Christians can be touched by such battle (despite the fact that Christians are exhorted to put on the full armor of God and to stand firm against the schemes of the devil). Still another teacher might not believe that God at some point in the future will bring forth widespread judgment on earth during a seven-year period of tribulation.

- the use of eisegesis rather than exegesis

    The practice of eisegesis reads a person's doctrinal position into a passage rather than using the passage itself to form the doctrinal position.

- A failure to determine the proper context of a passage

    Typically, a passage always has a "near" context—i.e., the immediate context or the context at hand. At times, however, a passage also has a "far" context—i.e., one which relates to the whole Biblical perspective. Evangelicals who contend a person can lose his salvation often include Matthew 24:13 as proof of their position: *"But the one who endures to the end, he will be saved."* The context of the passage, however, is not the Church Age, but the Tribulation period (Matt. 24:9-14). In these verses, Jesus informs his disciples that persons who (1) put their faith in Christ during the Tribulation period and who (2) survive the horrors of the Tribulation will be saved (i.e., not killed, v.9) and will enter the Millennial Kingdom (Matt. 25:31-34). They will also receive eternal life (Matt. 24:46). As can be seen in this example, an accurate determination of context thus sets up "guard rails," if you will, for a passage, so the interpreter doesn't wind up "off the tracks" with his interpretation.

- the use of "proof texting"—the practice of using an isolated or out-of-context verse or passage of Scripture to "prove" one's suppositions or biases.

  Dominion Theology, for example, believes that God has given Christians a mandate to take dominion over the earth and that the world's nations should be governed by Christians and Christian principles. The basis for belief, according to Dominionists, is supplied in the King James version of Genesis 1:28: *"And God blessed them, and God said unto them, 'Be fruitful, and multiply, and replenish the earth, and subdue it; and have dominion over the fish of the sea, and over the fowl of the air, and over every living thing that moves upon the earth.'"*

  In contrast, however, Christ tells Pilate the following: *"My kingdom is **not** of this world [emphasis added]. If My kingdom were of this world, then my servants would be fighting so that I would not be handed over to the Jews; but as it is, My kingdom is not of this realm."* Later, Christ makes clear to His disciples (and us) their mandate in His kingdom: *"Go, therefore, and make disciples of all the nations, baptizing them in the name of the Father, the Son, and the Holy Spirit"* (Matt. 28:19). Therefore, Christ's mandate for Christians has nothing to do with the well-meaning (but erroneous) Dominionist notion that the world's nations should be governed by Christians.

- holding to an interpretation that contradicts other Scriptures

  Reformed Theology's doctrine of "regeneration before faith," for example, contradicts Numbers 21:7-9 and John 3:14-15, which teach unequivocally that regeneration comes after the exercise of faith, not before. It also contradicts Genesis 15:6 and Romans 4:3.

- the use of deductive reasoning to develop a particular doctrine instead of an inductive exegesis of all passages relating to a topic

  Deductive reasoning starts with a premise and then attempts to prove it with Scripture. Inductive exegesis, in contrast, begins with the interpretation of all pertinent passages of Scripture on a particular topic, then draws its doctrinal conclusions.

- denominational dogmas

  Christians who grew up in and/or were saved in a particular denomination are particularly susceptible to accepting denominational teaching rather than examining all such beliefs in light of Scripture itself. For example, if you teach in a Reformed or Presbyterian church, you will be required to teach the doctrine of Limited Atonement, despite the fact that the doctrine contradicts fifteen passages of Scripture which teach Unlimited Atonement.

- tunnel vision; failure to see the big picture

  This condition can occur when a teacher become so enamored with dissecting the meaning of each word in a verse of Scripture that the overall context of the passage at hand becomes lost—and the overall meaning of the passage is perhaps missed or misinterpreted.

- a desire to make Christ in one's own image

    A teacher of a particular temperament, for example, may not like the idea of Christ also being a God of perfect justice in addition to being a God of perfect love.

- latent or underlying anti-Semitism

    For example, because of the Replacement Theology of the Catholic Church, a doctrine which was carried into the Protestant Reformation, those Evangelicals who still hold to Replacement Theology might teach that God is finished with the Jews and the nation of Israel due to the latter's corporate rejection of Christ. An honest evaluation of Scripture, however, teaches just the opposite: Though Israel has temporarily been set aside (Rom. 11:25-29), God at some point in the future will once again take up for Israel and will exalt her during the Millennial Age (Micah 4:1-3; Isa. 49:22-23; Isa. 60:13-15).

- deception from the enemy

    All Christian teachers must be on guard against the Satanic whisper of: "Indeed, has God said . . . ?" If a Christian leader, teacher, or theologian succumbs to this whisper, unsound doctrine might eventually enter the Church. Augustine's acceptance and promotion of amillennialism—despite early church's universal belief in premillennialism up to this point—is one such example.

3. **Subtracting from God's Word**

This condition exists when a teacher (1) doesn't believe certain parts of the Bible, (2) refuses to teach parts of the Bible, (3) waters down parts of the Bible, or (4) simply ignores parts of the Bible.

4. **Adding to God's Word**

This condition exists when Evangelical teachers resort to, or become enamored with, extra-Biblical revelation. Today, this reality often takes the form of "prophecies" or "prophetic words" which are deemed to be on par with, or even superseding, Scripture.

5. **Politicizing God's Word**

Dominionist and Kingdom Now Evangelicals believe that Christians have a mandate from God to take over the nations (or a nation's institutions) for Christ. Evangelical Progressive Christians, on the other hand, emphasize the need for social justice. As such, Progressives lobby "Caesar" (Western world human governments) to promote policies which call for socialism and an equitable redistribution of income. In sharp contrast to these political labors, Christ says: *"Go, therefore, and make disciples of all the nations, baptizing them in the name of Father, the Son, and the Holy Spirit, teaching them to observe all that I commanded you" (Matt. 28:19-20).*

6. **Deconstructing God's Word**

This condition arises when Evangelicals cavalierly teach and promote some form of moral and cultural relativism rather than the truths and moral absolutes of the Bible. This relativism in turn allows some Christians, for example, to condone homosexuality, transgenderism, and same-sex marriage. This relativism also allows other Christians to claim that a literal Hell does not exist. The doctrine which comes forth from this relativism always contradicts the Bible and, in doing so, rests on quicksand.

7. Failing to Discern Esoteric or Occult Teaching and Practices

Though this condition is not widespread in Evangelical circles, it nevertheless exists, as we will see in Chapter 37. For, example, the practice of being "slain in the spirit" seen in some charismatic and Pentecostal churches today is identical with demon-empowered Hindu practice known as "Shaktipat"—the transmission or conferring of "spiritual energy" from a Hindu guru to one of his followers.

Part IV

Understanding the Church Age and the Church

"I also say to you that you are Peter, and upon this rock I will build My church; and the gates of Hades will not overpower it." (Matt. 16:18).

"Go therefore and make disciples of all the nations, baptizing them in the name of the Father and the Son and the Holy Spirit, teaching them to observe all that I commanded you; and lo, I am with you always, even to the end of the age" (Matt. 28:19).

As He was sitting on the Mount of Olives, the disciples came to Him privately, saying, "Tell us, when will these things happen, and what will be the sign of Your coming, and of the end of the age?" (Matt. 24:3).

For I do not want you, brethren, to be uninformed of this mystery—so that you will not be wise in your own estimation—that a partial hardening has happened to Israel until the fullness of the Gentiles has come in (Rom. 11:25).

Part IV will enable the Christian to understand the nature of the Church and the Church Age. The Church Age, according to Daniel 9:24-27, is a "parenthesis" (or a pause) in God's dealings with Israel. This parenthesis allows for and involves the birth and growth of a *spiritual* kingdom (John 3:3; 8:36)—the Church—which is designed to take root in the hearts of all persons who put their faith in Jesus Christ for their sin problem (John 1:12; Acts 20:21). The Church Age began on the day of Pentecost, ten days after Christ's ascension back into heaven, and will end at the Rapture of the Church sometime in the future. Furthermore, during this God-ordained parenthesis the Good News of salvation through Jesus Christ will be offered primarily (but not exclusively) to the Gentiles "until the fullness of Gentiles has come in" (Rom. 11:25).

CHAPTER 16

Differentiating the Bible's Three Kingdom's of God/Heaven

The New Testament describes *three* separate "kingdoms of heaven" or "kingdoms of God." Because of the potential confusion over the timing and purpose of these three kingdoms, every Christian must understand the differences.

The first kingdom is the **Inter-Advent Kingdom.** Today this kingdom is known as Christianity or Christendom—and it deals with the sowing of, and response to, the Gospel message *between* the coming of the indwelling Holy Spirit on the day of Pentecost and Christ's still-future coming for His bride, the Church. [Note: by comparing the Sower and the Mustard Seed parables in Matthew, Mark and Luke, we can conclude that the terms "kingdom of heaven" (used in Matthew) and "kingdom of God" (used in Mark and Luke) are interchangeable terms.]

The resurrected Jesus Christ is king of this inter-advent kingdom. He reigns as its king from the right hand of the Father (Acts 2:32-33). Furthermore, Jesus teaches that admission into this kingdom comes solely by way of the new birth: *"Truly, truly, I say to you, unless one is born again, he cannot see the kingdom of God" (John 3:3)*. A person must put his faith in the kingdom's king to be a part of the kingdom; there is no other way. It must be noted, however, that this inter-advent kingdom includes *true* adherents and *counterfeit* adherents. The counterfeits call themselves "Christians," but they have not put their faith in the king (Jesus Christ) and have not come into the kingdom by way of new birth. We will review this phenomenon in Chapter 18.

It should also be noted that this inter-advent kingdom is a *spiritual* kingdom, not a social or political one (John 18:36). In addition, Christ mandates that the subjects of His spiritual kingdom *"go therefore and make disciples of all the nations, baptizing them in the name of the Father and the Son and the Holy Spirit, teaching them to observe all that I have commanded you" (Matt. 28:19-20)*. If a church or a missionary agency does not endeavor to make baptized disciples of Jesus Christ, then it is not pursuing the revealed will of God.

The second kingdom is the **Millennial Kingdom**, a kingdom which will be established and ruled over by the resurrected Jesus Christ after His Second Coming to the earth (Rev. 20:1-6)—in fulfillment of numerous Old Testament prophecies, including what's known as the Davidic Covenant (II Sam. 7:8-29).

The third kingdom is the **Eternal Kingdom**, a kingdom which will be established by God after the destruction of the present heavens and earth—and the creation of the new heavens and earth (where sin will no longer exist) (Rev. 21:1 - 22:5). This kingdom will include all resurrected believers from the entirety of human history. Not only will sin no longer exist in the Eternal Kingdom ("Heaven"), but Christ Himself *"shall wipe away every tear from their eyes; and there shall no longer be* *any death; there shall no longer be any mourning, or crying, or pain; the first things have passed away" (Rev. 21:4).*

At times a reader can determine from the text itself which kingdom is being presented. At other times the reader must determine the kingdom by the context. The Messianic (Millennial) Kingdom was widely prophesied in the Old Testament (see Appendix A). In contrast, the Inter-Advent Kingdom was a "mystery" (i.e., not revealed) in the Old Testament (Eph. 3:1-11; Col. 1:25-28).

THE TWO KINGDOMS OF GOD IN THE OLD TESTAMENT

- **The Messianic Kingdom**
  (Messiah's reign over the earth from Jerusalem)

- **The Eternal Kingdom**
  (The eternal home of every believer from all generations)

THE THREE KINGDOMS OF GOD IN THE NEW TESTAMENT

- **The Inter-Advent Kingdom**
  (Christ's kingdom on earth between His two advents. This kingdom was not revealed in the Old Testament [Eph. 3:1-11; Col. 1:25-28])

- **The Messianic (Millennial) Kingdom**
  (Christ's 1000-year reign over the earth from Jerusalem)

- **The Eternal Kingdom**
  (The eternal home of every believer from all generations)

Note: The New Testament teaches that the Eternal Kingdom is both different and distinct from the Millennial Kingdom in a number of ways:

1. The first heaven and first earth (on which the Millennial Kingdom will take place) will pass away after the Millennial Kingdom (Rev. 20:11; Rev. 21:1; II Pet. 3:10)—to be replaced by a new heaven, new earth, and new Jerusalem (Rev. 21:1-2).

2. The new earth will not have any seas (Rev. 21:1).

3. The new Jerusalem will be cube-shaped (as was the Holy of Holies in the wilderness tabernacle)—with dimensions of approximately 1,500 miles wide by 1,500 miles long by 1,500 miles high (Rev. 21:6).

4. The new Jerusalem will be pure gold (Rev. 21:18).

5. The new Jerusalem will have no temple, because God the Father and God the Son are its temple (Rev. 21:22).

6. The new Jerusalem will need no sun or moon to light it because the glory of God will illumine it (Rev. 21:23).

7. There will be no nighttime in the new Jerusalem (Rev. 21:25; 22:5).

8. God the Father and God the Son will be present in the new Jerusalem (Rev 21:22). Only the Son will be present in the Millennial Kingdom's Jerusalem (Rev. 19:11-21; Rev. 20:4).

9. Death will exist in the Millennial Kingdom (Isa. 65:20), but not in the Eternal Kingdom (Rev. 21:4).

Point of discernment: Any attempt to combine the Millennial Kingdom and the Eternal Kingdom into one kingdom is error. For example, by failing to distinguish between these two kingdoms, the best-selling 2004 book, *Heaven*, mixes the two and, regrettably, is replete with interpretive error.[1]

CHAPTER 17

Why It Matters

For fifteen hundred years the Catholic Church has taught amillennialism—the belief that Christ will *not* reign over the earth for a thousand years at some point in the future. Since the 10th century the Orthodox Church has taught the same thing. For five hundred years much of Protestantism has also believed in amillennialism. In contrast, the early church, during its first three hundred years, believed in and taught premillennialism—the belief that Christ would one day return bodily to the earth to rid the planet of His and Israel's enemies and subsequently reign over the earth for a thousand years as King of kings and Lord of lords.

Much confusion exists in the church today over the meaning of the New Testament's "kingdom of heaven" (or "kingdom of God"). During its first few centuries, however, the church had no such confusion. All early church leaders—because they interpreted Scripture in its plain, normal sense—were "Chiliast" (premillennial) in their understanding of the end times. Dozens of Old Testament prophecies picture Christ's earthly reign, and the New Testament tells believers (six times) the length of His reign—a thousand years. In short, the early church readily understood the differences between the Church Age, the Millennial Kingdom, and the Eternal Kingdom.

Because of Augustine's unfortunate allegorizing of the prophesied Millennial Kingdom, most of Christendom now holds to amillennialism. Yet, such a view is indefensible when one takes the Old Testament prophecies relating to Messiah's Kingdom at face value.

For example, Micah 4:1-3 reads as follows: *"And it will come about in the last days that the mountain of the house of the Lord will be established as the chief of the mountains. It will be raised above the hills, and the peoples will stream to it. Many nations will come and say, 'Come and let us go up to the mountain of the Lord and to the house of the God of Jacob, that He may teach us about His ways and that we may walk in His paths.' For from Zion will go forth the law, even the word of the LORD from Jerusalem. And He will judge between many peoples and render decisions for mighty, distant nations. Then they will hammer their swords into plowshares And their spears into pruning hooks; nation will not lift up sword against nation, and never again will they train for war."*

So, with Micah 4:1-3 in mind, let us ask the following: Is Mount Zion (Jerusalem) the chief of mountains today? Are the nations today saying, *"Come and let us go up to the mountain of the Lord and to the house of Jacob that He [Christ] may teach us about His ways and that we may walk in His paths"*? Are the Muslim nations saying this today? Are the Hindus of India saying this? Are Asia's Buddhists saying this? Are New Agers in the West clamoring for this? Are *Christians* around the world going to Jerusalem to learn from and to worship the resurrected Jesus Christ? The answer to all of these questions is no. Hence, the amillennial view contradicts the Micah passage at every turn.

Today, amillennialism is the official doctrine of the Roman Catholic Church (1.2 billion adherents), the Eastern Orthodox Church (300 million adherents), and much of Protestantism (700 million adherents). Indeed, most mainline Protestant denominations—including the Anglicans, Episcopalians, Lutherans, Congregationalists, Presbyterians, Methodists, and some Baptists—teach amillennialism.

During the past two hundred years, postmillennialism has also developed a significant following. Postmillennialists hold to one of two beliefs: (1) Christ will only return to the earth after the Gospel has been preached to all the nations, or (2) it is the job of Christians to set up a "Christian" world before Christ can return to judge the world and then take His people home to heaven. So the question must be asked: Does Scripture teach that the earth will be "Christianized" before Christ returns? The answer again is no. Christ teaches in His parable of the Sower (to be discussed in Chapter 20) that the Gospel will *not* be widely received during the Church Age. Indeed, though approximately thirty percent of the world's population today calls itself Christian, perhaps no more than fifteen percent have saving faith in Jesus Christ. To be sure, Christ asked his disciples rhetorically: *"When the Son of Man comes, will He find faith on earth?" (Luke 18:8)*. The implication of His question is that widespread faith will not exist.

In conclusion, amillennialism and postmillennialism amount to regrettable misinterpretations of Scripture, and both contradict the teachings of the apostles and early church leaders. Chapter 33 will examine these two errors more fully.

Point of discernment: amillennialists and postmillennialists fail to differentiate between the three kingdoms of God presented in Scripture. As a result, they rob their adherents of (1) understanding a significant component of the whole counsel of God's Word, specifically the culmination of God's recovery and renovation of our sin-wracked planet through the return and reign of Jesus Christ over the earth; (2) knowing the full purposes of God in and through Jesus Christ; (3) understanding that perfect justice will one day come to this planet through Jesus Christ; and (4) appreciating the glory reserved for Jesus Christ when He returns to reign over the earth.

CHAPTER 18

Matthew's Inter-Advent "Kingdom of Heaven" Parables

God's prophets in the Old Testament not only revealed the immediate future of the nation of Israel, but also her far-off future. This distant future would include the coming of Messiah to reign over the earth from Jerusalem and to rid Israel of her foreign oppressors (Micah 4:1-3; Zechariah 14:9; Daniel 2:36-44). It was this Messianic Kingdom that many of the Jews who saw and heard Jesus were expecting. Indeed, most who followed Christ were neither looking for, nor wanted, a Messiah who would save them from their sins. Instead, they wanted Jesus to set up the Messianic Kingdom to rid them of the yoke of Rome. To their dismay their hoped-for Messiah was crucified.

Consequently, the Jewish audience to whom Matthew writes wants to have one crucial question answered: "If Jesus Christ is Israel's Messiah, then why isn't He reigning from Jerusalem this very moment?" Matthew answers this question by unveiling in the second half of his Gospel the unforeseen *Inter-Advent* Kingdom of Messiah, a *spiritual* kingdom designed to take root in the heart of any person who puts his faith in Jesus Christ as Savior from sin. This kingdom had not been revealed to Israel's prophets.

Jesus discloses a number of the principal characteristics of this inter-advent kingdom through the use of twelve parables—similes which begin with the words "the kingdom of heaven is like" or "the kingdom of heaven is comparable to." These twelve parables are found in chapters 13, 18, 20, 22, and 25 of Matthew's gospel. Eleven of these parables describe a kingdom of Christ's which is to come forth on earth *between* His first and second comings. A twelfth parable describes an event which takes place immediately after Christ's second coming. Today this kingdom is known as Christianity or Christendom—and consists of all persons who call themselves Christians. Christianity stands in contrast to Islam or Buddhism or Hinduism, for example, whose adherents call themselves Muslims or Buddhists or Hindus. Let us take a brief look at nine of these parables.

The parable of the Sower explains that the Gospel message will be met with a continuum of response between the two advents of Christ—from outright rejection, to shallow profession, to carnal reception, to wholehearted belief. The parable of the Mustard Seed teaches that Christ's kingdom ("Christianity") will begin as the tiniest of movements but will grow to be the largest religion on earth before His second coming.* The parable of the Wheat and the Tares explains that Christ's kingdom will contain true adherents and counterfeit adherents. The parable of the Leaven makes it clear that Christ's kingdom will grow inexorably over time but will also become infiltrated with false teaching and destructive heresies. The parable of the Hidden Treasure and the parable of the Pearl of Great Value explain that a personal relationship with Christ will have incalculable value to the true adherent and is worth laying aside all other pursuits in order to have it to the fullest. The parable of the Landowner who Offers Work teaches that Christ's kingdom is available even to those who put their faith in Christ late in life. The parable of the Talents shows that Christ will reward faithful service in His kingdom. Significantly, the parable of the Ten Virgins not only pictures Christ's coming for born-again believers (His Bride) at the Rapture, but it also suggests that most of His followers will not be alert for his return.

Nevertheless, Christ makes it clear in the Gospels that this inter-advent kingdom of heaven (Christianity) is not a political kingdom: *"My kingdom is not of this world. If my kingdom were of this world, then My servants would be fighting, that I might not be delivered up to the Jews. But as it is, My kingdom is not of this realm" (John 18:36).* To repeat, Christ's inter-advent kingdom is a spiritual kingdom designed to take root (through the indwelling Holy Spirit) in the hearts of men and women— young and old, Jew or Gentile—who put their faith in Jesus Christ and His finished work on the Cross for their sin problem.

Point of discernment: Matthew's inter-advent "kingdom of heaven" parables provide a rich panorama of the nature of Christendom—including the condition of the hearts of those who hear the gospel message; the incalculable value of knowing Christ personally; the inexorable growth of the inter-advent kingdom to the ends of the earth; and the unfortunate reality of an infiltration of poor and false teaching into the kingdom.

---

* In 2020, Christianity is the world's largest religion with 2.2 billion who claim to be adherents. Islam ranked second with 1.5 billion. Hinduism ranked third with 1.1 billion.

Note: Some born-again theologians contend that Matthew's "kingdom of heaven" parables teach "new truths concerning the Millennial Kingdom" rather than unveiling of Messiah's "Inter-Advent" Kingdom.[1] Yet how accurate is this contention? Do the "kingdom of heaven" parables of Matthew 13 reveal new truths about the Millennial Kingdom?

In the parable of the Wheat and Tares (Matt. 13:24-30, 36-43) Jesus teaches that in the "kingdom of heaven" He (the Son of Man) is the one who sows the "wheat" (the good seed, the sons of the kingdom) in the world. But He also teaches that the enemy, the *devil*, sows the "tares" (the counterfeit seed, the sons of the evil one) in the world. Furthermore, Jesus teaches that both types of seed will be allowed to grow together until the harvest (v.30). Jesus also gives us the timeframe of the harvest and the judgment of the evil ones: the end of the age (vv.39-40). So, the question must be asked: Does this parable have the Millennial Kingdom in view? All Christians who interpret the Bible's words and figures of speech in their plain, normal sense would agree that Satan is bound during the Millennial Kingdom. Thus, it would be impossible for Satan to sow counterfeit seed during the Millennial Kingdom. As distasteful as this conclusion is to those who hold to the "new truths concerning the Millennial Kingdom" view, it is clear that the plain, normal interpretation of the parable of the Wheat and Tares rules out this interpretation.

In the parable of the Sower (Matt. 13:3-9, 18-23) Jesus teaches that the "word of the kingdom," when preached to unbelievers, will find a wide spectrum of response among those who hear the message. Once again, however, persons contending that the Millennial Kingdom is in view in this parable find themselves in an untenable position: *Satan* (v.19) is seen as the one who, in the case of the unreceptive hearer (v.20), "comes and snatches away what has been sown in his heart." Because Satan is bound during the Millennial Kingdom, it is difficult to see how Christ's Parable of the Sower could have a Millennial context. What interpretation is left? Most assuredly, the Parable of the Sower is dealing with the sowing of the Gospel of Christ—the good news that Christ died for the sinner and rose again on the third day—between Christ's two advents.

In conclusion, when one attempts a "new truths concerning the Millennial Kingdom" interpretation of Matthew's "kingdom of heaven" parables, he is forced to contradict Scripture in untenable ways—thus suggesting, to this writer at least, that an inter-advent understanding of the twelve parables is the best position.

MATTHEW'S INTERADVENT "KINGDOM OF HEAVEN" PARABLES

(In approximate chronological order, though the first eight overlap)

- **The Sower** [throughout the Church Age]
  (Matt. 13:3-9,18-23; Mark 4:3-8,14-20; Luke 8:5-8)

- **The Mustard Seed** [throughout the Church Age]
  (Matt. 13:31-32; Mark 4:30-32; Luke 13:18-19)

- **The Wheat & the Tares** [throughout the Church Age]
  (Matt. 13:24-30, 36-43)

- **The Leaven** [throughout the Church Age]
  (Matt. 13:33; Luke 13:20-21)

- **The Hidden Treasure** [throughout the Church Age]
  (Matt. 13:44)

- **The Pearl of Great Value** [throughout the Church Age]
  (Matt. 13:45-46)

- **The King who Settles Accounts** [throughout Church Age]
  (Matt. 18:23-35)

- **The Landowner who Offers Work** [throughout Church Age]
  (Matt. 20:1-16)

- **The Ten Virgins** [The Rapture]
  (Matt. 25:1-13)

- **The Talents** [The Judgment Seat of Christ, 25:19-23]
  (Matt. 25:14-30 [*The Great White Throne Judgment, 25:24-30*]

- **The Wedding Feast** [Revelation 19:7-9]
  (Matt. 22:2-14)

  [Christ's bodily return to the earth]

- **The Fishing Net** [Christ's post-return judgment of the nations]
  (Matt. 13:47-50)

  [The Beginning of Christ's 1,000-Year Reign over the Earth]

CHAPTER 19

The Parable of the Wheat & Tares

Through the use of a dozen parables in the second half of his Gospel, the apostle Matthew unveils a "kingdom of heaven" not previously revealed to the Old Testament prophets. Today this kingdom is known as Christianity, and it consists of all persons who call themselves "Christians."

Let us look more closely at two of these parables: The parable of the Wheat and Tares (in this chapter) and the parable of the Sower (in the next). Because they describe the overall composition of Christianity, both have crucial relevance to the topic of spiritual discernment.

The parable of the Wheat and Tares is recorded in Matthew 13:24-30. Christ explains its meaning in Matthew 13:36-43:

> *Then He left the multitudes, and went into the house. And His disciples came to Him, saying, "Explain to us the parable of the tares of the field." And He answered and said, "The one who sows the good seed is the Son of Man, and the field is the world; and as for the good seed, these are the sons of the kingdom; and the tares are the sons of the evil one; and the enemy who sowed them is the devil, and the harvest is the end of the age; and the reapers are angels. Therefore, just as the tares are gathered up and burned with fire, so shall it be at the end of the age. The Son of Man will send forth His angels, and they will gather out of His kingdom all stumbling blocks, and those who commit lawlessness, and will cast them into the furnace of fire; in that place there shall be weeping and gnashing of teeth. Then the righteous will shine forth as the sun in the kingdom of their Father. He who has ears, let him hear."*

Christ thus informs His disciples that two kinds of "Christians" will exist in this interadvent kingdom. He likens them to "wheat" and "tares." Wheat is the real item; the "tare" is a counterfeit. The tare looks like wheat, but in reality is a worthless weed. It is sobering to note that while Christ teaches that He Himself sows the wheat (the true Christians), He also states that Satan sows the tares (the counterfeit "Christians").

What, then, is the significance of the parable today? It is this: although twenty-first century Christianity represents the world's largest religion both numerically and geographically, Christendom contains both wheat and tares—**those who are born-again and those who are not born-again.** The wheat have put their faith in the finished work of Jesus Christ for their sin problem; the tares have not. The wheat are indwelled with the Holy Spirit; the tares are not. The wheat have come to Christ on the basis of a grace-faith belief system; the tares are trying to come to Christ on the basis of a law-works (or works-righteousness) system. The chart on page 92 highlights the contrasts between the wheat and the tares.

Sadly, the percentage of counterfeit Christians in the Western world outweighs the number of true Christians. In Protestant Great Britain, for example, eighty-five percent of the population is Anglican. Only ten percent of the population actually attends church, and approximately four to five percent of the country's "Christians" are born-again. In France, ninety percent of the population is Roman Catholic. Only two percent of the population attends church, and less than one-half of one percent is born-again. Thus, most of France's "Christians" are tares. In Greece, ninety-eight percent of the population is Greek Orthodox, yet less than one percent of the population is born-again. In short, it is important for a believer to understand that just because someone says he's a Christian, the person might not be a born-again believer sown by Christ, but instead might be a "tare" sown by Satan. Indeed, recognition of this reality is foundational to spiritual discernment.

As an aside, when Evangelical leaders today implore every so-called "Christian"—whether Protestant, Catholic, or Orthodox—to "join hands" for the "cause of Christ," such a plea stands in opposition to the Apostle Paul's admonition in II Cor. 6:14-15: *"Do not be bound together with unbelievers; for what partnership have righteousness and lawlessness, or what fellowship has light with darkness? Or what harmony has Christ with Belial [Satan], or what has a believer in common with an unbeliever?"* Tares are *counterfeits*—sown by Satan—and have no harmony with Christ. Accordingly, any ecumenical "Christian" partnership, because it inevitably includes both wheat and tares, opposes the revealed will of God.

Point of discernment: not everyone who claims to be a Christian is "wheat"—i.e., a true, born-again Christian sown by Jesus Christ. Instead, some are "tares" (counterfeits) sown by Satan. Most of today's Ecumenical Movement consists of tares.

THE MAKE-UP OF CHRISTIANITY TODAY	
"Wheat"	**"Tares"**
True Christians	Counterfeit Christians
Sown by Christ	Sown by Satan
Born-Again	Not Born-Again
Indwelled w/the Holy Spirit	Not indwelled with the H.S.
Saved	Not Saved
Empowered by the Holy Spirit	Empowered by the Flesh
Bear Authentic Fruit	Bear Counterfeit Fruit
Pruned	Cut-Off
"The Bride"	"The Harlot"
Will be Raptured	Will not be Raptured
Grace-Faith Doctrine	Law-Works Doctrine

CHAPTER 20

The Parable of the Sower

In the parable of the Sower we'll discover that the preaching of the gospel message—the Good News that God the Son, Jesus Christ, died for our sins, was buried, and was raised on the third day—will encounter a *continuum* of heart response from those who hear the message. Jesus likens this continuum to four types of soil: hard soil, rocky soil, thorny soil, or good soil. Because this parable describes the response of *every* person who hears the gospel message (including you the reader), it's perhaps the most powerful and convicting parable in the entire Bible.

The parable of the Sower is recorded in three of the Gospels—Matthew, Mark, and Luke. We'll use the Matthew account, where in Matthew 13:1-9 we see Christ's presentation of the story:

> *On that day Jesus went out of the house, and was sitting by the sea. And great multitudes gathered to Him, so that He got into a boat and sat down, and the whole multitude was standing on the beach. And He spoke many things to them in parables, saying, "Behold, the sower went out to sow; and as he sowed, some seeds fell beside the road, and the birds came and ate the seeds. And other seeds fell upon the rocky places, where they did not have much soil; and immediately they sprang up, because they had no depth of soil. But when the sun had risen, they were scorched; and because they had no root, they withered away. And still other seeds fell among the thorns, and the thorns came up and choked them out. And other seeds fell on the good soil, and yielded a crop, some a hundredfold, some sixty, and some thirty. He who has ears, let him hear."*

The parable of the Sower thus pictures a person sowing seed in several directions. Some of the seed falls on a road next to the field. Because this beaten-down soil is so hard, the seed can't enter. Eventually, birds come along and eat the seed. Next, some of the seed falls on rocky soil, where only a shallow layer of dirt covers the rocky areas. In short order the light, initial growth of the crop withers because it can't take root. Still other seed falls on potentially good soil. But the soil contains thorns, which in turn prevents it from yielding much of a crop. Finally, some of the seed falls on good soil—soil which yields a plentiful crop: parts of the soil thirty-fold, parts sixty-fold, and parts a hundred-fold.

In Matthew 13:18-23 Christ explains of the parable:

> *"Hear then the parable of the sower. When anyone hears the word of the kingdom, and does not understand it, the evil one comes and snatches away what has been sown in his heart. This is the one on whom seed was sown beside the road. And the one on whom seed was sown on the rocky places, this is the man who hears the word, and immediately receives it with joy; yet he has no firm root*

> *in himself, but is only temporary, and when affliction or persecution arises because of the word, immediately he falls away. And the one on whom seed was sown among the thorns, this is the man who hears the word, and the worry of the world, and the deceitfulness of riches choke the word, and it becomes unfruitful. And the one on whom seed was sown on the good soil, this is the man who hears the word and understands it; who indeed bears fruit, and brings forth, some a hundredfold, some sixty, and some thirty."*

The "sower" in this parable is Jesus Himself. After His ascension, the "sowers" are the apostles, then those who became Christians through the apostles, then those who hear these post-apostolic Christians, and so on through the centuries—up to our generation. A sower today is one who proclaims the Good News message of salvation from sin through Jesus Christ—the "word of the kingdom."

The **hard heart** does not understand the kingdom (v.19). Moreover, he likely doesn't want to understand it, because it either convicts him of sin (which he doesn't want to relinquish) or challenges him to submit his life to another authority, the Living God (which he doesn't want to do). As a result, this person rejects the message, and Satan's demons gladly come along and snatch away the Good News message from the surface of his heart. They likely do this through demonic whispers such as, "Don't believe that fairy tale," or "You'll have to give up all the vices you love," or "People will laugh at you."

The **rocky heart** receives the message with joy, but because the soil of this person's heart is shallow, the message finds insufficient root (v.21). This person perhaps likes the idea of being a "follower" of Jesus and perhaps living by a Golden Rule, but the person doesn't fully recognize that he is a *sinner* in desperate need of a Savior. The person likely doesn't understand that salvation is *not* a matter, for example, of intellectual assent to "follow" Jesus and his moral precepts. Instead, it is a supernatural transaction from above—being born-again (John 3:1-7)—when one recognizes his sin problem (which separates him from God) and then recognizes that God has provided the only way to bridge the chasm created by personal sin: faith in Christ's finished work on the Cross for man's sin problem. The chasm is bridged *not* by intellectual assent, or good deeds, or rituals, or performance of sacraments, but by a heart which turns to Christ and receives Him by faith alone. Because Christ makes no mention of this soil bearing fruit, we can conclude that the person with a rocky heart is not a saved individual. [Note: In Luke 8:13, Christ states that the person with a rocky heart has no root. Thus, if the seed of the message can't take root, by implication it can't bear fruit.]

The **thorny heart** receives the message by faith—and is born again. We can conclude from the words at the end of the following phrase that this person indeed is a saved individual: *"and the worry of the world, and the deceitfulness of riches choke the word, <u>and it becomes unfruitful</u> [emphasis added]."* The implication is that this person's life at one time had been fruitful for Christ as a result of Christ living through him. Yet the worries of the world and the deceitfulness of riches cause this believer to engage in double-mindedness—to have one foot in Christ's kingdom and one foot in the world. It is not a stretch to say that the majority of American born-again Christians as well as saved Christians in other affluent parts of the world struggle with these two enticements.

When falling prey to the worry of the world or the deceitfulness of riches, the thorny-hearted Christian does not lose his salvation, but he ends up building his Christian life out of "wood, hay, or straw." Paul teaches in II Corinthians 5:9-10 and I Corinthians 3:10-15 that each born-again Christian life will be evaluated by Christ on the basis of faithfulness with however much or little the Lord has called and gifted him to do: *"According to the grace of God which was given to me, as a wise master builder I laid a foundation, and another is building upon it. For no man can lay a foundation other than the one which is laid, which is Jesus Christ. Now if any man builds on the foundation with gold, silver, precious stones, wood, hay, straw, each man's work will become evident; for the day will show it, because it is to be revealed with fire; and the fire will test the quality of each man's work. If any man's work which he has built upon it remains, he shall receive a reward. If any man's work is burned up, he shall suffer loss; but he himself shall be saved, yet as through fire" (I Cor. 3:10-15).*

Paul assures us that there is no condemnation for the person who is in Christ Jesus (Rom. 8:1). Moreover, every Christian will receive an unimaginably grand eternal inheritance (I Pet. 1:3-4). However, Paul also reveals that Christ is going to evaluate every Christian's life at a special awards ceremony in heaven: *"Therefore also we have as our ambition, whether at home or absent, to be pleasing to Him. For we must all appear before the judgment seat of Christ, that each one may be recompensed for his deeds in the body" (II Cor. 5:9-10).* In short, Paul challenges all believers to lay aside the worry of the world and the deceitfulness of riches in order to build a Christian life on a foundation of whole-hearted devotion to Christ.

The **good heart** also receives the message by faith—and is born-again. Indeed, he "hears the word and *understands* it." Because his heart is fertile and receptive to the word of God, he understands the magnificence of the Gods' grace; the magnificence of his salvation; the importance and joy of putting Christ first in his life; the richness of loving Christ with all his heart, mind, strength, and soul; the importance of loving others with the same love that Christ has loved him; the blessing of servanthood, of thinking of others first; and the beauty of humility versus the insidiousness of pride. Moreover, he sees that his old nature needs to decrease and his new nature (Christ in him) needs to increase; he understands that the Christian life is Christ living his life through him; he learns the importance of being a blessing to others, beginning with his wife and children, his extended family, his friends, his employer, his co-workers; and he understands his role of being salt and light in his sphere of influence. Of course, none of this insight comes overnight, but is imparted by the Holy Spirit over time to the person who receives Christ and his Word with a fertile, tender, teachable, trusting heart.

So the questions you and I and every person who hears the Good News of Jesus Christ must ask are these: Which heart am I? Which heart do I want to be? If I'm not the heart I want to be, then what do I need to remove from my life—what snare, what attitudes, what misconceptions? None of us will ever be perfect Christians. But the parable of the Sower is not about perfection; it's about the condition, tenderness, and receptivity of our hearts toward Jesus Christ.

> **Point of discernment**: the Sower parable teaches the Christian that the gospel message encounters a *continuum* of response from those who hear it—from hard-hearted rejection, to shallow profession, to carnal reception, to whole-hearted devotion. It also teaches that the lives of believers in Christ will generate a *continuum* of fruit-bearing—from negligible fruit, to some fruit, to more fruit, to much fruit. These continuums (the range of response to the gospel message and the varying degrees of fruit-bearing among born-again Christians) help to explain why Christianity presents such a wide range of witness to the world—from the superficial, to the ritualistic, to the legalistic, to the worldly, to the genuinely transformed.

VARIOUS HEART RESPONSES TO THE GOSPEL

The "Hard" Soil:
- Anger
- Mockery
- Unbelief
- Disinterest
- Unwillingness to repent

The "Rocky" Soil:
- Intellectual assent / superficial reception / lukewarmness / hollow profession / "belief" on one's own terms, not God's

The "Thorny" Soil:
- Belief / faith (but varying degrees of double-mindedness)

The "Good" (Fertile) Soil:
- Belief / faith / receptive / teachable / devotion / awe

THE PARABLE OF THE SOWER (Matt. 13:3-9, 18-23)

UNBELIEVERS

1. The "hard" soil:
   - The hard, unreceptive heart to the Gospel and the things of God
   - Does not understand Christ's kingdom—and is not interested
   - Satan blinds the mind of this person (II Cor. 4:4)

2. The "rocky" soil:
   - The curious, but shallow heart with regard to the Gospel and the things of God
   - Is interested in Christ's kingdom, but on his terms, not Christ's
   - No supernatural transaction ever takes place; not born again

BELIEVERS

3. The "thorny" soil:
   - The receptive heart to the Gospel, but one which becomes distracted over time by the things of the world
   - The worries of the world and the deceitfulness of riches choke much of this heart's fruitfulness
   - Bears some spiritual fruit, but over time 'becomes unfruitful'
   - Builds his Christian life out of 'perishable' materials: wood, hay, or stubble (I Cor. 3:10-15)

4. The "good" soil:
   - The fertile, receptive heart to the Gospel and the things of God
   - Understands the word of Christ's kingdom; hungers and thirsts for Christ
   - Bears spiritual fruit '100, 60, or 30-fold'
   - Builds his Christian life out of 'imperishable' materials: gold, silver, or precious stones (I Cor. 3:10-15)

THE "THORNY" HEART VS. THE "FERTILE" HEART

Born-again "thorny" heart:

- A convert (loves Jesus)

- A mixed heart (assorted distractions)

- The Holy Spirit is being inhibited in his life

- Satisfied with the 'fire insurance'

- Seeks the approval of men

- Still largely conformed to the world

- Sometimes indistinguishable from the world

- A dimmer light to the world

- Mostly focused on the temporal

- Often trafficking in the world

- Often desires earthly treasures

- Bears little/some spiritual fruit

- Christ is more on the periphery of his life

- Builds his Christian life out of stubble, hay, or wood (i.e., fruit—1, 5, 10-fold??)

Born-again "fertile" heart:

- A disciple (loves Jesus—and wants to learn from Him, grow in Him)

- A single-minded heart (few distractions)

- The Holy Spirit is increasingly being released in his life

- Desires the sanctified life

- Seeks the approval of God

- Being transformed by the renewing of his mind

- Increasingly distinguishable from the world

- A brighter light to the world

- Increasingly focused on the eternal

- Increasingly hungering and thirsting for righteousness

- Desires intimacy with Christ

- Bears more/much spiritual fruit

- Christ is the focal point of his life

- Builds his Christian life out of precious stones, silver, or gold (i.e., fruit—30, 60, 100-fold)

Part V

Examining the Beliefs, Errors, Deceptions and Corrections in Church History

"I also say to you that you are Peter, and upon this rock I will build My church; and the gates of Hades will not overpower it." (Matt. 16:18).

"Go therefore and make disciples of all the nations, baptizing them in the name of the Father and the Son and the Holy Spirit, teaching them to observe all that I commanded you; and lo, I am with you always, even to the end of the age" (Matt. 28:19).

As He was sitting on the Mount of Olives, the disciples came to Him privately, saying, "Tell us, when will these things happen, and what will be the sign of Your coming, and of the end of the age?" (Matt. 24:3). . . . "Now learn the parable from the fig tree: when its branch has already become tender and puts forth its leaves, you know that summer is near; so, you too, when you see all these things, recognize that He is near, right at the door" (Matt. 24:32-33).

Part V continues our presentation of the nature of the Church and the Church Age. In this section the reader will learn what the early church believed; will be introduced to the "summer-fall-winter-spring" pattern of church history; will follow the inexorable downward slide of ever-larger portions of the church into error, deception and unsound doctrine during its first twelve hundred years; will see how far astray church doctrine had gone by 1200 A.D.; will follow the gradual return to sound doctrine in growing parts of the church over the past 800 years; and will receive an overview of present-day Christianity.

CHAPTER 21

What the Scriptures Teach about Deception in the Church

The New Testament teaches that spiritual deception will inevitably enter and buffet the church. Furthermore, it reveals the characteristics of the persons Satan uses for the task. As we will see below, those who infiltrate and deceive the church are identified variously as false teachers, false prophets, false apostles, false Christs, deceitful workers, deceivers, evil men, and imposters. Here are some of the passages.

- *But the Spirit explicitly says that in later times some will fall away from the faith,* ***paying attention to deceitful spirits and doctrines of demons*** *(I Tim. 4:1).*

[Some Christians will fall away from the faith and will knowingly or unknowingly give heed to seducing spirits (demons) and their doctrines. The history of the church is littered with examples of this reality (as we will see in upcoming chapters. Even today, certain parts of Evangelicalism have been seduced by, and engage in, occultic practices.]

- *Beloved, do not believe every spirit, but test the spirits to see whether they are from God,* ***because many false prophets have gone out into the world*** *(I John 4:1).*

[Satan has sent out false prophets into the world. These false prophets proclaim a message which contradicts or impugns all or parts of God's Word. Chapter 38 will reveal how to "test the spirits" to see if they are from God.]

- *But false prophets also arose among the people, just as there will also be* ***false teachers among you, who will secretly introduce destructive heresies****, even denying the Master who bought them, bringing swift destruction upon themselves (II Pet. 2:1).*

[False prophets and false teachers will surreptitiously introduce heresy into gullible, unsuspecting, or inattentive churches. Such churches contrast sharply with the Berean church, which compared all of Paul's teaching with Scripture (Acts 17:10-11).]

- *By this you know the Spirit of God: every spirit that confesses that Jesus Christ has come in the flesh is from God; and* ***every spirit that does not confess Jesus [that He has come in the flesh] is not from God; this is the spirit of the antichrist, of which you have heard that it is coming, and now it is already in the world*** *(I John 4:2-3).*

and

> *For **many deceivers have gone out into the world, those who do not acknowledge Jesus Christ as coming in the flesh.** This is the deceiver and the antichrist (II John 1:7).*

[Says one Evangelical commentator: "The time of the writing of I and II John is important. The Gnostic heresy was prominent. It taught that God was too pure to have anything to do with sinful flesh. Therefore, Gnosticism taught that Jesus could not be God in flesh. It was in this context and against this error that John was writing. Jesus, however, *is* God in flesh and to deny it is the spirit of antichrist."[1]]

- *But I am afraid that, **as the serpent deceived Eve by his craftiness**, your minds will be led astray from the simplicity and purity of devotion to Christ. For if **one comes and preaches another Jesus whom we have not preached, or you receive a different spirit which you have not received, or a different gospel which you have not accepted**, you bear this beautifully (II Cor. 11:3-4).*

[Just as Satan said to Eve, "Indeed, had God said, 'You shall not eat from any tree of the garden,'" Satan will send those who might say something like this to the church: "Indeed, has God said that salvation is by simple faith alone in Jesus Christ? Nonsense! It is by faith, plus your good works!" (i.e., a different gospel). In addition, such false teachers might inform the church that Jesus was not really God, or that Jesus's death on the cross didn't atone for anyone's sins (i.e., a different Jesus). Finally, some might enter the church and teach that one must open himself up to the "hidden or ancient wisdom" of the spirit world (i.e., a different spirit from the Holy Spirit).]

- *For such men are **false apostles, deceitful workers, disguising themselves as apostles of Christ** (II Cor. 11:13).*

[An Apostle of Christ had to have (1) been chosen by Christ personally, (2) witnessed a portion of the life and ministry of Christ and (3) been an eyewitness of the resurrection of Christ (Acts 1:21-22). Paul was personally called by, and witnessed, the resurrected Christ on the Damascus Road (Acts 9:1-8). Thus, Paul, in his second letter to the Corinthian church, branded certain men as "false apostles," men who claimed to be apostles but who had been undermining his teaching as a true apostle. He knew them to be false because they had not been called by Christ personally, had not seen Christ's ministry, and had not been eyewitnesses to His resurrection. Tragically, the Evangelical church has some in its midst today who likewise claim to be apostles of Christ (though none of them meet the Biblical qualifications of an apostle).]

- *No wonder, for even **Satan disguises himself as an angel of light.** Therefore, it is not surprising if **his servants also disguise themselves as servants of righteousness**, whose end will be according to their deeds (II Cor. 11:14-15).*

[Satan disguises himself as an angel of light, even though his goal is to deceive and destroy as many persons as possible (including Christians). Satan's "servants" are persons who either knowingly or naively have embraced demonic deception or demonic doctrine. The devil uses these persons as counterfeit "servants of righteousness." Their "deeds" will likely be humanitarian in nature—and will even appear to be "righteous" to the world. However, these counterfeit servants, because their "righteous deeds" have been done apart from a personal relationship with Christ, will perish in the end.]

- *I felt it necessary to write to you appealing that you contend earnestly for the faith which was once for all handed down to the saints. For certain persons have crept in unnoticed, those who were long beforehand marked out for this condemnation, **ungodly persons who turn the grace of God into licentiousness and deny our only Master and Lord, Jesus Christ** (Jude 1:3-4).*

[Part of the role of Evangelical church leadership is to contend earnestly for the faith. With regard to the two deceptions mentioned in the Jude passage, other Scriptures teach that though the Christian has liberty in Christ, he is not to turn that liberty in to license (I Cor. 8:9-13). Scripture also teaches that because Christ is holy, the believer should strive to become holy (I Peter 1:15-16; Eph. 5:27)—as Christ increases and self decreases in the Christian's life (John 3:30). The church, therefore, in contending for the faith, is to remove anyone in their midst who turns the grace of God into licentiousness or who denies the deity of Christ and His headship over the church.]

- *Enter through the narrow gate; for **the gate is wide and the way is broad that leads to destruction, and there are many who enter through it.** For the gate is small and the way is narrow that leads to life, and there are few who find it (Matt. 7:13-14).*

[Demonic doctrine attempts to convince people that there are many paths to God and many ways of salvation (the "wide" gate). God's Word, however, testifies that only one way of reconciliation with God exists: faith in the finished work of Jesus Christ (the "narrow" gate).]

- *Beware of the **false prophets, who come to you in sheep's clothing, but inwardly are ravenous wolves** (Matt. 7:15).*

[False prophets present themselves as God-fearers and perhaps even as "Christians." But their hearts (as ravenous wolves) are far from Jesus Christ—and their false and destructive message no doubt contradicts the Scriptures.]

- *As He was sitting on the Mount of Olives, the disciples came to Him privately, saying, "Tell us, when will these things happen, and what will be the sign of Your coming, and of the end of the age?" And Jesus answered and said to them, **"See to it that no one misleads you. For many will come in My name, saying, 'I am the Christ,' and will mislead many"** (Matt. 24:3-5).*

[Astonishingly, some persons will even claim to be Christ Himself. In recent times, dozens of people have claimed to be Christ incarnate, including such notables as Krishna Venta, Sun Myung Moon, Jim Jones, Marshall Applewhite (Heaven's Gate cult), and David Koresh.]

- *A little leaven leavens the whole lump of dough* (Gal. 5:9).

[It only takes a small error or deception in the church to derail key ingredients of God's truth. For example, Paul, in the book of Galatians, addresses the error—or "leaven"—of adding "good works" to the gospel of Jesus Christ (Gal. 1:6-9; Galatians 2; Galatians 3). This addition to the gospel destroys the true Biblical gospel.]

- *And even if our gospel is veiled, it is veiled to those who are perishing, in whose case* ***the god of this world has blinded the minds of the unbelieving so that they might not see the light of the gospel of the glory of Christ****, who is the image of God (II Cor. 4:3-4).*

[Satan blinds the minds of the unbelieving so that they cannot understand the truth of the good news of salvation through Jesus Christ.]

- ***I am amazed that you are so quickly deserting Him who called you by the grace of Christ, for a different gospel****, which is really not another; only* ***there are some who are disturbing you and want to distort the gospel of Christ*** *(Gal. 1:6-7).*

[The deception of false teachers, false prophets, and false Apostles always rejects the grace of God in the gospel of Jesus Christ for a different "gospel," one which invariably involves such things as good works, or faith plus good works, or infant baptism, or church membership, or partaking of the sacraments, and so on.]

- *Put on the full armor of God,* ***so that you will be able to stand firm against the schemes of the devil. For our struggle is not against flesh and blood, but against the rulers, against the powers, against the world forces of this darkness, against the spiritual forces of wickedness in the heavenly places.*** *(Eph. 6:11-13).*

[The Apostle Paul exhorts believers to put on the full armor of God in order to stand firm against the wiles of the devil. Throughout Scripture, Satan is shown to be proactive in his work of deception and destruction, employing assorted schemes. Furthermore, it is Satan and his fellow demons, not humans, who are the true enemy of believers.]

- *Be of sober spirit, be on the alert.* ***Your adversary, the devil, prowls around like a roaring lion, seeking someone to devour*** *(I Pet. 5:8).*

[Just as a lion targets the unsuspecting or inattentive animal in a herd, Satan looks for a Christian who is susceptible to deception. This person perhaps is not familiar with sound doctrine or finds himself questioning certain parts of the Bible. Still other Christians might be susceptible to demonic whispers because of their unwillingness to take all of Scripture at face value. In addition, Satan will not hesitate to plant temptation in front of unsuspecting believers in an attempt to derail their faith in Christ or their walks with Christ.]

- *From that time Jesus began to show His disciples that He must go to Jerusalem, and suffer many things from the elders and chief priests and scribes, and be killed, and be raised up on the third day.* ***Peter*** *took Him aside and began to rebuke Him, saying, "God forbid it, Lord! This shall never happen to You." But He turned and said to Peter, "Get behind Me, Satan! You are a stumbling block to Me; for you are not setting your mind on God's interests, but man's"* (Matt. 16:21-23).

[At opportune moments Satan can speak through a person (even a well-meaning Christian) in an effort to cause a believer to stumble. In order to recognize and withstand such attacks, it is vital for believers to grow in their understanding of God's Word and purposes.]

- *Do not be bound together with unbelievers; **for what partnership have righteousness and lawlessness, or what fellowship has light with darkness? Or what harmony has Christ with Belial, or what has a believer in common with an unbeliever?*** (II Cor. 6:14-15).

[Satan can defeat the truth by simply mixing truth with error. One of his principal means of accomplishing this goal is the use of syncretism—in this case, a partnership of believers with non-believers. The Old Testament prophets continually warned the children of Israel of the dangers of making covenants with the unbelieving nations surrounding her, lest Israel become seduced by their beliefs and idolatry (Deut. 7:2; Joshua 23:12-13; I Kings 18:21; Ezra 4:1-3; Ezra 9:1-2, 14). In like manner, the "bride" of Christ (Christ's true church of born-again believers) is not to partner together in ministry endeavors with unbelievers. Specifically, any intra-faith ministry efforts between the Bride ("wheat" sown by Christ) and the Harlot ("tares" sown by Satan)—no matter how well meaning—is forbidden in the Word because of the threat of syncretism. Furthermore, any inter-faith ministry efforts between the Bride and other religions (e.g., Muslims, Hindus, Buddhists) is likewise strictly forbidden. Tragically, some Evangelical churches and ministries blindly do both.]

- ***For the mystery of lawlessness is already at work***; *only he who now restrains will do so until he is taken out of the way.* (II Thess. 2:7).

[The ultimate source of lawlessness is Satan (II Thess. 2:8-10). Satan's efforts to promote lawlessness continue inexorably. Only the restraining influence of the Holy Spirit holds back universal lawlessness (II Thess. 2:1-7).]

Point of discernment: As it did in the first century, the Word of God warns Christians today about the danger of false teachers, false prophets, and false apostles entering into and seducing the church. The Word also warns about false Christs, deceitful workers, deceivers, evil men, and imposters. In short, throughout the New Testament, Christians are exhorted to be alert for error and deception in order to keep false teaching from entering the church. This can only happen when Christians stand on the firm ground of sound doctrine (Acts 17:10-11), which in turn enables them to discern unsound teaching.

THE MESSENGERS AND MESSAGE OF DECEPTION

The messengers of deception
- False teachers
- False prophets
- False apostles
- Deceitful workers
- Deceivers
- Evil men
- Imposters
- Deceitful or seducing spirits

The message of deception
- A different Jesus (not God in the flesh; not God the Son)
- A different Gospel (not salvation by faith alone in Christ alone)
- A broad way of salvation (universalism; many ways to God)
- A different spirit (legalism, license, syncretism, ecumenical)
- A different ethic (immorality, licentiousness, worldliness, compromise)
- Demonic doctrine rather than Biblical doctrine
- Someone proclaiming: "I am the Christ"
- The Satanic whisper: "Indeed, has God said . . .?"

THE MESSENGERS AND MESSAGE OF ERROR

The messengers of error
- Teachers who handle God's Word inaccurately

The message of error
- Unsound doctrine

CHAPTER 22

Christian Doctrine at the End of Paul's Ministry

I solemnly charge you in the presence of God and of Christ Jesus, who is to judge the living and the dead, and by His appearing and His kingdom: preach the word; be ready in season and out of season; reprove, rebuke, exhort, with great patience and instruction. For the time will come when they will not endure sound doctrine; but wanting to have their ears tickled, they will accumulate for themselves teachers in accordance to their own desires, and will turn away their ears from the truth and will turn aside to myths (II Tim. 4:1-4).

One of the best ways to know and recognize sound doctrine—and to hold firm to it—is to know what the early church believed. The following list summarizes what the apostles and the first generation of Christians wrote, believed and taught:

- The divine inspiration of Scripture (i.e., the Old Testament and the Apostles' teaching) (I Tim. 3:16)
- The inerrancy of Scripture (Matt. 5:18)
- A literal interpretation of Scripture, consistently applied (i.e., taking Scripture's words and figures of speech in their plain, normal sense)
- The sole authority of Scripture
- The power of Scripture ("the power of God unto salvation" and "living and active, sharper than a two-edged sword")
- The sufficiency of Scripture (I Tim. 3:16-17; Heb. 4:12)
- The free will of man (e.g., Joshua 24:15)
- Man's inherited and inherent sin nature (Ps. 51:5)
- Man's fallen nature: God's image in man is defaced, but not erased
- The universality of man's sin problem (Rom. 3:23)
- The deity of Jesus Christ—God in the flesh (John 1:1-18, et.al.)
- Christ's substitutionary atonement for mankind's sins
- The scope of Christ's atoning sacrifice: unlimited (i.e., for all mankind)
- The bodily resurrection of Christ
- The post-resurrection appearances of Christ

- The ascension of Christ back into heaven
- The necessity of the new birth (John 3:1-8)
- Salvation by faith alone in Christ alone (Rom. 3:21-28; Gal. 2:16; Acts 4:12; et.al.)
- Baptism by submersion (subsequent to salvation) as a public acknowledgment of faith in Jesus Christ (but having no efficacy in salvation)
- The future second coming of Christ to set up His Messianic kingdom on earth for a thousand years—a belief known as "Chiliasm."
- The reality of heaven and hell
- The Lord's supper as a remembrance of Christ's work on the Cross
- The headship of Christ over the church
- The Church as a spiritual kingdom in the hearts of Jewish and Gentile born-again believers, male and female
- The priesthood of all believers (I Pet. 2:4-9)
- Every believer having a spiritual gift for the common good of the body of Christ
- A local church leadership structure of spiritually-mature elders and deacons (Phil. 1:1; I Tim. 3:1-13)—elders tending to the body's spiritual needs, deacons to the body's temporal needs (Acts 6:1-4)

> **Point of Discernment:** Christian doctrine at the end of Paul's ministry and the doctrines commonly held by the first two generations of Christians should set the benchmark for sound doctrine throughout church history, including today. *Any deviation from first century doctrine should have set off alarms in the church over the centuries—and should set off alarms today.* Unfortunately, as we will see in the next four chapters, error and deception inexorably entered the church during its first twelve hundred years.

Note: The timing of the Rapture of the Church apparently was not as clearly understood or articulated in early church writings. Moreover, Daniel 12:8-9 indicates that the prophesied end-times events, including the timing of the Rapture, would not come into focus until these events drew near. The nearness of these events will be examined in Chapter 40. In addition, Christ's revelation of a pre-tribulation Rapture in the Olivet Discourse will be discussed in Appendix B.

Additional Note: the Old Testament scriptures, as well as the letters written by the Apostles, were *read* to the churches. This provides us with a clue that the Scriptures and letters were to be taken at *face value* and could be readily understood by hearers. First century hearers could not be expected to try to find some sort of "hidden meaning" or sophisticated allegory in what they heard—nor should we today.

CHAPTER 23

The Seven Churches of Revelation 2 & 3

I, John, your brother and fellow partaker in the tribulation and kingdom and perseverance which are in Jesus, was on the island called Patmos because of the word of God and the testimony of Jesus. I was in the Spirit on the Lord's day, and I heard behind me a loud voice like the sound of a trumpet, saying, "Write in a book what you see, and send it to the seven churches: to Ephesus and to Smyrna and to Pergamum and to Thyatira and to Sardis and to Philadelphia and to Laodicea (Rev. 1:9-11)."

In approximately 95 A.D. our resurrected Lord gave the Apostle John seven messages to be given to the fledgling church—one for each of seven designated churches in "Asia" (western Turkey). These messages described the spiritual condition of Christendom near the end of the first century, approximately sixty-five years after the Lord's resurrection and approximately thirty-five to forty years after the founding of these churches. The seven churches were predominately Gentile churches.

Each of the messages contains six elements: (1) a figurative description of Christ, who in each message is also identified as the one addressing the church; (2) a commendation (if any) for the church being addressed; (3) a rebuke (if any) of the church being addressed; (4) an exhortation for the church being addressed; (5) a promise from the Lord to believers (called "overcomers" in these messages); and (6) a challenge to hear (and take to heart) what the Holy Spirit is saying.

Although some Bible teachers contend that these seven messages also correspond to chronological eras of Christendom during the period of time between the first and second advents of Christ, such is not the case. Rather, the primary purpose of these messages is to describe the spiritual condition of the whole of Christendom at any point in time between the first and second advents of Christ. It can also be stated that the spiritual condition of twenty-first century Christendom can be readily seen in the strengths and weaknesses of these seven first century churches. Indeed, *all seven of these churches exist today throughout Christianity in type or substance*, and it can be asserted that Chapters 2 and 3 of Revelation help explain, to both critics and adherents alike, why Christendom has generated such a wide spectrum of witness over the past twenty centuries—from the transformed lives of some within its ranks to the more legalistic, worldly, and hypocritical lives of others.

[Note: it is imperative that the reader of Chapters 2 and 3 of Revelation recognize that Christ is describing the spiritual condition of *all* of Christianity in these seven messages. He is *not* simply describing the condition of the true Church (i.e., born-again believers in Jesus Christ). It is also imperative to understand, as has previously been stated, that "Christendom" (Christianity as a whole) at the end of the first century contained both born-again Christians (the "wheat" of Matt.

13:37-38) and counterfeit Christians (the "tares" of Matt. 13:38-39). Thus, when Jesus states in Revelation 3:20, *"Behold, I stand at the door and knock; if anyone hears My voice and opens the door, I will come in to him and will dine with him, and he with Me,"* He indeed is giving a gospel invitation. The lukewarm Laodicean church, the church to whom Christ gives the invitation (Rev. 3:14-22), was filled with "tares"—those who called themselves "Christian" but who in fact were not saved (Rev. 3:16, 18-19). To be sure, Christ in Revelation 3:20 describes His universal wooing of the sinner (in this case, those at Laodicea who were not yet born again), which encourages every sinner to open the door of his heart to Christ.]

Summaries of the Seven Churches . . . .

Summary of the church (and heart) at **Ephesus**: a persevering, doctrinally-sound, self-sufficient (rather than Christ-dependent) church, which no longer seeks Christ and His kingdom first, which no longer hungers and thirsts for Christ above all else, and which no longer has intimacy with Christ. This church, knowingly or unknowingly, has probably fallen into a pattern of prayerlessness and perhaps even legalism. This church is likely operating in the power of the flesh rather than the Spirit, and the Holy Spirit is being quenched.

Summary of the church (and heart) at **Smyrna**: a faithful, dependent, persecuted (but spiritually rich) church, which due to the fires of testing, persecution, and even martyrdom has great intimacy with Christ. [Note: The church at Smyrna reminds us of today's persecuted churches in China, Iran, the Sudan, and elsewhere.]

Summary of the church (and heart) at **Pergamum**: a Christ-proclaiming, steadfast church (despite Satanic surroundings), which nevertheless tolerates licentiousness and spiritual syncretism within its ranks. This church is being influenced by the world and the world's belief systems as much as it is by the Word. Some (if not many) in this church are worldly or carnal—and are grieving the Holy Spirit. Others in this church are attempting to marry the Word of God with the philosophies of men—and are quenching the Holy Spirit.

Summary of the church (and heart) at **Thyatira**: a loving, serving, steadfast, and persevering church, which nevertheless tolerates prophetic revelation that contradicts the Word of God. This church lacks Biblical discernment and some in the church are more enamored with extra-biblical revelation than with the living and active Word of God. To its discredit, this church even allows occult teaching and practices within its ranks ("the deep things of Satan"). [Note: the church at Thyatira exists today through the various strains of the "Prophetic Movement" and the New Apostolic Reformation. In addition, churches who countenance the practice of being "slain in the Spirit" are unknowingly allowing the Hindu (and demonic) practice of Shaktipat in their midst.]

Summary of the church (and heart) at **Sardis**: an apostate church which thinks it is alive but is dead spiritually. Though it calls itself "Christian," this church has no personal relationship with Christ. It is dead because the Holy Spirit does not indwell the persons at this church (with the exception of a few—

Rev. 3:4). This church contains many modern-day Pharisees—those who attempt to be rightly-related to God on the basis of ritual and good deeds rather than on new birth by faith alone in Jesus Christ. Salvation in this church is works-based rather than faith-based. It is a church permeated with false doctrine, and it is a church filled with tares (counterfeit Christians). [Note: the church of Sardis reminds us today of the Roman Catholic and Eastern Orthodox churches—both of whom have a name (and outward impression) of being alive, but who are dead (because they preach a false gospel of faith plus works for salvation—the Galatian error).]

Summary of the church (and heart) at **Philadelphia**: a steadfast, dependent, humble, faithful, evangelistic church which is used of God to go into the world with the gospel of Jesus Christ. This church, because it has little strength, is empowered richly by the Holy Spirit and has great intimacy with Christ. [Note: the church at Philadelphia reminds us of the churches around the world who preach and teach the word of God accurately and faithfully—and who send out missionaries to make disciples of all nations.]

Summary of the church (and heart) at **Laodicea**: an apostate church which attempts to have a relationship with Christ on its own terms rather than God's terms. It is apostate and lukewarm because the Holy Spirit does not indwell the persons at this church. This church contains modern-day Sadducees—those who deny many or all of the core beliefs of the Christian faith: the inerrancy of Scripture; the virgin birth of Christ; the Deity of Christ; the Resurrection of Christ; and the necessity of the new birth, among others. Salvation in this church is either works-based or universalism-based, rather than faith-based. It is a church filled with false doctrine, and it is a church filled with tares (counterfeit Christians). [Note: the church at Laodicea reminds us of the liberal Protestant movement today, which for the most part teaches a social gospel rather that the salvation gospel of Jesus Christ. It is a movement devoid of the Holy Spirit.]

SUMMARY OF CHRIST'S COMMENDATIONS

- Your good deeds (empowered by Christ)
- Your diligent toil for Christ
- Your sound doctrine
- Your abhorrence of those who practice evil
- Your discernment of false teaching
- Your endurance for the sake of Christ
- Your perseverance for the sake of Christ
- Your refusal to grow weary
- Your affliction for the cause of Christ
- Your richness in Spirit
- Your perseverance in the midst of persecution
- Your holding fast to belief in Christ despite persecution
- Your refusal to deny Christ in the midst of persecution
- Your demonstration of Christ's love to others
- Your walk by faith
- Your service to others
- Your increasing amount of service and good deeds
- Your rejection of extra-biblical revelation
- Your rejection of the deep things of Satan
- Your remaining steadfast in the faith
- Your having little strength

SUMMARY OF CHRIST'S REBUKES

- Your leaving your First Love (Jesus)
- Your tolerance of moral compromise and worldliness
- Your tolerance of spiritual compromise
- Your tolerance of spiritual syncretism
- Your tolerance of extra-biblical revelation
- Your tolerance of the so-called deep things of Satan (demonic-occultic teachings and practices)
- Your assumption that you are alive spiritually, when in reality you are dead
- Your lukewarm brand of Christianity

CHAPTER 24

The Summer-Fall-Winter-Spring Pattern of Church History:

The Parable of the Fig Tree—and the Sign of the End of the Age (Matthew 24:32-35)

> *³²"Now learn the parable from the fig tree: when its branch has already become tender, and puts forth its leaves, you know that summer is near; ³³even so you too, when you see all these things, recognize that He is near, right at the door. ³⁴Truly I say to you, this generation will not pass away until all these things take place. ³⁵Heaven and earth will pass away, but My words shall not pass away.*

In the Parable of the Fig Tree, Jesus informs the Christian how to discern when the "season" of His return is near: Just as a person knows that summer is near when leaves begin to burst forth in spring, so too a person can know that Christ's return is near when the "leaves" of world events begin to burst forth in ways which could allow for a literal fulfillment of the End-Times prophecies—including the death tolls to which Christ alludes when He states in Matthew 24:22a: *"and unless those days had been cut short, no life would have been saved"*).

In 1948, Israel once again became a nation. In the 1950s and 1960s, the nightmare of potential nuclear holocaust—and a potential *literal* fulfillment of the death tolls depicted in the Revelation—became a reality with the collective warhead and I.C.B.M capability of the United States and the Soviet Union. In 1967, Israel once again gained possession of Jerusalem. The 1970s saw the beginning of legalized abortion (Isa. 5:20) and the casting off of sexual restraint. The 1980s saw an explosion of pornography, the increasing acceptance of homosexuality and lesbianism as an "alternative lifestyle," global communications capabilities, and the emergence of the AIDS epidemic. The 1990s saw the maturation of global satellite TV (Rev. 13:8), the "safe sex" campaign, the threat of Islamic nuclear proliferation, microchip technology implanted into animals, and the global Internet. The twenty-first century has already seen the drive in the West to legalize same-sex marriage (Lev. 18:23), the revelation (in 2001) that China has eleven nuclear-tipped I.C.B.M.'s aimed at major U.S. cities, the sobering reality of radical Islam (and its call for the elimination of Israel and the Western world), the efforts of Iran to develop nuclear weapons, and the much publicized efforts of North Korea to test and perfect I.C.B.M.'s which could reach the west coast of the United States. Dozens of other "leaves" could be listed.

With the benefit of 20/20 hindsight it is reasonable to suggest that Jesus has in mind with this Fig Tree parable a "summer-fall-winter-spring" picture of the *entirety* of church history. Indeed, any big-picture overview of church history from today's twenty-first century perspective supports this premise. The Day of Pentecost—when Peter and the 120 are filled with the Holy Spirit and the 3,000 are "on fire" for Christ—thus represents the first hour of "summer" in Christ's parable. Next, given that nearly 2,000 years of church history has taken place and that the destruction of the Jerusalem temple took place forty years after Pentecost (or one-fiftieth into a 2,000-year church history), Titus's destruction of the temple in 70 A.D. thus occurs at the end of the first week of "summer" in this parable. During the next 240 years of church history a significant portion of the church is still largely hungering for and proclaiming Christ—hot, if you will, and alive in the Holy Spirit—though even this portion of the church begins to decrease in fervor as "summer" ends.

By 500 A.D., after Constantine's "Christianization" of the Roman Empire and the subsequent institutionalization of the church, the church enters into the cooler weather of "fall," if you will, and a period of an increasingly quenched Holy Spirit. The reality and efficacy of the "priesthood of all believers" diminishes substantially. By the time 1000 A.D. arrives, most of the church has entered into the long nights and frigid cold of "winter"—and a time of near lifelessness in the church. Five hundred years later, however, during the Reformation, the church age moves into early "springtime," and new life is breathed into parts of the church. A remnant of true believers once again begins to populate the church both in number and zeal.

Over these past five hundred years a significant portion of the church has grown ever warmer as "summer" approaches. In addition, the gospel moved into the Western Hemisphere, Africa, Asia, and recently into the Islamic Middle East. The "mustard seed" (Christianity) in the Parable of the Mustard Seed has now become the full-grown plant prophesied by Jesus nearly 2,000 years ago. To be sure, today's underground church in China is radically on fire for Christ and is probably the most vivid portrait of the early church seen by Christendom since the first century. During the past sixty years a significant number of Evangelical churches in America have seen the number of dedicated servant-believers increase dramatically. In certain parts of Christendom the reality of the priesthood of all believers once again has emerged, as millions of born-again Christians today use their spiritual gifts in the Body of Christ. As an aside, this easily recognizable "summer-fall-winter-spring" pattern to church history also points us to the conclusion that the springtime "leaves" of world events indeed now seem to be bursting forth in anticipation to Christ's coming at the end of "spring."

In the next chapter we'll trace the downward slide of a large portion of the church into error and deception as the church age moves from the beginning of "summer" into the middle of "winter."

CHAPTER 25

Downward Trends during the Church's First Twelve Hundred Years

> Summary of the list below: The systematic falling away of an increasing percentage of the church from its God-given first century mandate (given in the New Testament) into unsound doctrine, clericalism, institutionalism, secularism, and heresy. The result—after twelve hundred years—is a grand, counterfeit "Christian" church. Only a small remnant of born-again Christians remains.

- The entrance of the "Galatian error" into the early church—the teaching that salvation is not by faith alone in Christ alone, but by faith in Christ plus works (c. 54 A.D.). These "Judaizers" who attacked the Galatian church also represent the first Scriptural evidence of "tares" (counterfeit Christians sown by Satan) infiltrating the early church.
  [The Galatian error persists today in the Roman Catholic and Eastern Orthodox churches]

- The infiltration of additional doctrinal error into the early church by the end of the first century—including acceptance of moral license and spiritual syncretism (the church at Pergamum); toleration of extra-Biblical revelation (the church at Thyatira); and belief in works-based salvation (the church at Sardis) (c. 95 A.D.).
  [All of these errors persist today]

Note: All statements below stem from Bruce Shelley's 1982 book, *Church History in Plain Language*.[1]

- The development of the office of pastor in the local church—apparently promoted by Ignatius of Antioch (c. 110 A.D.)—thus superseding the Biblical pattern of elders and deacons in each local church.[2]
  [The beginning of clericalism]

- The establishment of the office of town bishop to oversee all local churches in a jurisdiction (c. 180 A.D.)[3]
  [The beginning of the episcopacy (i.e., the rule and government of the church by bishops); the beginning of a hierarchy of professional priests; and the beginning of the institutionalization of the church]

- The development by Origen of an "allegorical" method of interpreting Scripture (c. 230 A.D.). For Origen, there were "three levels of meaning in the Bible; the literal sense; the moral application to the soul; and the allegorical or spiritual sense, which refers to the mysteries of the Christian faith."[4]

[Heretofore, all Scripture had been taken at face value]

- The intense persecution of the church in 249-251 A.D., causing some of the persecuted to fall away from confessing Christ. Those who fell away in the face of martyrdom—even if one was a true believer—were now excluded from the church. Declared Bishop Cyprian of Carthage: "Outside the church there is no salvation."[5]

   [The increasing power of the bishops in the Western church over the "laity"—and the solidification of today's false doctrine in Catholic circles that there is no salvation outside of the Roman Catholic Church]

- The development of the policy of readmission to the church through "penance" (sorrow for sin)—so that sinners could be allowed to return to the Lord's Supper (c. 260 A.D.). A bishop could now extend forgiveness to the fallen, a practice nowhere taught in the New Testament.

- The conversion of the Roman Emperor, Constantine, to Christianity (312 A.D.)

   [The beginning of the secularization of the church]

- The eventual "conversion" of the Roman Empire to Christianity by Emperor Theodosius' imperial command (380 A.D.)

   [The beginning of the marriage of the sacred and the secular—as well as the marriage of the Roman Church and the Roman Empire]

- The endorsement of the efficacy of "sacrament Christianity" by Augustine, administered to the faithful by an ordained priest—an efficacy and practice nowhere taught in the New Testament

- The promotion by Augustine of the doctrine of predestination (c.400 A.D.), the teaching that God has pre-determined unconditionally those He will save.

   [Prior to Augustine all major church leaders believed in the free-will decision of each person to receive or reject Christ for salvation upon hearing the gospel message]

- The solidification of amillennialism as official church doctrine as a result of Augustine's *City of God* (c. 415 A.D.)

   [For the first three centuries church leaders had been premillennial, the teaching that Christ would return bodily to the earth (with all resurrected believers) to rule the earth from Jerusalem for a thousand years.]

- The beginnings of the Roman Papacy—through Bishop Leo of Rome, 455 A.D.—as a result of (1) the increasingly complex church structure during the third and fourth centuries, (2) the increased authority of Church councils, and (3) the authority of certain bishops over other bishops (because of the size and influence of four cities: Rome, Constantinople, Antioch, and Alexandria). In 451 A.D. at Chalcedon, a gathering of leading church bishops gave the bishop of Constantinople, as bishop of the "new Rome," authority equal to Leo's. This latter act was the genesis of the eventual split between the Roman Catholic Church and the Eastern Orthodox Church in 1054 A.D.[6]

- The solidification of additional core Catholic (and non-biblical) doctrine under Pope Gregory (590-604 A.D.): (1) winning merit with God through good works; (2) atonement for personal sins through penance (i.e., by such meritorious works as almsgiving, ascetic practices, and prayers at all hours of the day); (3) prayers to the saints of the Catholic church; (4) devotion to holy relics; (5) the intermediate state of Purgatory, where those with minor sins spend a season after death; and (6) the divine power of the Eucharist, which is offered by a priest for the sins of men.[7]

- The Holy Roman Empire begun by Charlemagne in 768 A.D. (and lasting in various forms until 1806 A.D.): the idea of church and state in harmonious interplay—with church and state being two equal aspects of an earthly "Christian" Empire[8] (versus Christ's admonition in John 18:36: *"My kingdom is not of this world"*).

- The rise of the Papal Monarchy (910–1198 A.D.)—and Pope Gregory's ideal of a Christian commonwealth under papal control. Gregory insisted (in 1073 A.D.) that church and state are not equal, but that the spiritual power is supreme over the temporal.[9]

    [Such papal authority over the state clearly foreshadows the attempted clerical authority of the end-times harlot church over the Antichrist's political empire, where the harlot is pictured as "riding" the beast (the Antichrist's empire) (Revelation 17). The Antichrist will countenance this charade for a time, but will eventually "devour" (slaughter) the harlot church (Rev. 17:16), apparently during the second half of the tribulation.]

- Pope Innocent III—and the height of Papal worldly power and arrogance (1198 – 1216 A.D.): the Pope is the judge of the world "set between God and man, below God and above man."[10]

    [Such a belief by Innocent III is utter heresy (vs. the priesthood of all believers— I Peter 2:4-5, 9-10). To be sure, Christ is the head of the church—Eph. 5:23, and the judge of the world—II Tim. 4:1, et.al.]

CHAPTER 26

The False Church in 1200 A.D.

In addition to its false teaching that faith alone in Christ alone was not sufficient for salvation (vs. Romans 1-8), the Roman Catholic Church over time developed a means by which other unbiblical teachings could be added to its beliefs and practices on the basis of "Church authority."

Says one team of Evangelical authors: "Examples of how such tradition works to deny what the Protestant Bible teaches are seen in the following list of dogmas and practices that have no biblical justification (as even some Catholics confess), and yet are accepted as having divine authority. Collectively these dates are given by several sources, are approximate, and refer to the time that such practices were either (1) first introduced, (2) formulated, (3) adopted by council, or (4) proclaimed by a pope."[1]

The Progression of Roman Catholicism Dogmas and Practices:

310 – the beginning of prayers for the dead

375 – the beginning of the worship of saints

394 – the adoption of the Mass

431 – the beginning of the worship of Mary, although it was not popularized for another 350 years

593 – the introduction of the doctrine of purgatory

606 – the taking root of the doctrine of papal supremacy

650 – the beginning of feasts in honor of the Virgin Mary

750 – the first incident of the pope assuming temporal power

787 – the beginning of the worship of images and relics

819 – the first observation of the Feast of Assumption [the belief that God assumed (carried) the body of Mary into heaven after her death]

850 – the invention of holy water

965 – the blessing of the bells

983 – the beginning of the canonization of saints

998 – the beginning of lent, advent, and abstinence of meat on Fridays

1003 – the introduction of the feasts for the dead

1074 – the introduction of the celibacy of the priesthood

- 1076 – the introduction of the concept of papal infallibility
- 1090 – the beginning of the use of prayer beads (cf. the Rosary)
- 1115 – the introduction of the practice of confession
- 1140 – the introduction of the doctrine of "seven sacraments"
- 1195 – the beginning of the sale of indulgences

None of these dogmas and practices are biblical. Indeed, to most born-again Christians such beliefs and practices not only seem nonsensical, but carry the obvious fingerprint of deception.

Point of discernment: Notice how far the Roman Catholic church, by 1200 A.D., had drifted from the core beliefs of the apostolic Church (Chapter 22).

Additional point of discernment: In Revelation 3:1 the resurrected Jesus Christ rebuked the church at Sardis as follows: *"I know your deeds, that you have a name that you are alive, but you are dead."* When Christ gave His seven messages to the Apostle John on the isle of Patmos, it seems reasonable to conclude that the seven churches of Revelation 2 and 3 were relatively equal in either size or influence—though some of the seven, including Sardis, had either stumbled or ventured away from Christ. By 1200 A.D., the ultimate successor to the "Sardis" church had become the Roman Catholic church. Had Christ penned a letter to the Roman Catholic church in 1200 A.D., He again would have said: *"I know you deeds, that you have a name that you are alive, but you are dead."* Unfortunately, the Roman church in 1200 A.D. had overwhelmed the offspring of the other six churches of Revelation 2 and 3 in both size and influence (though the six still existed). Today, five hundred years after the Protestant Reformation, the successors of these six churches have regained much of their footing relative to the Roman Catholic church (though the Roman church is still the largest in numerically). [Note: the Eastern Orthodox church is likewise a successor of the church at Sardis.] See the charts on pp. 124-126.

Sadly, error and deception in Catholic doctrine and practice continued to march on after 1200 A.D.:[2]

- 1215 – the beginning of the dogma of transubstantiation (by Pope Innocent III)
- 1216 – the acceptance of auricular confession of sins to a priest
- 1220 – the acceptance of holy water
- 1226 – the beginning of the elevation and adoration of the wafer
- 1274 – the confirmation of Purgatory as official doctrine at the Second Council of Lyons

1303 – the proclamation of the Roman Catholic Church as the only true Church where salvation can be found

1316 – the introduction of the Ava Maria

1414 – the declaration that priests alone can say the mass and partake of the wine

1438 – the official acceptance of Purgatory and the seven sacraments by the Council of Florence

1546 – the placing of Roman tradition and the Apocrypha on the same level as Scripture by the Council of Trent

1547 – the rejection of salvation by faith alone by the Council of Trent—and the upholding of salvation by faith-works

1562 – the acceptance of the Mass as a propitiatory offering

1854 – the announcement and acceptance by Pope Pius IX of the immaculate conception of the Virgin Mary

1870 – the proclamation by Vatican I of Papal infallibility

1950 – the proclamation by Pope Pius XII of the bodily assumption and personal corporeal presence of the Virgin Mary in heaven

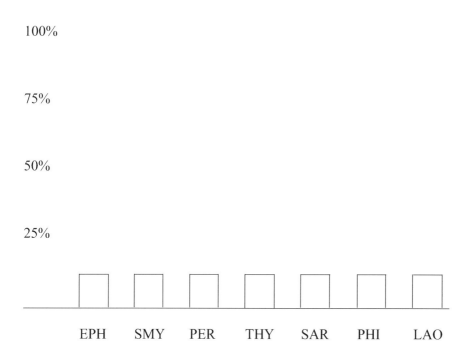

In 95 A.D., the seven archetypical churches of Revelation 2 & 3 readily embody the salient characteristics (including strengths and weaknesses) of Christianity that will exist throughout the inter-advent Age. At this point, each church is likely equal in its representation of Christianity to the world—whether that witness be a true faith, a carnal faith, a gullible faith, or a name-only, non-existent faith.

OFFSPRING OF THE SEVEN CHURCHES (1200 A.D.)

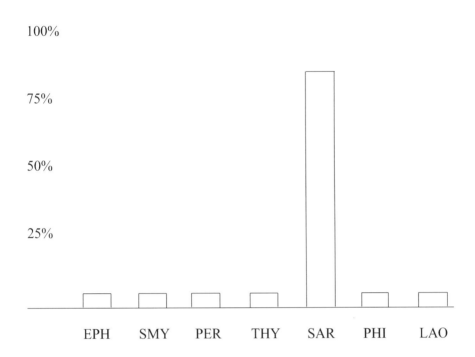

By 1200 A.D., the apostate, dead Roman Catholic Church (the "Sardis" church) dominates Christianity, perhaps representing 85% of Christendom at the time. The other six archetypical churches have a minimal presence.

OFFSPRING OF THE SEVEN CHURCHES (2020 A.D.)

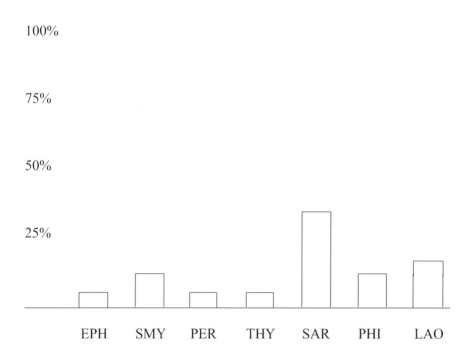

Today, the apostate Roman Catholic and Eastern Orthodox Churches ("Sardis") and the apostate liberal Protestant churches ("Laodecia") perhaps represent 50% of Christendom throughout the world. The persecuted church ("Smyrna") and the faithful church ("Philadelphia") perhaps represent 25% of Christendom. The other three archetypical churches—"Ephesus," "Pergamum," and "Thyatira"—have a smaller witness. The "Sardis" and "Laodecian" churches for the most part consist of tares; the "Ephesian," "Smyra," "Pergamum," "Thyatira," and "Philadelphia" churches largely consist of wheat. It is this writer's view that Christendom (worldwide) in 2020 likely contains 50% wheat and 50% tares. This percentage would be consistent with the Parable of the Ten Virgins (Matt. 25:1-13). [Note: Christendom in the Western world, however, likely contains no more than 10% wheat. In contrast, the percentage of wheat in Chinese Christendom is likely as high as 90%.]

CHAPTER 27

Upward Trends During the Next Eight Hundred Years

> Summary of the list below: The gradual restoration of increasing portions of Christianity to its God-given first-century mandate (laid out in the New Testament)—and away from heresy, secularism, institutionalism, clericalism, and unsound doctrine.

- The decline of the Papacy (1296-1505), beginning in 1296 when King Edward I of England and King Philip in France outmaneuvered Pope Boniface VIII in a battle over taxation—and ending in 1503 after the papacy of the grossly immoral Alexander VI. Hereafter, some Christians began to think in terms of national churches rather than a universal Catholic Church.[1]

- The beginnings of protest: John Wyclif (1378) and John Hus (1412). Wyclif emphasized the spiritual freedom of the believer and the personal relationship between God and man, making the mediating priesthood and the sacrificial masses of the medieval church unnecessary. Wyclif also insisted that the pope should be the shepherd of the flock and the preacher who brings men to Christ, rather than a master of men by way of political or temporal power. Wyclif argued that Christ alone is head of the church not the pope—and that the church is a unity that knows nothing of papal primacies, hierarchies, or sects of monks, friars, and priests. In addition, Wyclif asserted the right of every man to examine the Scriptures for himself. Finally, Wyclif rejected the traditional Roman Catholic doctrine of transubstantiation.[2]

- The inventions of the printing press and moveable type (mid-1400s)—and William Tyndale's Bible (1526): the beginning of God's Word being disseminated to the laity

- The Protestant Reformation (initiated by Martin Luther on October 31, 1517), including: (1) justification by faith alone (rather than faith plus works); (2) the authority of Scripture alone (rather than the proclamations of the popes or councils of the Catholic Church); and (3) the priesthood of all believers (rather than a professional priesthood).[3]

- Martin Luther's attacks on the papacy and Rome's sacramental system.

- The radical protest of the Anabaptists (1525): the call for a return to believer's baptism and for the separation of church and state.[4]

- John Calvin's Reformed Theology (1536) and its rejection of several key Roman Catholic beliefs, including the Roman Church's belief in salvation by faith plus works, its definition of "justification," its belief that it is the only true church, its belief that the pope has authority over the church by direct apostolic succession from Peter, its belief that the pope when speaking *ex cathedra* can never err, and its belief that it has the final say regarding any interpretation of Scripture.[5]

- Jacobus (James) Arminius's efforts to reform Calvin's deterministic theology (c. 1609)—and the beginnings of Arminianism.

- The development of Protestant national churches in lieu of the Roman Catholic Church: i.e., the German Lutheran Church, the Dutch Reformed Church, the English Anglican Church, and others—along with the gradual development of denominations (rather than national churches) over the next century, particularly in the religiously-diverse American colonies.[6]

- The development of Protestant "Covenant Theology" by Johannes Cocceius in 1648. Covenant Theology was (and is) an attempt by theologians to provide an "overarching, unifying theme" to the Bible—in this case, on the basis of two covenants: a covenant of works and a covenant of grace. Some Covenant theologians add a third covenant—the covenant of redemption. The importance of Covenant Theology at this point in the church age is its steadfast emphasis on a salvation transaction based on faith alone (rather than the faith plus works heresy of the Catholic Church).

- The re-emergence of a literal hermeneutic in Protestant theology (vs. the dual hermeneutic of Origen and the Catholic, Orthodox, and Reformation Protestant churches) by such men as Joseph Mede (1586-1638), Increase Mather (1639-1723), Cotton Mather (1663-1728), Morgan Edwards (1722-1792), and Robert Haldane (1764-1842). Among other things, this literal hermeneutic—consistently applied to the words and figures of speech in Scripture—began the restoration of premillennialism to a growing portion of the Protestant church. [Note: to this writer, the re-emergence of a literal hermeneutic, consistently applied, is nothing less than an unrecognized or de facto *second* Protestant Reformation]

- The Great Awakening in America (1720-1740)—and the call to personal conversion (led by Jonathan Edwards and America's first mass evangelist, George Whitefield).

- The British Isles revival led by John Wesley, featuring Wesley's passion for the conversion of the lost through the preaching of the gospel to all (1739-1789). Also, Wesley's rejection of the Reformation doctrine of predestination—believing instead that God longs for the salvation of all men and that men have enough freedom of will to choose or refuse divine grace, thus opening the door for today's moderate Calvinism and moderate Arminianism as Biblical alternatives to the Reformation's five-point Calvinism.

- The development of Protestant "Dispensational Theology" (progressively refined by Pierre Poiret [1687], John Edwards [1699], Isaac Watts [c.1720], and J. N. Darby [c.1840]—and popularized by C. I. Scofield [c.1900]).

- J.N. Darby's teaching that Israel and the true Church are separate entities—and his repudiation of "Replacement Theology." [Replacement Theology teaches (erroneously) that, because Israel crucified her Messiah, God has now given all of Israel's Covenant promises to the Church.]

- The re-emergence of premillennialism (in some Protestant circles) during the eighteenth and nineteenth centuries—including, in the 20th century, "dispensational premillennialism" (led by Dallas Seminary).

- The late-nineteenth century prophecy conferences in the U.S. and England, causing some in the Church to be alert for the return of Christ—and causing many others to have a renewed interest in prophetic Scripture. Some of the conferences featured speakers who saw in Scripture that Jews around the world would eventually be regathered into their land. This regathering indeed soon began (in the early twentieth century) and even saw Israel, after nineteen hundred years of dispersion, once again became a nation.

- The American and European missions movement: taking the Gospel of Christ to unreached parts of the world

- The rapid proliferation of Bible study resources (printed in English) during the twentieth century—including study Bibles, commentaries, devotionals, and Christian books on assorted topics—which provided hungry-hearted Christians with an increased measure of spiritual understanding. Some of these materials in turn were translated into other languages, thus providing additional spiritual food for non-English speaking believers throughout the world.

- The explosive growth of the underground church in China (1949-1990): the priesthood of all believers in practice, not just in Reformation rhetoric.

- The Billy Graham evangelistic crusades: sharing the Gospel of Christ with much of the world through the Biblical and compelling message that each person must be born again in order to be saved.

- The emergence of the independent Protestant church movement in America (churches now independently governed rather than governed by the bishops of a denomination)—and the widespread opportunities for the priesthood of all believers to use their gifts in many of these churches.

- The parachurch movement in the American and British Evangelical church: filling the ministry gaps and needs not being met by the local church—and using the priesthood of all believers to accomplish it (e.g., the Navigators, Campus Crusade for Christ, InterVarsity Christian Fellowship, Trans World Radio, Far East Broadcasting, Bible Study Fellowship, Precepts, Community Bible Studies, and Prison Fellowship)

- The explosive growth of the Calvary Chapel movement (born during the Jesus Movement of the 1970s)—boldly proclaiming the whole counsel of God, including the pre-tribulation Rapture and the pre-millennial return of Christ.

- The supernatural work of God in the Middle East (late 20th century and early 21st century) to call out a people for His name (including His use of dreams and the internet in closed societies).

> **Point of discernment**: Despite all these positive moves during and after the Protestant Reformation to bring a significant portion of the church out of the heresy, secularism, institutionalism, clericalism, and unsound doctrine of the Roman Catholic Church, error and deception still exists today in segments of Evangelicalism. This phenomenon will be examined in Chapters 35 and 36.

CHAPTER 28

Covenant Theology and Dispensational Theology

Evangelical Bible colleges and seminaries today typically teach one of two main systems of theology (both developed after the Protestant Reformation): Covenant Theology or Dispensational Theology. Neither system existed at the time of the Apostolic church.

Covenant Theology

Covenant Theology was formulated by Johannes Cocceius in 1648. As mentioned in the previous chapter, it was an attempt to provide an overarching, unifying theme to the Bible on the basis of two covenants: a covenant of works and a covenant of grace. (Some Covenant theologians add a third covenant—the covenant of redemption.) The significance of Covenant Theology in post-Reformation church history is its emphasis on a salvation transaction based on faith alone, rather than the faith-plus-works heresy of the Catholic Church. Nevertheless, the premise that God's dealings with man can be found in and tied together by these two (or three) covenants is a man-made construct rather than a clearly-delineated biblical truth.

According to its adherents, the first of these suppositions—**the covenant of works**—was made in the Garden of Eden between God and Adam, who represented all mankind as the federal (or representative) head of all mankind (Romans 5:12-21). God offered Adam a perfect and perpetual life if he didn't violate God's single command [eating from the tree of the knowledge of good and evil]. God also warned Adam of the consequences if he disobeyed this command. Unfortunately, Adam broke the covenant, and sin entered into mankind for the first time.[1] **The covenant of grace**, in turn, promises eternal life for all people who put their faith in Jesus Christ for their sin problem. Christ is the substitutionary covenantal representative fulfilling the covenant of works on man's behalf. Christ's work on the cross is the historical expression of the eternal covenant of redemption offered to man in Genesis 3:15.[2] Indeed, the major focus of Covenant Theology is the salvation and redemption of man.

Though Covenant Theology employs the moniker "covenant," most of its theologians choose to marginalize the five biblical covenants given to Israel by allegorizing or spiritualizing them—and teach instead that God, in the New Covenant of grace, has now given all these covenant promises to the Church.

The major weaknesses of Covenant Theology are as follows:

- Its proponents use a grammatical-historical-literal hermeneutic, *inconsistently* applied. Much of prophetic Scripture is therefore allegorized or spiritualized.

- Most of its adherents are amillennial in their eschatology; some are postmillennial; a few are premillennial. Only those who are premillennial grasp the Father's plan to glorify the resurrected Christ after the Son's return to the earth.

Its amillennial and postmillennial adherents hold to Replacement Theology

- It insists on reading much of Scripture into these two (or three) covenants, rather than letting Scripture alone (including the five Biblical covenants) bring forth sound doctrine.

- Most Covenant theologians, either consciously or unconsciously, make no attempt to teach the whole counsel of God—and instead focus on the redemption of man and the Christian life.

Dispensational Theology

Developed in the 1700s sometime after Covenant Theology, Dispensational Theology is likewise an attempt by theologians to provide an overarching, unifying theme to the Bible. Like Covenant Theology, Dispensational Theology is a man-made construct. A "dispensation" is usually defined as "God's distinctive and different administrations or out-workings in directing the affairs of the world."[3] In each dispensation, man has certain responsibilities given to him by God—along with consequences for failure. In addition, Dispensationalists see the culmination of human history as the future establishment of Christ's millennial kingdom on earth. During this time, the glory of God in and through Jesus Christ will be displayed on earth.[4]

Today, Dispensationalists would typically put forth the following seven dispensations:[5]

1. The dispensation of **Innocence** [Adam to the Fall]. Adams' responsibilities involved "maintaining the garden of Eden and not eating of the fruit of the tree of the knowledge of good and evil. He failed the test about eating and, as a result, far-reaching judgments were pronounced on him, his wife, mankind, the serpent, and the creation. At the same time God pronounced judgment, He also graciously promised a Redeemer and made immediate provision for the acceptability of Adam and Eve in their sinful condition before God."[6]

2. The dispensation of **Conscience** [the Fall to the Flood]. "During this stewardship, man was responsible to respond to God through the promptings of his conscience, and part of a proper response was to bring an acceptable blood sacrifice as God had taught him to do (Gen. 3:21; 4:4). We have a record of only a few responding, and Abel, Enoch, and Noah are especially cited as heroes of faith. We also have a record of those who did not respond and who by their evil deeds brought judgment on the world. Cain refused to acknowledge himself as a sinner even when God continued to admonish him (Gen. 4:3,7). . . . The longsuffering of God (I Peter 3:20) came to an end, and He brought the Flood as judgment on the universal wickedness of man. But at the same time God graciously intervened; Noah found grace in His sight (Gen. 6:8), and he and his family were saved."[7]

3. The dispensation of **Civil Government** [Noah to Babel]. "The new revelation of this time included animals' fear of man, animals given to man to eat, the promise of no further global floods, and the institution of capital punishment. It is the latter that gives the distinctive basis to this dispensation as that of human, or civil, government. God gave man the right to take the life of man, which in

the very nature of the case gave man the authority to govern others. Unless government has the right to the highest form of punishment, its basic authority is questionable and insufficient to protect those it governs. . . . Failure to govern successfully appeared on the scene almost immediately. The people, instead of obeying God's command to scatter and fill the earth, conceived the idea of staying together and build the tower of Babel to help achieve their aim. Fellowship with man replaced fellowship with God. As a result, God sent the judgment of the tower of Babel and the confusion of languages."[8]

4. The dispensation of **Promise**, or Patriarchal Rule [Abram to Moses]. "The title *Promise* comes from Hebrews 6:15 and 11:9, where it is said that Abraham obtained the promise and sojourned in the land of promise. . . . The governmental feature of the economy is best emphasized by the designation *Patriarchal Rule*. Until this dispensation, all mankind had been directly related to God's governing principles. Now God marked out one family and one nation, and in them made a representative test of all. The responsibility of the patriarchs was simply to believe and serve God, and God gave them every material and spiritual provision to encourage them to do this. The Promised Land was theirs, and blessing was theirs as long as they remained in the land. But, of course, there was failure soon and often. Finally, Jacob led the people to Egypt, and soon the judgment of slavery was brought on them."[9]

5. The dispensation of the **Mosaic Law** [Mt Sinai to the Cross]. "To the children of Israel through Moses was given the great code that we call the Mosaic Law. It consisted of 613 commandments covering all phases of life and activity. It revealed in specific detail God's will in that economy. The period covered was from Moses to the death of Christ, or from Exodus 19:1 to Acts 1:26. The people were responsible to do all the law (James 2:10), but they failed. As a result, there were many judgments throughout this long period. . . . All during their many periods of declension and backsliding, God dealt with them graciously from the very first apostasy of the golden calf to the gracious promises of final regathering and restoration in the millennial age to come. . . . We are also told clearly in the New Testament (Rom. 3:20) that the law was not a means of justification but of condemnation."[10]

6. The dispensation of **Grace** [Pentecost to Christ's Second Coming]. "Under Grace the responsibility of man is to accept the gift of righteousness that God freely offers to all (Rom. 5:15-18). There are two aspects of the grace of God in this economy: (1) the blessing is entirely of grace and (2) the grace is for all. God is no longer dealing with just one nation as a sample but with all mankind. The vast majority have rejected Him and as a result will be judged. The dispensation will end with the Second Coming of Christ since the tribulation period is not a separate dispensation but is a judgment on those living persons who are Christ rejecters at the end of the present dispensation. The Scripture involved is Acts 2:1 to Revelation 19:21."[11]

7. The dispensation of the **Millennium** [Christ's 1000-year reign over the earth]. "After the second advent of Christ the millennial kingdom will be set up in ful-

fillment of all the promises given in both Testaments and particularly those contained in the Abrahamic and Davidic covenants. The Lord Jesus, who will personally take charge of the running of the affairs of the world during that age, will be the chief personage of the dispensation. It will continue for a thousand years, and man will be responsible for obedience to the King and His laws. Satan will be bound, Christ will be ruling, righteousness will prevail, overt disobedience will be quickly punished.[12]

In addition to proposing the existence of seven divine Dispensations (vs. two Covenants), Dispensational Theology also repudiates the dual hermeneutic of the Catholic Church and the Protestant Reformers in favor of a single hermeneutic, consistently applied to Scripture throughout. Moreover, unlike their peers in Covenant Theology, most Dispensationalists attempt to teach the whole counsel of God (Acts 20:27).

The earliest form of post-Reformation Dispensational Theology is often credited to Pierre Poiret in 1687. John Edwards [1699] and Isaac Watts [1720] also produced rudimentary Dispensational models. J. N. Darby [1830] is usually considered to be the father of modern Dispensationalism. Darby also popularized the pre-tribulation Rapture in the 1830s. Darby's teaching influenced C.I. Scofield, whose Scofield Reference Bible catapulted Dispensationalism into the Evangelical mainstream during the early 1900s. In 1908, a Scofield contemporary (and fellow Dispensationalist), William A. Blackstone wrote the classic book, *Jesus is Coming*. Blackstone's book not only delineated the pre-tribulation Rapture, the seven-year tribulation period, the second coming of Christ, and the Millennial kingdom, but it also foresaw from Scripture the necessity of the permanent restoration of Israel to Palestine. His diagram of events is virtually identical to those produced in the second half of the twentieth century by John Walvoord and Charles Ryrie.

Though the arrangement of the seven dispensations can and has been debated, there can be little debate that dispensations ("God's distinctive and different administrations or out-workings") exist in Scripture (Matt. 12:32, Mark 10:30, Luke 18:30). To be sure, Scripture presents three separate "kingdoms of heaven"—the Inter-advent Kingdom (the Church Age), the Millennial Kingdom, and the Eternal Kingdom. Each of these kingdoms is a different "economy" or out-working in the accomplishment of God's overall purposes. The first two dispensations—Innocence and Conscience—are likewise clearly-defined (but different) administrations in early human history. As well, it is clear that God has revealed His purposes *progressively* over time. The writer of Hebrews states: *"God, after He spoke long ago to the fathers in the prophets in many portions and in many ways, in these last days has spoken to us in His Son, whom He appointed heir of all things, through who also He made the world" (Hebrews 1:1-2).*

In this writer's view, the major contributions of Dispensationalism to an Evangelical's understanding of the Bible derive not so much from its presentation of seven dispensations, but from (1) its use of a consistently-applied G-H-L hermeneutic, (2) its delineation of the progressive revelation of God's purposes in human history, (3) its delineation of Scripture's progressive revelation of Jesus Christ, (4) its clear distinction between national Israel and the Church (which includes born-again Jews), and (5) its contention that ultimate goal of human history is the glory of God in and through Jesus Christ. [In contrast, Covenant Theology (for the most part) uses an inconsistently-applied G-H-L hermeneutic, believes that the Church has inherited Israel's covenant promises, and believes that the principal goal of human history is the redemption of man.]

Nevertheless, for all its strengths in helping Evangelicals understand God's overall purposes in human history, the major weakness of Dispensationalism (again, in this writer's view) lies in its delineation and explanation of the fourth, fifth, and sixth dispensations. For example, the fourth and fifth dispensations deal only with Israel rather than all mankind. The sixth dispensation (Grace), which once again deals with all mankind, is said to begin on the day of Pentecost and to end with Second Coming of Christ. However, the existence of the Tribulation period in this dispensation creates the following problem: the first sixty-nine weeks of Daniel's prophecy takes place in the fifth dispensation (Law), while the seventieth week takes place in the sixth dispensation (Grace)—yet all seventy weeks are a judgment upon Israel ("to finish the transgression"—Dan. 9:24). Such is the difficulty of delineating dispensations with complete precision.

In short, it is easy to identify God's two major out-workings before the Flood (Innocence and Conscience) as well as His major out-workings in the Church Age, the Millennial Kingdom, and the Eternal Kingdom. It is more difficult, however, to tie together clearly-defined dispensations after the tower of Babel up to the beginning of the Church Age. One could argue, for example, that God—through His calling of Abram, Isaac, and Jacob—has a unique and completely different mission for Israel than He has for the "nations" (the Gentiles). Thus, should there be parallel (but different) dispensations/economies for the Jews and the nations? Alternatively, it could be proposed that God's dealings with Israel have taken place (and will take place) in stages or periods: e.g., selected; covenanted with; grown; enslaved; delivered; set apart; tested; planted; seduced—restored / seduced—restored; blessed; divided; captured & scattered; chastened (for 483 years); set aside temporarily (during the Church Age); chastened (for 7 years); rescued and saved; exalted (for 1000 years) [see page 58]. Should these stages or periods in Israel's history in some way be incorporated into the post-Babel dispensations?

To be sure, however, Dispensationalism remains far ahead of Covenant Theology in terms of proclaiming God's overall purposes in human history (culminating in Christ's reign future over the earth for a thousand years) and unabashedly attempting to teach the whole counsel of God.

Contrasts between Covenant Theology and Dispensationalism

Covenant Theology	**Dispensationalism**
Overarching construct: Two (or three) covenants	Overarching construct: Seven dispensations
Hermeneutic: G-H-L, *inconsistently* applied	Hermeneutic: G-H-L, *consistently* applied
Overarching theme of the Bible: The salvation of man	Overarching theme of the Bible: The glory of God in Jesus Christ
Teaching Emphasis: Salvation and sanctification	Teaching Emphasis: The whole counsel of God (including salvation and sanctification)

Note: The covenants articulated in Covenant Theology have nothing to do with the Biblical covenants given to Israel in the Old Testament. The Biblical covenants are:

- **The Abrahamic Covenant** (Gen. 12:1-7; 13:14-17; 15:1-7; 15:18-21; 17:1-8; 22:16-18; 26:2-5; 28:11-15; 35:9-14). Among other things, God promises to make Abraham's seed (through Isaac and Jacob) a great nation; to make Abraham's name great; to bless Abraham; to enable Abraham to be a blessing; and to give Abraham's descendants (through Isaac and Jacob) the land of Canaan. In addition, God promises to bless those who bless Abraham and curse those who curse Abraham.

- **The Mosaic Covenant** (Exodus 19:3-8). God makes a conditional promise to the Israelites (through Moses) that if they obey His voice and keep His commandments, then they will be His possession among the nations; and they shall be a kingdom of priests and a holy nation.

- **The Palestinian Covenant** (Deut. 30:1-10). God reveals that He (at a time subsequent to the writing of Deuteronomy) will banish the Jews from the land of Israel to other nations because of their disobedience, but He also promises to bring them back to the land of Canaan after this banishment. In addition, God promises to prosper them after returning them to the land, and He promises to circumcise their hearts with a deep love for Him.

- **The Davidic Covenant** (II Sam. 7:8-16). God prophesies that He will make David's name great and that He will one day give Israel a place of safety and rest from her enemies, never to be disturbed again. God also prophesies that He will establish a house, an eternal kingdom and an eternal throne with one of David's descendants (the Lord Jesus Christ).

- **The New Covenant** (Jer. 31:31-34; Hebr. 8:7-13; Rom. 3:19-28; 6:14-15; Gal. 2:16; 3:8-14; 3:16-18; 3:24-26; 4:21-31; Hebr. 10:11-17; Isa. 61:8-9; Ezek. 37-21-28; John 1:17; Matt. 26:27-28; II Cor. 3:5-6; Hebr. 10:17-17). God promises, in this new covenant with Israel, to put His law within them and to put His law on their hearts; and He shall be their God, and they shall be His people; and they shall know the Lord, from the least of them to the greatest of them; and He will forgive their iniquity, and He will no longer remember their sin.

Of the five Biblical covenants, only the Mosaic Covenant is conditional (i.e., it is conditioned on Israel's obedience to the Law). The other four covenants are unconditional: God will accomplish for Israel what He has promised.

CHAPTER 29

The De Facto Second Protestant Reformation

Despite all the positive developments of the Protestant Reformation, especially with regard to the doctrine of salvation, the Reformers nevertheless failed to shed several notable Roman Catholic practices and beliefs: (1) the continued allegorization of prophetic Scripture; (2) the belief that the Church has replaced Israel in God's plans and purposes (Replacement Theology); and (3) its belief in amillennialism. Indeed, much of Evangelicalism maintains these Roman Catholic beliefs today, including the following denominations and movements:

- Evangelical Reformed and Presbyterian churches
- Evangelical Lutheran churches
- Evangelical Wesleyan and Methodist churches
- Evangelical Anglican and Episcopalian churches
- Evangelical Congregational churches
- Amillennial Evangelical Baptist churches
- Amillennial Charismatic churches

For the first three hundred years of the early church (with the exception of Origen in 250 A.D.), all church leaders interpreted the words of Scripture in their plain, normal sense. None believed that the church had replaced Israel in God's plans and purposes. And all believed in a literal thousand-year reign of Christ over the earth.

Unfortunately for the Church, Augustine of Hippo, in approximately 390 A.D., became enamored with Origen's allegorical approach to interpreting prophetic Scripture. Soon thereafter, Augustine jettisoned his previously-held literal interpretation of prophetic Scripture in favor of one which saw different levels of meaning, namely a literal meaning as well as moral and spiritual meanings. Eventually, he wrote the influential book, *City of God*, after the sacking of Rome by the Visigoths in 410 A.D. In *City of God*, Augustine argued that Christianity should be concerned with the mystical, heavenly city—the New Jerusalem—rather than earthly politics.[1] Due to his efforts, amillennialism replaced premillennialism almost overnight as official doctrine in the increasingly powerful Roman church. At the same time, the use of an inconsistently applied hermeneutic (Chapter 13) became entrenched in theological circles. Amillennialism remains to this day as the official doctrine of the Roman Catholic Church and the Eastern Orthodox Church. It is also the most widely-held belief among Evangelicals.

However, in line with what one would expect in the "summer-fall-winter-spring" pattern of church history, an increasing number of Evangelical theologians—beginning approximately three hundred years ago—began once again to interpret *all* of Scripture in its plain, normal sense. These men rejected Replacement Theology and saw the born-again church and Israel as separate and distinct bodies. They also returned to the early church's belief in premillennialism. Such men included Pierre Poiret (1700-1800), Isaac Watts (1700-1800), Morgan Edwards (1722-1792), and Robert Haldane (1764-1842). Following their pathfinding, others arose over the next decades who likewise embraced a consistently applied, grammatical-historical-literal hermeneutic when interpreting Scripture, most notably J. N. Darby (1800-1882), William Blackstone (1841-1935), and C. I. Scofield (1843-1921).

The influence of the consistently-applied hermeneutic utilized by these men then exploded onto the scene in the twentieth century, contributing in turn to the rapid growth in the number of dispensational Bible churches, dispensational Community churches, and the entire Calvary Chapel movement. Early twentieth century notables included R.A. Torrey, Clarence Larkin, Arno Gabelein, Lewis Sperry Chafer, M.R. DeHaan, and Harry Ironside. The second half of the twentieth century included J. Vernon McGee, John Walvoord, Dwight Pentecost, Charles Ryrie, Roy Zuck, Donald K. Campbell, Ray Stedman, Earl Radmacher, Tim LaHaye, Chuck Smith, and Dave Hunt.

This return by an increasing number of Evangelicals to a consistently-applied hermeneutic—though virtually unrecognized by church historians—in retrospect amounts to nothing less than a **Second Protestant Reformation**. Today, well-known Evangelicals who use a consistently-applied, G-H-L hermeneutic include Hal Lindsey, Kay Arthur, Charles Stanley, John MacArthur, David Jeremiah, T.A. McMahon, Arnold Fruchtenbaum, Anne Graham Lotz, Renald Showers, Lon Solomon, Grant Jeffrey, Roger Oakland, David Reagan, Jobe Martin, Robert Jeffress, Jan Markell, Paul R. Wilkinson, and Mark Hitchcock. Perhaps one-third of American Evangelicals have returned to the premillennialism and the consistently-applied literal hermeneutic of the Apostolic Church. This movement in turn has come to be known as "Biblical Christianity."

CHAPTER 30

Present-Day Christianity

Christianity presently has three main branches: Roman Catholic, Eastern Orthodox, and Protestant. Roman Catholicism moved to the forefront of Christianity in approximately 500 A.D. The Eastern Orthodox Church spun off from Roman Catholicism in approximately 1000 A.D. Protestantism emerged on the scene shortly after 1500 A.D.

Protestantism's most important early proponents were Martin Luther (a German Catholic professor, priest, and monk) and John Calvin (a French theologian and pastor who fled to Switzerland). Luther's famous Ninety-Five Theses were nailed to the door of All Saints' Church in Wittenberg in protest to what he viewed as questionable Catholic practices. Luther and Calvin both worked to reform the Catholic Church—hence, the movement's eventual label: The Protestant Reformation.

As noted in a previous chapter, early Protestantism initially saw the development of Protestant national churches—the German Lutheran Church, the Dutch Reformed Church, the English Anglican Church, and others—in lieu of the Roman Catholic Church. A century later the Protestant church also began to see the emergence of denominations—groups of believers who were not necessarily aligned to a particular nationality, but who instead held to certain doctrinal distinctions. Denominations gained major footholds in the American colonies. National churches and large Protestant denominations still exist throughout Christianity.

Since the middle of the nineteenth century, the Protestant church has seen two other phenomena emerge: (1) the schism between the "evangelical" and "liberal" wings of Protestantism, and (2) the growth in "Christian" cults. As a result, Christendom today actually consists of five clearly definable groups: Evangelical Protestants, Liberal Protestants, Christian cultists, Roman Catholics, and Eastern Orthodoxes. The chart on the next page shows these five groups—and identifies the "wheat vs. tare" composition of each. Those Christians who are born-again believers in Jesus Christ are His Bride (the wheat). Christians who are not born-again are the counterfeits (the tares). The World Council of Churches—an ecumenical group of liberal Protestants, Roman Catholics, and Orthodoxes—will comprise the bulk of the "harlot" church described in the book of Revelation. These "Christians" (with the exception of a few—Rev. 3:4) have not to come to Christ on *His* terms, i.e., by a grace-faith transaction, but instead have attempted to come by such inefficacious notions as good works, infant baptism, ethical living, or church membership.

CHRISTENDOM TODAY

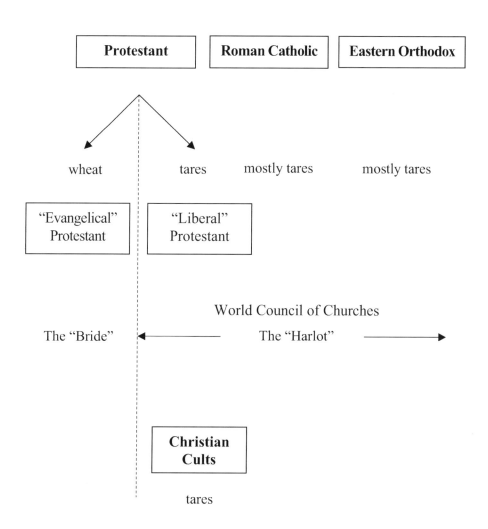

MAJOR DOCTRINES OF THE CHRISTIAN FAITH

BIBLIOLOGY [The Nature of the Bible]

THEOLOGY [The Nature of God]

CHRISTOLOGY [The Nature of Christ]

PNEUMATOLOGY [The Nature of the Holy Spirit]

ANGELOLOGY [The Nature of Angels]

DEMONOLOGY [The Nature of Demons]

ANTHROPOLOGY [The Nature of Man]

HAMARTIOLOGY [The Nature of Sin]

SOTERIOLOGY **[The Nature of Salvation]**

ISRAELOLOGY [The Nature of Israel]

ECCLESIOLOGY [The Nature of the Church]

ESCHATOLOGY [The Nature of Future Things]

Point of Discernment: The principal dividing line between Evangelicals and non-Evangelicals (Catholics, Orthodoxes, Liberal Protestants, and Christian Cults) has to do with their **soteriology**—their respective salvation beliefs (although Evangelicals and non-Evangelicals would also have significantly different views on bibliology, anthropology, hamartiology, and ecclesiology). All Evangelicals believe that a person must be born again to be saved—i.e., a supernatural transaction from above takes place (the Holy Spirit instantly indwells a person) when that person receives Christ into his life through faith in Christ's atoning death (attested to by His resurrection). Non-Evangelicals variously teach that man is saved by such things as faith plus works, good works, ethical living, infant baptism, partaking of sacraments, church membership, or universalism.

THE MAJOR DOCTRINES AND EVANGELICALISM

BIBLIOLOGY   [The Nature of the Bible]

THEOLOGY   [The Nature of God]

CHRISTOLOGY   [The Nature of Christ]

PNEUMATOLOGY   [The Nature of the Holy Spirit]

ANGELOLOGY   [The Nature of Angels]

DEMONOLOGY   [The Nature of Demons]

ANTHROPOLOGY   **[The Nature of Man]**

HAMARTIOLOGY   [The Nature of Sin]

SOTERIOLOGY   [The Nature of Salvation]

ISRAELOLOGY   **[The Nature of Israel]**

ECCLESIOLOGY   [The Nature of the Church]

ESCHATOLOGY   **[The Nature of Future Things]**

Most of the doctrinal differences in Evangelicalism involve bibliology, anthropology, Israelology, and eschatology. These differences will be reviewed in upcoming chapters. Moreover, though all Evangelicals believe that a person must be born again in order to be saved, Evangelicals nevertheless have conflicting views regarding the roles of God and man in the salvation transaction. These differences—consisting of four competing views—will be discussed in Chapter 32

PROTESTANTISM TODAY

"Evangelical" Protestant [1]

all Calvary Chapels
all dispensational Bible
all dispensational Community
all Conservative Baptist
all P.C.A. Presbyterian
all Assemblies of God
all Southern Baptist
all Evangelical Free
most Nazarene
most Charismatic
most independent Methodist
some Lutheran
a few Anglican
a few Episcopalian
a few Congregational

"wheat"

born again

"Liberal" Protestant [1]

most Anglican
most Episcopal
most Congregational
most Presbyterian USA
most United Methodist
many Lutheran
some Nazarene
some Baptist

"tares"

not born again

Note: Virtually every Evangelical church at times will have "tares" in attendance, and virtually every liberal Protestant church will likely have some "wheat" as members. The "wheat" and "tares" demarcations above thus relate to the salvation doctrine of the churches/denominations and the overall composition of their memberships.

[1] Not an all-inclusive list. Other churches/denominations could be included.

FURTHER DISTINCTIONS AMONG THE "WHEAT"

- Various stages of growth:
    - New believers
    - Growing believers
    - Maturing believers
    - Stunted believers
    - Backsliding believers

- Varying degrees of "fruit bearing":
    - 1-fold (negligible fruit)
    - 5-fold
    - 10-fold (some fruit)

    - 30-fold (more fruit)   (Matt. 13:8,23; Mark 4:8,20)
    - 60-fold (still more fruit)   (Matt. 13:8,23; Mark 4:8,20)
    - 100-fold (much fruit)   (Matt. 13:8,23; Mark 4:8,20)

- Different spiritual gifts (I Cor. 12:4,7) [for the common good]

- Different ministries (I Cor. 12:5)

- Various effects (I Cor. 12:6)

- Varying magnitudes of assignment (Matt. 25:14-30)

Point of Discernment: Evangelicalism contains within its ranks a wide spectrum of spiritual maturity, fruit bearing, giftedness, and ministry callings.

OTHER OBSERVATIONS ABOUT THE "WHEAT"

- The Father's goal for the believer: to be transformed into the image of Christ (Rom. 8:29)

- The greatest in Christ's kingdom is the one who is last of all and servant of all (Mark 9:35)

- The Parable of the Talents: equal reward for equal faithfulness with however much or little Christ has called you to do (Matt. 25:14-30)

- Christ's calling for every believer:
    - To love God with all your heart, mind, strength, and soul
    - To love others as much as God loves you (John 13:34)
    - To seek first the kingdom of God and His righteousness
    - To trust the Lord with all your heart
    - To let the Word of God dwell richly on your heart
    - To love one another
    - To serve one another
    - To lay aside your own rights
    - To lay down your life for others
    - To consider others to be more important than yourself
    - To be salt and light to a hurting world
    - To be ready to give an account for the hope within you
    - To be an ambassador for Christ
    - To endure hardship
    - To forgive those who have hurt you
    - To rejoice always
    - To pray without ceasing
    - To give thanks in everything
    - To be content with what you have
    - To be a cheerful giver
    - To go and make disciples of all the nations

Point of Discernment: God's goal and calling for the believer contrasts sharply with what the world deems to be life and "success."

CHAPTER 31

Today's Apostolic Counterpart: Biblical Christianity

In today's Evangelical Church, "Biblical Christianity" represents the brand of Christianity which most readily attempts to (1) handle God's Word accurately and (2) teach the whole counsel of God's Word. The movement is a byproduct of the de facto Second Protestant Reformation some two to three hundred years ago. Accordingly, it uses a consistently-applied, grammatical-historical-literal hermeneutic to interpret Scripture. Its doctrine in turn most closely mirrors the teaching of the apostles and their immediate successors. Biblical Christianity's doctrine, however, differs in part from other forms of Evangelicalism. These differences (some slight, some not so slight) will be reviewed in the Chapters 35 and 36. As its name suggests, the Bible is Biblical Christianity's sole source of authority. Its beliefs and positions are as follows:

Biblical Christianity . . .

- Is based on "sola Scriptura"—Scripture alone
- Places little or no emphasis on the post-Reformation creeds of the church
- Eschews "decretal theology"
- Interprets Scripture's words and figures of speech in their plain, normal sense
- Uses a Grammatical-Historical-Literal hermeneutic, consistently applied throughout Scripture
- Sees a progressive revelation and eventual glorification of Jesus Christ in God's overall plan for human history
- Sees a clear distinction between Israel and the Church
- Rejects "Replacement Theology"
- Believes in a pre-tribulation Rapture of the Church (see Appendix B)
- Believes in a still-future, seven-year Tribulation period on earth
- Believes in a premillennial return of Jesus Christ
- Believes that the resurrected Jesus Christ will reign over the earth for a thousand years
- Sees three "kingdoms of heaven" in Scripture
- Believes that man—though dead in his trespasses and sins—nevertheless has the capacity to hear and respond to the gospel message

- Believes that the Bible is inspired, inerrant, authoritative, and sufficient
- Believes that God is one, but triune in nature: Father, Son, and Holy Spirit
- Believes that the six creation days are literal, 24-hour days
- Believes that man was created on the sixth day of creation
- Believes that man was created in the image of God
- Believes that man's image was effaced at the Fall, but not erased.
- Believes that death entered the world upon Adam's sin, not before
- Is based on the inductive study of Scripture rather than man-made presuppositions or deductive reasoning
- Sees two ordinances in Scripture: (1) water baptism and (2) communion (in remembrance of Christ)
- Believes in the local governance of each church by elders and deacons (with elders tending to the spiritual needs of the flock and deacons tending to the temporal needs)
- Believes that Christ died for the sins of all mankind
- Believes in the necessity of the new birth
- Believes that salvation is a gift, bestowed by God's grace, to those who put their faith in God's gracious provision—Jesus Christ
- Believes that salvation is by faith alone in Christ alone
- Believes that spiritual regeneration comes immediately after the exercise of saving faith
- Believes that repentance unto salvation is the turning of one's mind and heart away from any previous belief system to an embracing of the gospel of Jesus Christ for salvation. Furthermore, it also believes that repentance and faith are often simultaneous transactions
- Believes that a believer cannot lose his salvation once he is born again
- Believes that lifestyle repentance—the forsaking of sin and sin habits in one's life—is a sanctification issue, not a salvation (justification) issue
- Believes that salvation has three tenses: past, present, and future—or justification, sanctification, and glorification
- Believes that faith in Jesus Christ is the only way of salvation
- Believes that though the gospel is exclusive and the only way of salvation, it is likewise inclusive in *scope*: it is offered to *all*

Within 21st century Evangelicalism, Biblical Christianity's distinctives and beliefs are embraced by all Calvary Chapels, all dispensational non-denominational churches, all Conservative Baptist churches, all Regular Baptist churches, all Plymouth Brethren churches, some Southern Baptist churches, and any church which utilizes a grammatical-historical-literal hermeneutic, consistently applied.

Part VI

Sharpening Your Discernment

Be diligent to present yourself approved to God as a workman who does not need to be ashamed, accurately handling the word of truth (II Tim 2:15).

Examine everything carefully (I Thess. 5:21a).

Part VI will examine Evangelicalism's four major views of the salvation transaction and several areas where Evangelical teaching or practice fails to line up with Scripture. It will also show the believer how to "test the spirits" in order to discern the source and substance of a message or teaching.

CHAPTER 32

Salvation Approaches in the Evangelical Church Today

This chapter assesses the four major views of the salvation transaction held by Evangelicals today. Three of the four emerged from the Protestant Reformation, while the fourth (according to its proponents) has antecedents dating back to the church fathers and has had adherents throughout Church history. The four views are as follows:

1. Reformed Theology (Strong Calvinism) (5-point)
2. Moderate Calvinism (3.5-point or less)
3. Arminianism
4. Neither Calvinist nor Arminian ("Inductive Mediate Theology")

The fourth approach—Neither Calvinist nor Arminian (or "Inductive Mediate Theology")—presents itself as an intermediate position (hence the term "mediate") between Calvinism and Arminianism. However, many adherents of Mediate Theology contend that it is neither Calvinist nor Arminian—or is beyond Calvinism and Arminianism. Advocates of Mediate Theology point out that during the first three centuries of the church (1) no church father taught "the predestination and divine election of individuals to salvation," (2) all church fathers taught that man has a free will, and (3) salvation was considered to be a free-will decision on the part of the person hearing the Good News of Jesus Christ.[1]

Reformed Theology, **Moderate Calvinism**, **Arminianism,** and **Mediate Theology (i.e., neither Calvinist nor Arminian)** represent the salvation views of perhaps ninety-six percent of all believers today. This writer would also submit that each of the four has an approximate one-fourth share of the ninety-six percent figure.

[Note: Hyper Calvinism, Amyraldianism, and Open Theism are three lesser views in the Evangelical church today, representing no more than four percent of believers in total. Hyper Calvinists not only hold to 5-point Calvinism, but also teach that God determines *all* events and that God is therefore the author of evil. (This latter belief is anathema to 99% of all born-again Christians). Amyraldians reject the Limited Atonement of 5-point Calvinism, and therefore call themselves 4-point Calvinists. Open Theists assert that God knows most of, but not all of the future. They contend that God cannot possibly know all of man's future choices lest man be devoid of a free will. This view limits God's omniscience, however, and is rejected by virtually all born-again Christians.]

REFORMED THEOLOGY (STRONG CALVINISM) (5-POINT)

All Calvinists believe in the predestination and divine election of certain individuals to salvation.

Reformed theologians believe in "decretal theology"—a theological approach which teaches that "God, in eternity, decreed the salvation of a select and definite number. Those chosen are the elect while those rejected are the reprobate."[2] Most Reformed theologians see the eternal decrees as the starting point for studying salvation and the works of God.

Reformed Theologians use the familiar "TULIP" acronym to explain their system, and they define the five points as follows:[3]

1. (T) **Total Depravity**: Because sinful man is totally depraved, he cannot understand or receive the gospel. Persons "dead in trespasses and sins" (Eph. 2:1) are incapable of doing anything with regard to salvation. Indeed, to the Strong Calvinist, man is totally unable to hear or respond to the gospel. Thus, God must regenerate those whom He has sovereignly predestined to salvation before they can believe.

2. (U) **Unconditional Election**: As a result of man's total depravity, he is unable (and unwilling) to come to God for salvation. Therefore, God must sovereignly choose those who will be saved. His decision to elect individuals for salvation is unconditional. It is not based on anything that man is or does but solely on God's grace. In Reformed Theology, regeneration *precedes* faith. However, to the Reformed adherent, man—once regenerated and saved by God—is capable of making free-will decisions to do good, though his whole sanctification process at times involves a struggle between doing good or doing evil. Unregenerate man, on the other hand, has no such struggle—and continually does evil.[4]

3. (L) **Limited Atonement**: The scope of Christ's atoning sacrifice on Calvary's cross includes only the elect, rather than all men.

4. (I) **Irresistible Grace**: Those whom God has predestined cannot resist God's saving grace.

5. (P) **Perseverance of the Saints**: One who is predestined by God for salvation will persevere in the faith until his death.

Reformed Theology/Strong Calvinism (unlike Hyper Calvinism) does not believe that every act or action of man is predetermined by God. Regenerate man has some freedom of will.

Notable proponents include: B.B. Warfield, John Gerstner, J.I. Packer, R.C. Sproul, Michael Horton, John Piper, Tim Keller

Important books: *Chosen by God*, R.C. Sproul; *Grace Unknown*, R.C. Sproul

Assessment:

- At its core, Reformed Theology is based on deductive reasoning rather than inductive exegesis of Scripture. Its deductive logic goes like this: Because man is "dead" in his trespasses and sins, it is impossible for him to respond to God. Thus, God has to regenerate certain people before they can "hear" the Gospel. Accordingly, in eternity past, God has sovereignly chosen certain people (the "elect") for salvation. Those whom He has chosen, He calls unconditionally to Himself by giving them the faith to believe. This calling unto salvation is irresistible because these persons have been predestined from eternity past. Finally, because of this election, Christ's atoning sacrifice is limited to the "elect."

- In contrast, inductive exegesis of Scripture reveals that man, though he is "dead" in his trespasses and sins, can nevertheless respond—in his fallen state—to the gospel message (Acts 2:37-38 and others). In addition, Scripture teaches that all men—in their fallen state—have a knowledge of good and evil (Romans 1:19) and can clearly see God's invisible attributes, His eternal power, and His divine nature through what has been made (Romans 1:20). As a result, a person using inductive exegesis—because he does not have to force a conclusion onto a presupposition—can conclude correctly that the "deadness" of man in his trespasses and sins does not prevent him from being able to hear and respond to the saving gospel of Jesus Christ (Romans 10:14-17), nor does it excuse him from recognizing God's general revelation of Himself in creation (Romans 1:18-20).

- The "divine election and predestination of individuals"—based on God's autonomous choice—was not taught during the first several hundred years of church history (and draws into question why it is being taught today). The doctrine of the divine election and predestination of individuals first came to the forefront through the teachings of Augustine near the end of the fourth century.[5] The doctrine received a chilly response in general,[6] and double predestination (i.e., the predestination of some to salvation and others to reprobation) was rejected by the Second Council of Orange in 529 A.D.[7] After remaining mostly dormant for the next one thousand years, the doctrine of predestination was revisited by Martin Luther, John Calvin, Huldryck Zwingli, Theodore Beza, and others during the Protestant Reformation. Soon thereafter, the doctrine took substantial root.

- Though many Reformed theologians attempt to deny that their belief system teaches double predestination, others would contend that the inescapable logic of some persons being "passed over" suggests that it does: if a person has not been unconditionally predestined to salvation by God Himself, then he has no chance of being saved. Consequently, any person having no chance of being saved has a *de-facto* predetermined fate in hell. The only way around such a conclusion would be for Strong Calvinists to say that though God predestines and chooses those whom He will save, He nevertheless gives those not "predestined" a chance to hear and believe. This, however, the Strong Calvinist does not do. Hence, Strong Calvinism ultimately teaches double predestination.

Where Reformed Theology Fails to Line Up with Scripture:

- Reformed Theology is **not** a grace-faith system; rather, it is a grace-grace system. When it comes to the salvation transaction in Reformed Theology, God does it all; man does nothing. Man's saving "faith" is given to the predestined sinner by God Himself as a divine act of grace. Scripture, on the other hand, sets up a contrast between "law-works" and "grace-faith" with regard to human responsibility (Romans 3 and elsewhere). In the grace-faith (New Covenant) arrangement, God has graciously provided the *provision* of salvation through Jesus Christ, but man's responsibility is to receive it by *faith*, not through the performance of good works. To be sure, Reformed Theology unwittingly contradicts the *sola fide* ("faith alone") of the Protestant Reformation.

- Reformed Theology's limited atonement contradicts a number of verses which state that Christ died for the sins of all mankind (e.g., John 1:29; 3:14-17; 12:32; 16:8; Romans 5:18; II Cor. 5:14-15; 5:19; I Tim. 2:3-6; 4:10; Titus 2:11; Hebrews 2:9; II Peter 3:9; I John 2:2; 4:14).

- Reformed Theology's belief that man is so "dead" that he cannot possibly hear the gospel message unless God first regenerates that person contradicts numerous verses in both the Old and New Testaments. In the Old Testament the word "hear" is used hundreds of times. The phrase, "Hear, O Israel!" is used dozens of times. When the Israelites heard the word of the Lord from Moses, it is clear they understood the message: *"All the words which the Lord has spoken we will do!" (Exo. 24:3)*. Thus, the problem was not that the Israelites were so dead that they could not *hear* the Word, but that they could not *keep* the Word. In the New Testament, Jesus several times exhorts His audience with the expression, "he who has ears to hear, let him hear." Such Old and New Testament exhortations would be meaningless if man was so "dead" he had no capacity to hear and understand what God was saying.

- Christ's parable of the Sower teaches a continuum of response to the gospel—from outright rejection, to shallow profession, to carnal reception, to wholehearted reception. This continuum strongly implies that man has the capacity to hear and understand the gospel *before* regeneration (Acts 2:37-38 and others)—in complete opposition to the teaching of Reformed Theology.

- Reformed Theology, by teaching that God must regenerate an "elect" person before he can exercise faith, contradicts the salvation analogy used in Numbers 21:4-9 and John 3:14-15 (which teach that salvation comes *after* the exercise of faith). It also contradicts Genesis 15:6, which states that Abram was declared righteous by God *after* his exercise of belief.

MODERATE CALVINISM (3.5-POINT)

All Calvinists believe in the predestination and divine election of certain individuals to salvation.

Moderate Calvinists believe that Christ died for the sins of *all* mankind (Unlimited Atonement); therefore, they use only four ("TUIP") of the five points of the familiar "TULIP" acronym. Moreover, the definitions developed and used by Moderate Calvinists for the TUIP differ significantly from the definitions used by 5-point and 4-point Calvinists—and are as follows:

1. (T) **Total Depravity**: Though sinful man is totally depraved, he nevertheless *can* understand and receive the gospel.[8] Thus, according to Moderate Calvinists, those whom God has sovereignly predestined to salvation will put their faith in the gospel message and at that moment will be born again. In Moderate Calvinism (unlike Reformed Theology), faith *precedes* regeneration.[9]

2. (U) **Unconditional Election [/ Conditional Election]**: Salvation is given by God alone (to whom He has predestined). Nevertheless, salvation is conditioned upon man hearing and putting his faith in the gospel message that Christ died for him. In short, from *God's* standpoint, the salvation transaction is unconditional ("chosen before the foundation of the world"); from *man's* standpoint, the transaction is conditional ("whosoever believes").[10] [Note: It is this "unconditional/conditional" explanation which causes some to label this version of Moderate Calvinism "3.5-point Calvinism."]

3. (I) **Irresistible Grace**: Those whom God has predestined cannot resist God's saving grace. "Grace is irresistible on the willing but does not force the unwilling."[11]

4. (P) **Perseverance of the Saints**: All those who are regenerate will, by God's grace, persevere to the end and be saved.[12]

Moderate Calvinism rejects Reformed Theology's Limited Atonement; rather, it believes that Christ died for the sins of all mankind (Unlimited Atonement)—and, like Amydraldism (4-point Calvinism), teaches that the efficacy of Christ's atonement is applied to those who believe.

Proponents include: Lewis Sperry Chafer, John Walvoord, Charles Ryrie, Dwight Pentecost, Roy Zuck, Norman Geisler

Important books: *Chosen But Free*, Norman Geisler

Assessment:

- Moderate Calvinism eschews the deductive reasoning of Reformed Theology and instead interprets salvation Scripture inductively. Using inductive exegesis, Moderate Calvinism concludes (1) that, despite his fallen nature, man has the capacity to hear, understand and receive the gospel; (2) that Christ's atoning sacrifice is for all (Unlimited Atonement); and (3) that faith precedes regeneration.

- Moderate Calvinism attempts to harmonize what it sees as the twin truths of God's sovereignty and man's responsibility. "God's predestination and human free will are a mystery, but not a contradiction. They go beyond reason, but not against reason."[13]
- Moderate Calvinism is "in accord with" God's foreknowledge, not "in spite of" God's foreknowledge (Hyper and Strong Calvinism) or "based on" God's foreknowledge (Arminianism).[14]
- Moderate Calvinism teaches that election, from God's standpoint, is based on His choosing of the man (in accord with His foreknowledge); but that from man's standpoint, election is based on the man's choosing of God (upon hearing the gospel message of salvation through faith in Jesus Christ).
- Moderate Calvinism's view that sinful man has the capacity to understand and receive the gospel (1) was the view of the early church fathers, (2) is supported in Romans 1:18-20 and Acts 2:14-41 (among others), (3) is the view of three-fourths of Christians today, and (4) opposes the doctrine of man's "total inability" to understand and receive the gospel taught in 5-point Calvinism and Reformed Theology.
- Moderate Calvinism's belief in Unlimited Atonement was the view of the early church fathers and is the view of three-fourths of Evangelicals today.
- Moderate Calvinism contends that Reformed Theology has a defective view of the love of God: "The stark truth of the matter is that the God of Hyper and Strong Calvinism is not all-loving. Limited atonement necessarily means God has only limited love. In a redemptive sense, He loves only the elect. He does not really love all sinners and desire them to be saved."[15]

ARMINIANISM

Arminianism believes that divine election is based on God's foreknowledge of a person's free will decision to receive Christ after hearing the Gospel message.

Jacobus (James) Arminius responded to John Calvin's "five points" with the following five points (Arminius's words are in quotation marks):[16]

1. God elects on the basis of His "eternal, unchangeable purpose" only "those who, through the grace of the Holy Spirit, shall believe on His Son Jesus." He also wills "to leave the incorrigible and unbelieving in sin and under wrath." Therefore, God's election of certain humans is conditioned on their (1) responding to God's drawing and (2) believing in Jesus Christ for their salvation—i.e., **conditional election.**

2. Christ "died for all men and for every man, so that he has obtained for them . . . redemption and forgiveness of sins; yet that no one actually enjoys the forgiveness of sins except the believer. . . ." Therefore, Christ's atonement is **unlimited** in extent, but is effective for only those who believe.

3. "That man has not saving grace of himself, nor of the energy of his free will . . . can of and by himself neither think, will, nor do anything that is truly good (such as saving faith eminently is); but that it is needful to be born again of God in Christ. . . ."

4. "That this grace of God is the beginning, continuance, and accomplishment of all good, even to this extent, that the regenerate man himself, without prevenient or assisting awakening, following, and co-operative grace, can neither think, will, nor do good. . . ." He adds: "But as respects the mode of operation of this grace, it is not irresistible. . . ." Therefore, **resistible grace.**

5. "That those who are incorporated into Christ by a true faith . . . have thereby full power to . . . win the victory . . . but whether they are capable . . . of becoming devoid of grace, that must be more particularly determined out of the Holy Scriptures, before we ourselves can teach it with the full persuasion of our minds."

The following five points offer a more contemporary version of Arminianism (rather than Arminius's own words above). These five points represent a response to the five points of Reformed Theology's TULIP:[17]

1. Although human nature was seriously affected by the fall, man has not been left in a state of spiritual helplessness. God graciously enables every sinner to repent and believe, but He does not interfere with man's freedom. [Therefore, **Depravity** rather than Reformed Theology's Total Depravity/Total Inability.]

2. Each sinner possesses a free will, and his eternal destiny depends on how he uses it. Man's freedom consists of his ability to choose good or evil in spiritual matters; his will is not enslaved to his sinful nature. The sinner has the power either to cooperate with God's Spirit and be regenerated or to resist God's

grace and perish. The lost sinner needs the Spirit's assistance, but he does not have to be regenerated by the Spirit before he can believe, for faith is man's act and precedes the new birth. Faith is the sinner's gift to God; it is man's contribution to salvation. [Therefore, **Conditional Election**]

3. Christ's redeeming work made it possible for everyone to be saved but did not actually secure the salvation of anyone. Although Christ died for all men and for every man, only those who believe on Him are saved. His death enabled God to pardon sinners but it did not actually put away anyone's sins. Christ's redemption becomes effective only if man chooses to accept it. [Therefore, **Unlimited Atonement**]

4. The Spirit calls inwardly all those who are called outwardly by the gospel invitation; He does all that He can to bring every sinner to salvation. But inasmuch as man is free, he can successfully resist the Spirit's call. The Spirit cannot regenerate the sinner until he believes; faith (which is man's contribution) precedes and make possible the new birth. Thus, man's free will limits the Spirit in the application of Christ's saving work. The Holy Spirit can only draw to Christ those who allow Him to have His way with them. Until the sinner responds, the Spirit cannot give life. God's grace, therefore, is not invincible; it can be, and often is, resisted and thwarted by man. [Therefore, **Resistible Grace**]

5. Those who believe and are truly saved can lose their salvation by failing to keep up their faith. [Therefore, **Fallen from Grace**]

The majority of Arminians contend that election is individual and based on God's foreknowledge of an individual's faith.[18] Nevertheless, a second perspective warrants mention: Some Arminians reject the concept of individual election, preferring to understand the doctrine in corporate terms. According to the corporate election view, God never chose individuals to salvation, but rather He chose to elect the believing church to salvation.[19] These scholars also maintain the Jesus was the only human ever elected and that individuals must be in Christ (Eph. 1:3-4) through faith to be part of the elect.[20] Hence, to some in contemporary Arminianism, "predestination" is not the predetermination of who will believe, but the predetermination of a believer's future inheritance. Believers are therefore predestined to sonship through adoption, glorification, and eternal life.[21]

Assessment:
- Arminianism accentuates the love of God (John 3:16 and others), whereas Reformed Theology emphasizes the sovereignty of God.
- Arminianism believes that although God is sovereign over His creation, He nevertheless has granted man a free will—the freedom to make choices in life, including spiritual choices.
- Salvation in Arminianism is based on God's foreknowledge, not in spite of God's foreknowledge (Reformed Theology) or in accord with God's foreknowledge (Moderate Calvinism).

- Arminianism rejects Reformed Theology's contentions that (1) man is totally unable to hear or respond to God because of his depravity and that (2) God must therefore regenerate man before he can hear the Gospel and be saved. It also emphatically rejects Reformed Theology's belief in unconditional election and irresistible grace.
- Arminianism rejects Reformed Theology's belief in limited atonement.
- Arminianism believes that a Christian can "fall from grace"—and in doing so, lose his salvation. As a result, many Arminians live their Christian lives with little or no assurance of salvation.

Where Arminianism Fails to Line Up with Scripture:
- Arminianism's belief that a Christian can "fall from grace" and, in doing so, can lose his salvation does not line up with key New Testament passages. In John 3:1-8, Jesus teaches that a person must be born again in order to have eternal life; he must have a spiritual birth by the Holy Spirit ("that which is born of the Spirit is spirit"). Accordingly, for the new-birth analogy to hold true, a person cannot be unborn spiritually (just has a human baby cannot be unborn). Next, in II Corinthians 5:17, the born-again Christian is said to be a new creature. Thus, once a person has become a new creature spiritually, he cannot become an "un" new creature. In Ephesians 1:13-14 the born-again Christian is said to be sealed in Christ. Nowhere in the New Testament is it taught that a born-again Christian can be "unsealed" and taken out of Christ. In addition, the born-again Christian has been redeemed by the blood of Christ; he has been purchased by Christ's blood. Nowhere does the New Testament state that God returns the purchase price of a sinning or back-sliding born-again Christian. Romans 8:38-39 unequivocally teaches that *nothing* can separate the believer from the love of God which is in Christ Jesus. John 10:27-28 states: "My sheep hear My voice, and I know them, and they follow Me; and I give eternal life to them, and they will never perish; and no one will snatch them out of My hand."

Neither Calvinist nor Arminian

A substantial number of Evangelicals today (perhaps one-fourth of all Evangelicals) are neither Calvinist (in any form) nor Arminian. This belief system can be seen in books such as *The Other Side of Calvinism*; *What Love is This?*; and *Beyond Calvinism & Arminianism: An Inductive Mediate Theology of Salvation*. Though this belief system has no formal name, some are now calling it "Inductive Mediate Theology" (based on the book just cited by C. Gordon Olson). Others simply call it "Neither Calvinist nor Arminian." Mediate Theology is also the likely intuitive set of beliefs of many Christians who have read the Bible but who have never been exposed to the other three views of the salvation transaction just presented.

Laurence M. Vance, the author of *The Other Side of Calvinism* who is neither Calvinist nor Arminian, states the following: "The philosophical speculations of Calvinism, although they have been debated for hundreds of years, have masqueraded as sound Bible doctrine for much too long. The resultant theological implications, under the pretense of orthodoxy, have been the dominant influence in all facets of theology. They have been accepted as authoritative, but only to the detriment of the Scriptures."[22]

Explains the author of *Beyond Calvinism & Arminianism*, C. Gordon Olson:

> Indeed, there is significant evidence that John Calvin did not hold to what passes today for Calvinism, and Jacob Arminius never really became "Arminian" before his untimely death. Thus, it was their followers who significantly polarized the traditions. Luther's views were quite paradoxical, virtually self-contradictory, and Lutheranism reflects that tension.
>
> Rather than persisting in going back to them as touchstones of truth, we must go beyond them and their followers' systems and do a fresh and more careful study of Scripture as the sole foundation of our theology. Only *after* we have developed a doctrine of salvation inductively from the Bible may we go back to Christian history to find any confirmation of our conclusions.[23]

In short, Inductive Mediate Theology (i.e., neither Calvinist nor Arminian) places little emphasis on what the Reformers taught, but instead examines all passages of Scripture dealing with salvation—and then through the use of inductive reasoning (rather than the deductive approach taken by five-point Calvinists) forms its conclusions with regard to how salvation takes place.

NEITHER CALVINIST NOR ARMINIAN

Inductive Mediate Theology rejects Calvinism's belief that God predestines certain individuals to salvation and reprobates or passes by others—and instead believes that God foreknows those who, on a free-will basis, will believe in Jesus Christ

In the words of C. Gordon Olson, the architect and chief proponent of Inductive Mediate Theology:

> We are proposing a mediate theology of salvation, intermediate to Calvinism and Arminianism. The thesis of this book [*Beyond Calvinism & Arminianism*] is that any sinner can be saved by grace only through explicit repentant faith in the finished work of Christ alone. This means that the gospel is a valid offer for every human being, available by God's unmerited favor apart from human performance either before or after conversion. It is the privilege of every true believer to have assurance of present and ultimate salvation. Christ is the only way of salvation, and no one can be saved apart from explicit trust in the merits of His person and work. Although the new birth and right standing with God are given instantaneously upon the exercise of saving repentant faith, there is a process by which unbelievers come to Christ for salvation.[24]

Mediate Theology holds to the following overarching principles and conclusions:[25]

- God's image in fallen man (Gen. 9:6; I Cor. 11:7a) implies an ability to respond to God
- Christ died for all, but only believers are saved
- Salvation must be proclaimed on God's terms, unadulterated by human traditions and philosophies
- The Spirit's conviction is necessary and required to prepare sinners' hearts for faith
- Repentant faith is the only condition for the new birth
- True believers are eternally secure in Christ
- God's calling to salvation is not irresistible
- Christian history is full of mediate antecedents
- World witness was restored by non-determinists [i.e., by non 5-point Calvinists]

    Note: "repentance" [in Mediate Theology] is defined as "a change of heart, mind, will, attitude, or mind-set about sin, self, and the Savior."[26] *Thus, coming to faith in Christ must include a change of heart, mind, and attitude toward Christ, His person, and His work.*

The following **plan of salvation** emerges from Mediate Theology's principles and conclusions above:[27]

- God made an eternal plan for the cross, church, and kingdom

- God foreknew those who would repent and believe in Christ
- God appointed the church in Christ to be set apart for service and a future inheritance based upon His foreknowledge
- Sinners are summoned—and are responsible to repent and trust Christ
- Conviction by the Spirit prepares human hearts through human instrumentality as the word of God is proclaimed
- Justification and new birth are conditioned on repentant faith alone
- Believers are marked out as children of God for an eternal inheritance
- Outward conversion results from justification and regeneration
- The justified and regenerate believer's salvation is eternal
- Discipleship and progressive sanctification are a believer's responsibility by the Spirit's power and will be rewarded in the kingdom

Proponents include: C. Gordon Olson

Favorably disposed: Tim LaHaye, Laurence Vance, Dave Hunt, Paige Patterson, Leith Anderson, John Minnema, Earl Radmacher, Edward P. Meadors

Important books: *Beyond Calvinism & Arminianism: An Inductive Mediate Theology of Salvation*, C. Gordon Olson; *The Other Side of Calvinism*, Laurance M. Vance; and *What Love is This?*, Dave Hunt

Assessment:
- Mediate Theology is based on inductive exegesis of Scripture. Rather than starting with certain biblical or philosophical presuppositions (as does Reformed Theology), Mediate Theology first looks at all passages which relate to a topic or a doctrine and then draws a conclusion as to its meaning.
- Mediate Theology has a more Biblical/balanced view of God's sovereignty than 5-point Calvinism. Indeed, one of Mediate Theology's greatest contributions, in this writer's view, is its presentation of God's sovereignty over human history in terms of (1) God's direct intervention; (2) God's indirect orchestration; and (3) God's delegation of free will to His creatures. [See chart on page 166]
- Mediate Theology has a more Biblical/balanced view of God's love than 5-point Calvinism. For example, John 3:16 (*"For God so loved the world that He gave His only begotten Son so that whoever believes in Him shall not perish but have everlasting life"*) overwhelms any tender-hearted believer with the magnitude and depth of God's love. In addition, II Peter 3:9 (*"The Lord is not slow about His promise, as some count slowness, but is patient toward you, not wishing for any to perish but for all to come to repentance"*) conveys the overwhelming inclusiveness of God's love—a love that desires for none to perish and for all to come to repentance.
- Mediate Theology rejects the notion of predestination of individuals to salvation. Instead, it believes that Christ died for the sins of all mankind (Unlimited Atonement); believes that man has free will; believes in the convicting ministry of the Holy Spirit upon the sinner; believes that sinners are summoned

through human instrumentality as the gospel is proclaimed; believes that salvation is contingent upon repentant faith in Jesus Christ; believes in the eternal security of the born-again Christian; and believes that discipleship is not a salvation issue but a sanctification issue.

- Mediate Theology believes that, in the New Testament, "predestination" (better, to pre-appoint or to foreordain) applies not to individuals but to God's foreordained corporate blessing and purposes for *believers*: e.g., the adoption of believers into Christ's family; providing believers with every spiritual blessing; transforming believers into the image of Christ, and providing believers with an eternal inheritance, the down payment being the indwelling Holy Spirit.[28]
- Mediate Theology is a grace-faith system: God, in His grace, freely provides the Person (Jesus Christ) and way of salvation (through Christ's substitutionary and atoning sacrifice); God the Father, in His grace, employs God the Spirit to convict sinners of their need for salvation (John 16:8-11 and others). Man's one responsibility is to receive the gift of salvation through faith in Jesus Christ.
- Mediate Theology corresponds more closely with the beliefs of the apostolic church and the church fathers than do the beliefs of Calvinism and Arminianism.[29]
- Mediate Theology has had antecedents throughout church history.[30]

Inductive Mediate Theology's Model of God's Sovereignty:[31]

God's Direct Intervention

e.g., God's creation of the universe; the curse on creation due to Adam's sin; the ejection of Adam and Eve from the garden; God's delegating rule/regency to Adam; God dealing directly with Cain; the translation of Enoch; the worldwide flood; the commissioning of the Patriarchs; Isaac's miraculous birth; the Exodus of Israel from Egypt; the miraculous conquest of the land; the miracles of Elijah, Elisha, Daniel; the virgin birth of Christ; Christ's many miracles; the resurrection of Christ; the Spirit's coming at Pentecost; the many apostolic miracles; the continued revelation of the NT through the Apostles.

God's Indirect Orchestration

e.g., Joseph brought into Egypt; David's providential survival from Saul; the Assyrian and Babylonian captivities; Israel's return from exile under Ezra and Nehemiah; God's providence with Mordecai and Ester; God's providences in the life of Daniel; the political ascendency of governments; God's judgments on nations; God's orchestrating the Cross through godless men; God's providences in the apostolic church; God's providences in the lives of all believers; God's orchestration of the end-time events preparatory to the return of Christ, including Israel's restoration as a nation.

God's Delegation of Free Will to His Creatures

e.g., Satan's revolt against God; the sin of Adam and Eve; all human sin; Cain's disobedience and murder of Abel; the godless Cainite civilization; Lamech's sin; the escalation of human violence before the Flood; the unrepentance of all except Noah's family; the sin of Canaan; the tower of Babel; the sins of Abraham, Isaac, Jacob, and Jacob's sons; Pharaoh's self-hardened heart and Egypt's idolatry; Israel's sins in the wilderness; Israel's sins in the land under the Judges; David's sin with Bathsheba; Israel's continuing apostasy before and after the exile; the legalism of the Pharisees and the rationalism of the Sadducees; the sins of Judas, Jewish leaders, Herod, Pilate, and the Romans through Satan and the flesh; and Hitler's Satan-inspired holocaust.

Note: To this writer, a principal weakness in all current salvation approaches among Evangelicals is their "either/or" conclusions with regard to the doctrine of election. As currently taught in Evangelical circles, only two alternatives exist: either all persons are saved ("elected") on an *unconditional* basis (5-point and 4-point Calvinism) or a *conditional* basis (Moderate Calvinism, Arminianism, and Inductive Mediate Theology). However, an inductive exegesis of Scripture indicates that at least some persons are selected and saved on an *unconditional* basis (in some cases even before birth). New Testament examples of the latter would be John the Baptist (Luke 1:5-25) and the Apostle Paul (Gal. 1:15). Thus, this writer would suggest that though conditional election far and away is *normative* in Scripture, unconditional election (the exception) is sometimes used by God to ensure that His purposes are accomplished. Apparently, the possibility that God could use *both* conditional and unconditional election—with conditional election being normative—has rarely been discussed or postulated over the past five hundred years.

CHAPTER 33

Major Doctrinal Errors in the Evangelical Church Today

*And when they had prayed, the place where they had gathered together was shaken, and they were all filled with the Holy Spirit and began to speak the word of God with boldness. And the congregation of those who believed were of **one heart and soul** [emphasis added] (Acts 4:31-32).*

*Day by day continuing with **one mind** in the temple [emphasis added], and breaking bread from house to house, they were taking their meals together with gladness and sincerity of heart, praising God and having favor with all the people (Acts 2:46-47a).*

*"I do not ask on behalf of these alone, but for those also who believe in Me through their word; **that they may all be one** [emphasis added], even as You, Father, are in Me and I in You, that they also may be in Us, so that the world may believe that You sent Me" (John 17:20-21).*

"Indeed, has God said . . . ? (Gen. 3:1).

Satan does not want Christ's Church to be a unified body having one mind, heart, and soul. Instead, through subtle deception, he continuously works to divide it—in order to diminish its witness to the world.

What is Satan's primary method of deception? It is the same approach he used with Eve in Genesis 3:1—"Indeed, has God said . . . ?" This simple challenge to the Word of God has deceived undiscerning Christian theologians throughout the Church Age, deceptions which in turn have brought error into the church. Though doctrinal errors are now many, this chapter will focus on seven of the major ones in Evangelicalism today:

- Limited Atonement
- Amillennialism
- Postmillennialism
- Replacement Theology
- Preterism
- Regeneration before faith
- Loss of salvation

It can be stated unequivocally that Evangelicalism would be much closer to the one heart, mind, and soul that Jesus desired for His flock if these seven errors could be eliminated from the church. Let us examine each.

Limited Atonement

Reformed theologians and other 5-point Calvinists believe that Christ's atoning sacrifice is limited in scope to the elect. Such a belief, however, contradicts fifteen passages of Scripture—Isaiah 53:6; John 1:29; John 3:14-17; John 4:42; John 12:32; John 16:8; II Cor. 5:14-15; II Cor. 5:19; I Tim. 2:3-6; I Tim. 4:10; Titus 2:11; Hebrews 2:9; II Peter 3:9; I John 2:2; and I John 4:14—which teach the Christ died for the sins of all mankind, not just the elect.

John the Baptist heralds the beginning of Christ's ministry with the words, *"Behold, the lamb of God who takes away the sin of the world!"* (John 1:29). The Apostle John proclaims in his first epistle, *"and He Himself is the propitiation for our sins; and not only for ours, but also for those of the whole world"* (I John 2:2). The Apostle Paul explains the following to Timothy: *"For there is one God, and one mediator also between God and man, the man Jesus Christ, who gave Himself as a ransom for all"* (I Tim. 2:5-6). Paul shares this truth with Titus: *"For the grace of God has appeared, bringing salvation to all men"* (Titus 2:11). To be sure, in the New Testament, Jesus is presented as the atonement, ransom, and propitiation for the sins of *all* mankind—a sacrifice which becomes efficacious when a person puts his faith in Christ (John 1:12; John 3:16; John 20:31; Rom. 10:19; Rev. 3:20; Rev. 22:11, et. al.).

For those Evangelicals who interpret Scripture in its plain, normal sense, such overwhelming evidence against the Limited Atonement beliefs of 5-point Calvinism and Reformed Theology is both troubling and bewildering. How can any Evangelical scholar hold a doctrinal position which contradicts the unambiguous teaching of fifteen passages of Scripture? Is not such a position grievous error?

In addition, the doctrine of Limited Atonement seriously impugns the breadth of Christ's love for man and the depth of His suffering on behalf of man. According to the testimony of the fifteen verses listed above, God—in perfect love—sent His Son to provide the way of reconciliation for *all* mankind, for *all* sinners. To be sure, Satan gets a considerable public relations victory if he can convince portions of the church that Christ simply died for persons the Father "pre-determined" to save. The unbelieving world would have every right to ask, "What kind of love is that?"

In short, the Limited Atonement doctrine of 5-point Calvinism and Reformed Theology is an indefensible mishandling of God's Word, which Satan has used to divide the Church. Should not our 5-point and Reformed brethren lay aside this doctrine immediately?

Amillennialism

Widespread belief in and adoption of amillennialism began with Augustine of Hippo around 400 A.D. Before Augustine, the premillennial position was held by all in Christendom, with the exception of Origen.[1] Having been influenced by Origen's allegorizing of Scripture and his subsequent search for hidden and mystical meaning, "Augustine found Origen's allegorical method of interpretation a helpful tool in side-stepping the teachings of certain millennial passages. So Augustine came to reject the premillennial idea of an earthly reign of Christ, which had been held in the church for several centuries."[2]

Two basic forms of amillennialism exist today: The Augustinian view and the "heavenly millennium" view. The Augustinian view (the majority view) teaches that the Millennium "is being fulfilled in the present age in the church and is on earth."[3] The basic element of Augustinian amillennialism "is the belief that the Millennial Kingdom began at the first coming of Christ and will continue until the second coming. Christ is today reigning in the church in the hearts of believers, as well as over the souls of believers in heaven."[4] Other significant elements of Augustinian amillennialism include (1) the binding of Satan (Rev. 20:1-3) at the time of Christ's first coming; (2) belief that the Rapture and the Second Coming of Christ are simultaneous events; (3) belief that at the time of Christ's second coming there will be one general resurrection and one general judgment.[5]

The "heavenly millennium" view (the minority view) teaches that the Millennium "is being fulfilled only in heaven as Christ reigns over the glorified saints. The Millennium . . . has to do with the blessed condition of the saints in heaven. The Millennium, therefore, is not something that finds fulfillment on this earth."[6]

Unfortunately, several problems buffet amillennialism:

- Amillennialism contradicts the straightforward teaching of the Bible, which asserts that Christ will reign over the earth for a thousand years (Rev. 20:1-6). Furthermore, numerous Old Testament prophecies describe a literal reign of Messiah over the earth (see Appendix A.)

- Jesus teaches the apostles that "in the regeneration when the Son of Man sits on His glorious throne, you also will sit upon twelve thrones, judging the twelve tribes of Israel" (Matt. 19:28). Because sin will not exist in the Eternal Kingdom (Heaven), no one at that time will need to judge the twelve tribes of Israel. As well, the twelve apostles have not yet been resurrected, so the passage cannot be referring to the current Church Age. Thus, the context of Christ's teaching in the Matthew 19 verse is an earthly Millennial Kingdom.

- Scripture teaches that Satan is the god of this world today (II Cor. 4:3-4) until Christ returns to the earth to bind him for a thousand years (Rev. 20:2-4)—and eventually cast him into the Lake of Fire forever (Rev. 20:7-10).

- If Christ is reigning over the earth from heaven today, then—considering the rampant sin and unrighteousness throughout the earth—one would have to conclude that He's doing a poor job of it, an obviously foolish notion. Without debate, it cannot be said the Christ is ruling over the earth today with a rod of iron (Rev. 2:17; 12:5; 19:15), nor can it be said that righteousness exists from sea to sea (Ps. 22:27-28; 72:7-8).

- Amillennialism either rejects or ignores the prophecies of Daniel, which teach that Messiah Himself will destroy man's final earthly kingdom, replacing it with His own (Dan. 2:36-45).

- Amillennialism eliminates a substantial portion of the glory due Christ after His return—an earthly glory prophesied in both Testaments (Ps. 24:7-10; 29:1-11; 72:11; 72:18-19; Ps. 96:7-13; 145:10-13; Rev. 19:16).

The whisper of Satan says: "Indeed, has God said that Christ will reign over the earth for a thousand years?" When Origen and Augustine took the bait and began to doubt God's Word, the error of amillennialism was birthed. In short, as with Limited Atonement, the doctrine of amillennialism is an indefensible mishandling of Scripture on the part of Christians who refuse to take God's Word at face value—the result being an unnecessary and heartbreaking division in the Church.

Postmillennialism

Two basic forms of postmillennialism exist today: 'Classic' postmillennialism and 'liberal' postmillennialism. 'Classic' postmillennialism "takes seriously the doctrines of the Scriptures and the need to spread the gospel throughout the world. The belief is that the church of Jesus Christ, operating in the power of the Holy Spirit will bring dramatic and transforming changes to the world. . . . Their optimism was born out by a belief in the triumph of the gospel in the world and the work of the Holy Spirit in bringing in the kingdom."[7] 'Liberal' postmillennialism "focuses on societal transformation rather than on personal conversion. Their 'social gospel' sees the saving of society from social evil as the great purpose of the church. The mission of the church is not to preach the gospel but, rather, to liberate mankind from poverty, racism, disease, war, and all kinds of injustice. It has the unbiblical view that people are not sinners in need of Christ's redeeming work but are inherently good."[8]

The basic elements of classic postmillennialism consist of the following:

- It teaches that "the return of Christ will take place *after* the Millennium. Thus, the Millennium ends with the personal, bodily return of Jesus Christ."[9]

- It posits that "the 'thousand years' mentioned six times in Revelation 20 is not to be taken in a literal way but instead represents a "long period of time." In this regard, postmillennialism is similar to amillennialism. However, some postmillennialists believe that during the present church age "there will emerge a golden age of spiritual blessing that flows out of the church age and will be in existence when Christ returns."[10]

- It believes that "the kingdom is spiritual and not a literal, earthly reign of Christ. Instead, it is the rule of Christ in the hearts of believers. When an individual believes in Christ and commits to obey Him, the kingdom is present. As the percentage of Christians grows in proportion to the total world population, the Kingdom of God expands and the promised blessings of peace and righteousness begin to fill the earth. Eventually conflict will cease between nations, racial groups, and social classes, and the fulfillment of the lion and lamb lying down together will take place (Isa. 11:6)."[11]

In recent years, newer forms of classic postmillennialism have surfaced in the Evangelical church. These include Theonomy, Reconstructionism, Dominion Theology, and Kingdom Now Theology.[12] These newer views populate the New Apostolic Reformation movement (to be discussed in Chapter 36).

To be sure, however, the same interpretive problems facing amillennialism also face postmillennialism:

- Postmillennialism contradicts the straightforward teaching of the Bible, which teaches that Christ will reign over the earth for a thousand years (Rev. 20:1-6). As stated previously, numerous Old Testament prophecies describe this literal reign of Messiah over the earth.

- Postmillennialism rejects or ignores the prophecies of Daniel, which teach that Messiah Himself will destroy man's final earthly kingdom, replacing it with His own (Dan. 2:36-45)—the premillennial view.
- Postmillennialism eliminates a substantial portion of the glory due Christ upon His return—an earthly glory prophesied in both Testaments (Ps. 24:7-10; 29:1-11; 72:11; 72:18-19; Ps. 96:7-13; 145:10-13; Rev. 19:16).

To their credit, many postmillennialists have a zeal for evangelism and a desire to Christianize the world. Nevertheless, an accurate handling of the Scriptures must always be a Christian's goal. In short, the doctrine of Postmillennialism, like Amillennialism, is an unfortunate mishandling of Scripture on the part of Christians who refuse to take God's Word at face value, the result being division in the Church.

Replacement Theology

What is Replacement Theology, and what are its interpretive problems? According to GotQuestions.org:

> Replacement Theology essentially teaches that the church has replaced Israel in God's plan. Adherents of replacement theology believe that the Jews are no longer God's chosen people and that God does not have specific future plans for the nation of Israel. . . .
>
> Replacement Theology teaches that the church is the replacement for Israel and that the many promises made to Israel in the Bible are fulfilled in the Christian church, not Israel. The prophecies in Scripture concerning the blessing and the restoration of Israel to the Promised Land are spiritualized or allegorized into promises of God's blessing for the church.
>
> Major problems exist with this view, including the continuing existence of the Jewish people throughout the centuries and especially the revival of the modern state of Israel: If Israel has been condemned by God and there is no future for the Jewish nation, then how do we explain the supernatural survival of the Jewish people over the past 2,000 years despite the many attempts to destroy them? How do we explain why and how Israel reappeared as a nation in the 20th century after not existing for 1,900 years.
>
> The view that Israel and the church are different is clearly taught in the New Testament. Biblically speaking, the church is distinct from Israel, and the terms church and Israel are never to be confused or used interchangeably. We are taught from Scripture that the church is an entirely new creation that came into being on the day of Pentecost and will continue until it is taken into heaven at the rapture (Eph. 1:9-11; I Thess. 4:13-17). The church has no relationship to the curses or blessings for Israel. The covenants, promises, and warnings of the Mosaic Covenant were valid only for Israel. Israel has been temporarily set aside in God's program during the past 2,000 years of dispersion (see Romans 11).[13]

In contrast to the teachings of Replacement Theology, the Apostle Paul declares passionately in Romans 11:1: *"I say then, God has not rejected His people [Israel], has He? May it never be! [emphasis added]"* He later adds in v.11: *"I say then, they [the Jews] did not stumble so as to fall, did they? May it never be! But by their transgression, salvation has come to the Gentiles, to make them [the Jews] jealous."* Paul closes his argument that God has not rejected Israel as follows: *"For I do not want you, brethren, to be uninformed of this mystery—so that you will not be wise in your own estimation—that* **a partial hardening has happened to Israel until the fullness of Gentiles has come in** *[emphasis added]; and so all Israel will be saved; just as it is written, 'the Deliverer will come from Zion, He will remove ungodliness from Jacob. This is My covenant with them, when I take away their sins.' From the standpoint of the gospel they are enemies for your sake, but from the standpoint of God's choice they are beloved for the sake of their fathers; for the gifts and the calling of God are **irrevocable** [emphasis added]"* (Romans 11:25-29).

Regrettably, the belief in Replacement Theology wholly contradicts Paul's teaching on God's inter-advent relationship with Israel in Romans 11. Moreover, Replacement Theology promotes a form of anti-Semitism and simultaneously robs Israel of her prophesied future glory.

Preterism

Christianity's analysis of the Bible's prophesied Tribulation period has become more fully developed over the past two to three hundred years as growing numbers of Christians began to take a more literal view of Eschatology and Christian theologians from different Eschatological leanings increasingly weighed in on the subject. Today, most Christians embrace one of four clearly defined Tribulation views: the Preterist view, the Historicist view, the Futurist view, or the Idealist view. Evangelical theologian Thomas Ice provides this summary of the four views:

> One of the most important, but seemingly little recognized, aspects of the proper interpretation of Bible prophecy is the role of timing. When will a prophecy be fulfilled in history? There are four possibilities, and they reflect the only four possibilities in relation to time: past; present; future; and timeless. The *preterist* (past) view believes that most, if not all, prophecy has already been fulfilled, usually in relation to the destruction of Jerusalem in A.D. 70. The *historicist* (present) view sees much of the current age as equal to the Tribulation period. Thus, prophecy has been and will be fulfilled during the current church age. *Futurists* (future) believe that virtually all prophetic events will take place in the future Tribulation, second coming, or millennium. The *idealist* (timeless) view does not believe that the Bible indicates the timing of events, or that we can determine their timing in advance. Therefore, idealists think that prophetic passages mainly teach that great ideas or truths about God are to be applied regardless of timing.[14]

With regard to the Preterist view, it must be noted that Preterism has developed into two distinct groups of followers—one group adhering to what is called "Full Preterism" and the other group adhering to what is called "Partial Preterism."

Full Preterism believes and teaches the following: all prophecy was fulfilled with the destruction of Jerusalem, including the resurrection of the dead and Jesus' Second Coming or *Parusia*. Full Preterism is also known by several other names: Consistent Preterism, Covenant Eschatology, Hyper-Preterism, and Pantelism. Full Preterism holds that Christ's Second Coming is to be viewed not as a future-to-us bodily return, but rather a "return" in glory manifested by the physical destruction of Jerusalem and her temple in AD 70 by foreign armies in a manner similar to various Old Testament descriptions of God coming to destroy other nations in righteous judgment. In addition, the New Heavens and New Earth are also equated with the New Covenant and the fulfillment of the Law in A.D. 70 and are to be viewed in the same manner by which a Christian is considered a "new creation" upon his or her conversion. In short, Full Preterists believe that the Tribulation period is a *past* event (taking place in the A.D. 70 timeframe), not a future one.[15] Most Full Preterists are amillennial; a few are postmillennial; none are premillennial.

The Theopedia encyclopedia provides the following summary of Partial Preterism:

> Partial Preterism holds that prophecies such as the destruction of Jerusalem, the Antichrist, the Great Tribulation, and the advent of the Day of the Lord as a "judgment-coming" of Christ were fulfilled c. A.D. 70 when the Roman general (and future Emperor) Titus sacked Jerusalem and destroyed the Jewish Temple, putting a permanent stop to the daily animal sacrifices. It identifies "Babylon the Great" of Revelation 17 & 18 with the ancient pagan city of Rome or Jerusalem.
>
> Most Partial Preterists also believe that the term "last days" refers not to the last days of planet Earth or the last days of humankind, but rather to the last days of the Mosaic Covenant, which God employed exclusively with the nation of Israel until the year A.D. 70. As God came in judgment upon various nations in the Old Testament, Christ also came in judgment against those in Israel who rejected him. These last days, however, are to be distinguished from *the* "last day," which is considered still future and entails the Second Coming of Jesus, the Resurrection of the righteous and unrighteous dead physically from the grave in like manner of Jesus' physical resurrection, the Final judgment, and the creation of a literal (rather than covenantal) New Heavens and New Earth, free from the curse of sin and death which was brought about by the fall of Adam and Eve. . . .
>
> Partial Preterists hold that the New Testament predicts and depicts many "comings" of Christ. They contend that the phrase "Second Coming" means the second of a like kind of series, for the Scriptures record other "comings" even before the judgment-coming in A.D. 70. This, they contend, would eliminate the A.D. 70 event as the "second" of any series, let alone the second of a series in which the earthly, physical ministry of Christ is the first. Partial Preterists believe that the new creation comes in redemptive progression as Christ reigns from His heavenly throne, subjugating His enemies, and will eventually culminate in the destruction of the "last enemy," physical death (I Cor. 15:20-24). If there are any enemies remaining, the resurrection event cannot have occurred.[16]
>
> Nearly all Partial Preterists embrace amillennialism or postmillennialism. Many postmillennial Partial Preterists are also Theonomic in their outlook—the belief that the Mosaic Law should be observed by modern societies.[17]

The most obvious problem with both types of Preterism is that they contradict known human history—and do so utterly and completely. Indeed, Preterism (Full or Partial) must be confronted head-on with the following historical realities: During the seven-year period surrounding or bisecting 70 A.D.,

- Did ten powerful nations subrogate their respective national sovereignties and form a ten-nation world empire (Dan. 7:24)? **No.**

- Did a Western political leader [the Antichrist] rise to power to lead these ten powerful nations (Dan. 7:24-25; Rev. 17:12-13)? **No.**

- Did men and women throughout the earth make an idol or image of a world political leader to worship (Rev. 13:11-19)? **No.**
- Did men and women throughout the earth receive the mark of the beast on their right hand or forehead (Rev. 13:11-19)? **No.**
- Were men and women throughout the earth forbidden to buy or sell goods unless they had the mark of the beast on their right hand or forehead (Rev. 13:11-19)? **No.**
- Was one-fourth of the earth's population killed (Rev. 6:7-8)? **No.**
- Did every mountain and island move out of its place (Rev. 6:12-17)? **No.**
- Did men and women throughout the earth hide in caves and mountains out of sheer fright (Rev. 6:12-17)? **No.**
- Was another one-third of the earth's population killed (Rev. 9:15-18)? **No.**
- Was a third of the earth burned up (Rev. 8:7)? **No.**
- Was a third of the earth's green grass burned up (Rev. 8:7)? **No.**
- Were a third of the earth's trees burned up (Rev. 8:7)? **No.**
- Did a third of the earth's seas become blood (Rev. 8:8-9)? **No.**
- Did a third of the earth's sea creatures die (Rev. 8:8-9)? **No.**
- Were a third of the world's ships destroyed (Rev. 8:8-9)? **No.**
- Did a third of the earth's rivers and lakes become bitter, causing many men to die from these waters (Rev. 8:10-11)? **No.**
- Was a third of the earth prevented from seeing the sun, moon, and stars (Rev. 8:12)? **No.**
- Did two Jewish witnesses, having the power to shut up the sky and to smite the earth with every plague, prophesy in Jerusalem for three and a half years (Rev. 11:3-6)? **No.**
- Did the Antichrist double-cross and destroy Apostate Christendom (the "Harlot") (Rev. 17:15-18)? **No.**
- Did the Antichrist subdue three of his ten heads of state (Rev. 7:24)? **No.**
- Was the Antichrist's Empire judged and destroyed in one hour, causing wailing and lament among the earth's shipmasters and merchants (Rev. 18:9-20)? **No.**
- Did the earth's oceans turn to blood and every living thing in the seas die (Rev. 16:3)? **No.**
- Did the earth's fresh water supply turn to blood (Rev. 16:4-7)? **No.**
- Did mankind find itself scorched with fierce heat, causing men and women throughout the earth to blaspheme God (Rev. 16:8-9)? **No.**
- Did men and women throughout the Antichrist's Empire gnaw their tongues and blaspheme God because of intense pain (Rev. 16:10-11)? **No.**

- Did the Euphrates River dry up, enabling the kings and armies of the East to gather in northern Israel (Rev. 16:12-16)? **No.**
- Did a world-wide earthquake take place during which all the cities of the nations fell (Rev. 16:18-19)? **No.**

What does a Preterist do with these numerous contradictions to known human history? He either allegorizes them, ignores them, or redefines the meaning and scope of words (e.g., one-third of Israel was burned up, not one-third of the earth). To support their use of an inconsistent hermeneutic, Preterists sometimes like to accuse Futurists of "wooden literalism" when interpreting end-times events and the second coming of Christ (even though the Preterist uses the same "wooden literalism" with regard to all prophecies relating to Christ's first coming).

Because of Preterism's refusal to take Christ's teaching on the Tribulation period at face value, two questions must be asked. First, why would any twenty-first century Christian, in view of the obvious contradictions listed above, want to accept the Preterist's assertion of an A.D. 70 Tribulation timeframe? Second, is not the Preterist's denial of Christ's prophetic voice a dangerous precedent and a serious quenching of the Holy Spirit? The Futurist position, in contrast, contains none of these contradictions. Every Futurist, because he believes that all Second Advent prophecies will be fulfilled literally (just as all prophecies relating to Christ's First Advent were fulfilled literally), contends that all of the questions listed above—at some point in the future—will be answered with a "yes."

Regeneration Before Faith

5-point Calvinism and Reformed Theology teach that God must regenerate a person *before* he can believe. How did this teaching come about? 5-point Calvinism and Reformed Theology begin with the supposition that man is so dead spiritually that he cannot possibly hear or respond to the gospel message. Thus, 5-point and Reformed theologians *deduce* that God must first regenerate a spiritually dead person before he can hear the gospel and exercise faith in its good news.

However, the Reformed doctrine of "regeneration before faith" wholly contradicts Numbers 21:7-9 and Christ's teaching to Nicodemus in John 3:14-15. In both passages it is clear that deliverance (in Exodus) and salvation (in John 3:14-15) comes *after* the exercise of faith on the part of the individual. Because a doctrinal position must never contradict Scripture, 5-point Calvinists and Reformed theologians have thrust a major error onto the Evangelical Church.

The doctrine of "regeneration before faith" also contradicts Genesis 15:1-6: *After these things the word of the LORD came to Abram in a vision, saying, "Do not fear, Abram, I am a shield to you; Your reward shall be very great." Abram said, "O Lord GOD, what will You give me, since I am childless, and the heir of my house is Eliezer of Damascus?" And Abram said, "Since You have given no offspring to me, one born in my house is my heir." Then behold, the word of the LORD came to him, saying, "This man will not be your heir; but one who will come forth from your own body, he shall be your heir." And He took him outside and said, "Now look toward the heavens, and count the stars, if you are able to count them." And He said to him, "So shall your* *descendants be." **Then he believed in the LORD; and He reckoned it to him as righteousness** [emphasis added].* Because Abram believed, God imputed righteousness to Abram. Romans 4:3, Galatians 3:6, and James 2:23 all refer to this seminal transaction in Genesis 15 to teach salvation by faith: When man believes God's gracious provision of Christ for his sin problem, God imputes His righteousness. Romans 10:9-10 corroborates the "faith first, subsequent regeneration" principle: *"If you confess with your mouth Jesus as Lord, and believe in your heart that God raised Him from the dead, you will be saved; for with the heart a person believes, resulting in righteousness, and with the mouth he confesses, resulting in salvation."*

In the Old Testament and New, God imputes His righteousness to a person *after* the exercise of faith. Indeed, no evidence exists in either Testament which supports the notion that God regenerates a person before he can exercise faith. This latter position invaded Evangelicalism as a result of the flawed supposition and resultant erroneous deduction mentioned above. Unfortunately, 5-point Calvinists and Reformed theologians, being misled by this flawed supposition and their deductive (rather than inductive) approach to the Bible, refuse to acknowledge that their "regeneration before faith" doctrine contradicts the straightforward teaching of Scripture.

Loss of Salvation

The belief by some Evangelicals that a born-again believer can lose his salvation does not line up with Scripture. In John 3:1-8, Jesus teaches that a person must be born again in order to have eternal life; he must have spiritual birth by the Holy Spirit ("that which is born of the Spirit is spirit"). Accordingly, for the new-birth analogy to hold true, no believer can ever be *un*born spiritually (just has a human baby can never be *un*born physically). In Ephesians 1:13-14 the born-again Christian is said to be sealed in Christ. Nowhere does the New Testament teach that a born-again Christian can be "unsealed" and taken out of Christ. In addition, the born-again Christian has been redeemed by the blood of Christ; he has been purchased by Christ's blood. Nowhere does the New Testament state that God returns the purchase price of a sinning or backsliding born-again Christian. Yes, a Christian can fall away from his first love [Jesus] (Rev. 2:4) and can even fall into heinous sin [e.g., King David]. But such a "falling away" will result in loss of reward (I Cor. 3:12-15), not loss of salvation (I Cor. 3:15). Finally, Jesus explicitly told his disciples that the Holy Spirit would not only indwell them, but would be with them *forever* (John 14:16-17). If the Holy Spirit is with the born-again believer forever, he cannot lose his salvation.

Point of Discernment: The first century Apostolic Church knew nothing of Limited Atonement, Amillennialism, Postmillennialism, Replacement Theology, Preterism, regeneration before faith, and loss of salvation—nor should you. All seven of these errors exist in the church today because of a refusal on the part of their proponents to take Scripture at face value. Moreover, let it again be stated that Evangelicalism would be much closer to the one heart, mind, and soul that Jesus desires for His flock, if these seven doctrinal errors were eliminated from the church.

CHAPTER 34

"Origins" Errors in Evangelicalism

In the beginning, God created the heavens and the earth (Genesis 1:1)

Introduction

Until two hundred years ago, virtually all Christians accepted the authority of the Bible's creation narrative and held (1) that the earth was young and (2) that God created the heavens and the earth—and all life upon the earth—in six, literal 24-hour days. Since then, however, these views have steadily come under attack by humanist and naturalist scientists.

The first assault on the Biblical account came with the development of modern geology in the 18th and 19th centuries, when naturalists argued that the earth's geological strata and fossil sequences suggested an earth which could be millions of years old, not thousands. The next assault came in the form of Darwinian evolution, which utilized geology's "millions of years" hypothesis to popularize the notion of biological evolution of all life on earth—including a "molecules-to-man" process over long periods of time for humans. Both the "millions of years" and the "molecules-to-man" theses contradict the plain, normal sense of the Biblical record. In short, man's word now challenged God's word in the matter of origins.

Today, the Old Earth thesis and Biological Evolution are taught as fact in the world's academic institutions. Biblical creationism, in turn, is universally belittled by academia as being abjectly "unscientific." Thus, the minds of countless high school and college-age students have been conditioned to doubt not only the veracity of the Bible's creation account, but the very authority of the Bible itself.

Attempts by Christians to Harmonize Old Earth and Evolutionary Beliefs with the Bible

Christians buffeted by the apparent scientific "proofs" of an Old Earth and biological evolution have put forth (over the past decades) various interpretive schemes in an effort to harmonize "science" with the Biblical account of our origins. Creationist author, Ken Ham, recently surveyed these attempts:[1]

1. **The Gap Theory**: This view claims that a huge time gap (perhaps several millions or billions of years) exists between Genesis 1:1 and Genesis 1:2. The most popular version of the Gap Theory—the ruin and reconstruction version—contends that Satan during this time gap rebelled and led a pre-historic creation in rebellion against God. As a result, God destroyed this original creation—and Genesis 1:2 describes the condition of the world following this ruin. **Major Problems** with this view: (1) Nowhere does Scripture hint of a pre-Adamic race of humans. (2) Because the sun (which is needed to heat the earth for human

survival) was not created until the fourth day, no pre-Adamic race could have existed or survived in a Genesis 1:1-2 timeframe; (3) most versions of the Gap Theory put death and suffering long before Adam's sin (see Romans 5:12).

2. **Theistic Evolution**: This view claims that God used evolution as a means of bringing about His creation. As such, Adam and Eve evolved from ape-like creatures. **Major Problems** with this view: (1) It attacks the idea that Adam was created in the image of God (Genesis 1:26-27) and made from the dust of the earth (Genesis 2:7). (2) It means that millions of years of death and suffering occurred before Adam's sin, in complete contradiction to Romans 5:12.

3. **The Day-Age Theory**: Proponents of this view claim that each of the days of creation was an extremely long period of time. In support of this view, proponents quote Psalms 90:4 and II Peter 3:8, which state that "one day is as a thousand years . . ." **Major Problems** with this view: (1) The Hebrew word for "day" in Genesis 1 is used throughout the Old Testament to mean a literal 24-hour day. (2) Certain types of plants and flowers created on the third day require unique types of birds or insects (created on the fifth day) for pollination and survival. If such birds and insects were not created for another million years, then certain plants and flowers could not have survived, let alone exist today. But they do. In contrast, all of them could have survived for two 24-hour days without being pollinated.

4. **Progressive Creation**: This view contends that each of the creation days was a long period of time. However, rather than accepting biological evolution, progressive creationists believe that God created in stages over many millions of years. They believe, for example, that God created certain animals millions of years ago and then they died out. Then God created more animals that died out. Eventually, he made humans. **Major Problem** with this view: it teaches that millions of years of death and suffering occurred before Adam's sin. Again, see Romans 5:12.

5. **The Literal-Day-With-Gaps View**: As its name implies, this view contends that each creation day was a literal 24-hour day, but that long periods of time took place between each 24-hour creation day. **Major Problems** with this view: (1) Certain types of plants and flowers created on the third day require unique types of birds or insects (created on the fifth day) for pollination and survival. If such birds and insects were not created for another million years, then certain plants and flowers could not have survived, let alone exist today. But they do. In contrast, all of them could have survived for two 24-hour days without being pollinated. (2) Millions of years of death and suffering would have occurred in the bird and fish kingdoms (both created on the fifth day) before the creation of Adam—and Adam's subsequent sin.

Today, however, could it be that such interpretive schemes are not only unbiblical but *unnecessary*? Could it be that God has brought forth to His church new evidence which both contradicts current scientific dogma and supports the Biblical record? The answer is yes.

The Unreliability of Radiometric Dating

Tens of millions of impressionable young people over that past decades have either studied or heard that radiometric dating techniques now "prove" that the earth is millions or billions of years old. Here's how these "clocks" work. Radioactive atoms, such as uranium (the parent isotopes), decay into stable atoms, such as lead (the daughter isotopes), at a measurable rate. To date a radioactive rock, geologists first measure the parent radioisotope, such as uranium-238 or potassium-40. They also measure the daughter isotope, such as lead-206 or argon-40 respectively. Based on these observations and the known rate of radioactive decay, they then estimate the time for the daughter isotope to accumulate in the rock. However, the reliability of these radioactive "clocks" is subject to three *unprovable* assumptions.[2]

Assumption 1: No daughter isotopes are present at the formation of the rock.

Dr. Andrew Snelling, a noted Australian geologist, notes the considerable problems with this assumption as follows:

> No geologists were present when most rocks formed, so they cannot test whether the original rocks already contained daughter isotopes alongside their parent radioisotopes. For example, with regard to the volcanic lavas that erupted, flowed, and cooled to form rocks in the unobserved past, evolutionary geologists simply assume that none of the daughter argon-40 atoms were in the lava rocks.
>
> For the other radioactive "clocks," it is assumed that by analyzing multiple samples of rock body, or unit, it is possible today to determine how much of the daughter isotopes (lead, strontium, or neodymium) were present when the rock formed (via the so-called isochron technique, which is still based on the unproven assumptions 2 and 3 below.)
>
> Yet lava flows that have occurred in the present have been tested soon after they erupted, and they invariably contain much more argon-40 than expected. For example, when a sample of the lava from the Mt. Saint Helens crater (which had been observed to form and cool in 1986) was analyzed in 1996, it contained so much argon-40 that it had a calculated "age" of 350,000 years. Similarly, the lava flows on the sides of Mt. Ngauruhoe, New Zealand, known to be less than 50 years old, yields "ages" of up to 3.5 million years.
>
> Therefore, it is logical to conclude that if recent lava flows of known age yield incorrect old potassium-argon ages due to the extra argon-40 they inherited from the erupting volcanoes, then the ancient lava flows of unknown ages could likewise had inherited extra argon-40—and, as a result, yield excessively old ages.[3]

Assumption 2: No contamination of the rock with other substances has occurred (versus, for example, conduit wall-rocks intermixed with lava flowing through the conduit).

Dr. Snelling reveals the problems with this assumption as well:

> The problems with contamination are already well-documented in the textbooks on radioactive dating of rocks. Indeed, the radioactive "clock" in rocks is open to contamination by gain or loss of parent or daughter isotopes because of (1) waters flowing in the ground from rainfall and (2) from the molten rocks beneath volcanoes. Similarly, as molten lava rises through a conduit from deep inside the earth to be erupted through a volcano, pieces of conduit wallrocks and

their isotopes can mix into lava and contaminate it. Because of such contamination, the less than 50-year-old lava flows at Mt. Ngauruhoe, New Zealand yield a rubidium-strontium "age" of 133 million years, a samarium-neodymium "age" of 197 million years, and a uranium-lead "age" of 3.908 billion years.[4]

Assumption 3: Radioactive decay occurs at a constant rate.

Dr. Snelling discusses the tenuous nature of this assumption:

Physicists have carefully measured the radioactive decay rates of parent isotopes in laboratories over the last one hundred years or so and have found them to be essentially constant (within the measurement error margins). Furthermore, they have not been able to change these decay rates significantly by heat, pressure, or electric or magnetic fields. So geologists have assumed these radioactive decay rates have been constant for billions of years. However, this is an enormous extrapolation of seven orders of magnitude back through immense spans of unobserved time without any concrete proof that such an extrapolation is credible. Nevertheless, geologists insist the radioactive decay rates have always been constant, because it makes these radioactive clocks "work."

New evidence, however, has recently been discovered that can only be explained by the radioactive decay rates not having been constant in the past. For example, the radioactive decay of uranium in tiny crystals in a New Mexico granite yields a uranium-lead "age" of 1.5 billion years. Yet the same uranium decay also produced abundant helium, but only 6,000 years worth of that helium was found to have leaked out of the tiny crystals. This means that the uranium must have decayed very rapidly over the same 6,000 years that the helium was leaking. Therefore, the rate of uranium decay must have been at least 250,000 times faster than today's measured rate.[5]

After presenting the inherent (and substantial) weaknesses of the assumptions on which radiometric dating is based, Snelling thus concludes:

The assumptions on which the radioactive dating is based are not only unprovable but plagued with problems. As the three points above illustrate, rocks may have inherited parent and daughter isotopes from their sources, or they may have been contaminated when they moved through other rocks to their current locations. Or inflowing water may have mixed isotopes into the rocks. In addition, the radioactive decay rates may not have been constant. So, if these clocks are based on faulty assumptions and yield unreliable results, the scientists should not trust or promote the claimed radioactive "ages" of countless millions of years." To be sure, the woeful inaccuracy of the argon-40 clocks employed in dating the recent lava flows from Mt. St. Helens and Mt. Ngauruhoe proves the tenuous nature of science's "millions or billions of years" conclusions.[6]

The Impossibility of Macroevolution

First, thanks to human genome advances in the 21st century, medical science has proven Biological Evolution and its molecules-to-man thesis to be utterly impossible: the genetic code in a human cell is far too intricate to have evolved from a simpler form over time. Man had to have been created.

Second, a contemporary researcher has demonstrated that certain animals, fish and insects could not possibly have evolved, but indeed had to have been created. For example, this researcher states the following about the bombardier beetle:

> Evolutionary theory has big problems when attempting to explain the existence and complexity of the bombardier beetle by means of random, chance happenings. Each stage in the development of its special self-defense chemicals would have led to its destruction. This one-half inch insect mixes chemicals that violently react to produce something similar to an explosion. How could the bombardier beetle have evolved such a complex means of defense without killing itself in the process? This problem has the members of the evolutionary establishment scratching their heads. Evolutionary says that you lose it if you don't use it. But how do you use it unless you have it in a completed and fully-functional form?
>
> We have two options. One is to believe that a mindless, random, chance process brought into existence exactly what would be essential for the creature to maintain life and defend itself. The other option is that God, in his sovereign wisdom, designed and created precisely what was needed for the welfare of the creature and encoded the information in its genes. With godless evolution, a new enzyme or chemical or organ or fin or beak or bone will have to evolve randomly, mindlessly, unexplainably until the creature gains its new improvement. As creationists, we would say that God created it just like it is—a discreet, fully functional little bug with an incredibly complex defense mechanism.[7]

Conclusion

The universally accepted Old Earth and biological Evolution views have been savaged by recent scientific discoveries. Accordingly (as has always been the case over the past five hundred years), scientific discoveries eventually support the Bible's presentation of science—and the Creation vs. Evolution debate is no exception. Today, Christians need not cower over Old Earth and Evolution dogmas, but instead can point to the recent scientific evidence from Mount St. Helens, Mt. Ngauruhoe, and the intricacy of the human genetic code, evidence which proves the authority and reliability of the Bible.

Point of discernment: Every Christian can arm himself with the following three truths: (1) the dating methods use to "prove" an old earth are embarrassingly inaccurate, (2) the genetic code in the human cell is far too intricate to have evolved, and (3) numerous animals, insects, birds, and fish could not possibly have evolved.

CHAPTER 35

Evangelical Movements that Differ from Biblical Christianity

Evangelicals believe that a person must be born again in order to be saved. A supernatural transaction from above takes place when one puts his or her faith in Jesus Christ for salvation; he or she is born anew and is a new creation in Christ the moment saving faith takes place.

As proposed in Chapter 31, Biblical Christianity most closely represents the beliefs of the "wheat" (the true church) in Paul's day. It also most likely mirrors the beliefs of the Smyrna and Philadelphia churches in 95 A.D. Biblical Christianity believes in the inspiration, inerrancy, authority, and sufficiency of Scripture. It interprets the Bible's words and figures of speech in their plain, normal sense—and it uses a Grammatical-Historical-Literal hermeneutic, consistently applied throughout Scripture. It attempts to know and teach the whole counsel of God's Word, and it works diligently to teach God's Word accurately. It does not add to or subtract from God's Word, nor does it attempt to politicize or deconstruct God's Word.

Today's Evangelical Church, however, includes movements that use other interpretive approaches, which in turn causes them to arrive at different beliefs in certain areas of doctrine. Each of these movements varies from Biblical Christianity—some in minor ways, others in larger ways (to be discussed below). The brands/movements surveyed in the next two chapters (not an all-inclusive list) are as follows:

1. Historic (or Covenant) Premillennialism
2. Reformed/Presbyterian Churches
3. Polite Evangelicalism (The Purpose Driven Church)
4. Polite Evangelicalism (The Seeker Sensitive Movement)
5. Lutheran Evangelical Churches
6. Anglican/Episcopal Evangelical Churches
7. Progressive Christianity
8. The New Apostolic Reformation
9. The Positive Confession (or Word-Faith) Movement
10. Emergent Christianity

I. The Movement Closest to Biblical Christianity:

1. Historic (or Covenant) Premillennialism

- What it is: Historic Premillennialism (sometimes called Covenant Premillennialism) is based on Covenant Theology rather than the biblical covenants found in Scripture. Historic Premillennialism (as its name suggests) believes in a Second Coming of Christ to establish His reign of a thousand years over the earth. However, unlike Biblical Christianity, it doesn't see as clear a distinction between the Church and Israel as does Biblical Christianity.[1] In addition, some in the movement hold to 5-point Calvinist salvation beliefs.

- View of the Bible: Most in the movement have a high view of Scripture and believe in the inspiration, inerrancy, and authority of Scripture.

- Interpretive approach: Historical Premillennialism utilizes a Grammatical-Historic-Literal hermeneutic, but at times applies it inconsistently. With regard to eschatology, for example, many in the movement teach a mid-tribulation or post-tribulation Rapture.[2] To do this, they must ignore or allegorize Christ's teaching on an "any moment" return (e.g., Matt. 24:32-42; 24:43-44; 25:1-13). The movement also fails to recognize Christ's teaching of two, mutually-exclusive comings of the Son of Man in the Olivet Discourse—one being the pre-tribulation Rapture and the other being Christ's second coming to the earth (see Appendix B). Moreover, some in the movement do not fully utilize Old Testament scripture to fill in the details of the Millennial Kingdom, and others at times spiritualize Old Testament prophecy.[3]

II. Movements Somewhat Farther from Biblical Christianity:

2. Evangelical Reformed/Presbyterian Churches

- What it is: Evangelical Reformed and Presbyterian churches believe in the divine predestination and election of man. In addition, Reformed and Presbyterian salvation is monergistic: God does it all, including giving His elect the faith to believe; man does not freely cooperate in the salvation transaction.

- View of the Bible: Most in the movement have a high view of Scripture and believe in the inspiration, inerrancy, and authority of Scripture.

- Interpretive approach and beliefs:
    - Uses a dual hermeneutic
    - Is based on Covenant Theology
    - Chooses to spiritualize or allegorize certain prophetic passages rather than taking them at face value

- Other beliefs:
    - For the most part holds to Replacement Theology
    - For the most part holds to amillennialism—and does not believe that Christ will one day return to reign over the earth
    - Holds to Limited Atonement, a belief that contradicts numerous passages of Scripture
    - Teaches that regeneration precedes faith, a belief which contradicts Genesis 15:6 and Christ's teaching in John 3:14-15

- o Places great emphasis on the Westminster Confession of 1647

3. **Polite Evangelicalism (The Purpose Driven Church)**

- What it is: The Purpose Driven Church movement focuses on God's purposes, not a pastor's ideas for ministry. "There's no particular formula or way of doing church; it's the Purpose Driven focus and intentionality that's important, not the method."[4] Purpose Driven churches share twelve characteristics, including having "a Purpose Statement (in their own words) that describes their commitment to building the church around five New Testament purposes: worship, evangelism, fellowship, discipleship, and ministry."[5]
- View of the Bible: Many in the movement have a high view of Scripture and believe in the inspiration and inerrancy of Scripture.
- Interpretive approach:
  - o Uses a dual hermeneutic
  - o Is based on Covenant Theology
  - o Chooses to spiritualize or allegorize certain prophetic passages rather than taking them at face value
- Other beliefs:
  - o Holds to Replacement Theology
  - o Does not believe that Christ will one day return to reign over the earth
  - o De-emphasizes and downplays the topic of eschatology
  - o Countenances ministry partnerships with non-Christian religions (in direct disobedience to II Cor. 6:14-15) in an effort, for example, to wipe out poverty

4. **Polite Evangelicalism (The Seeker-Sensitive Movement)**

- What it is: The Seeker-Sensitive Movement gears its worship services to the "seeker" or the newcomer in such a way that it eschews using Christian words and phrases which might alienate or offend the seeker.
- View of the Bible: Many in the movement have a high view of Scripture and believe in the inspiration and inerrancy of Scripture.
- Interpretive approach:
  - o Uses a dual hermeneutic
  - o Is based on Covenant Theology
  - o Chooses to spiritualize or allegorize certain prophetic passages rather than taking them at face value
  - o Waters down certain parts of Scripture, e.g., will not talk about the shed blood of Christ lest a seeker be offended. This watering down of Scripture amounts to a de facto weakening of the authority of the Bible
- Other beliefs:
  - o Holds to Replacement Theology

- o Does not believe that Christ will one day return to reign over the earth
- o Its founding church (Willow Creek Community Church) supports Christian Palestinianism, an anti-Semitic belief

5. **Lutheran Evangelicalism**

- What it is: Lutheran Evangelicalism leans heavily on the Reformation teachings of Martin Luther—including his notions of "grace alone, "faith alone," and "Scripture alone."
- View of the Bible: Many in the movement have a high view of Scripture and believe in the inspiration and inerrancy of Scripture. Parts of Lutheran Evangelicalism, however, only pay lip service to the authority of Scripture, as evidenced by the ordination of female pastors/ministers.
- Interpretive approach:
  - o Uses a dual hermeneutic
  - o Chooses to spiritualize or allegorize certain prophetic passages rather than taking them at face value
- Other beliefs:
  - o Holds to Replacement Theology
  - o Does not believe that Christ will one day return to reign over the earth
  - o Is typically more liturgical than other brands of Evangelicalism (with the exception of Anglican/Episcopal Evangelicalism)

6. **Anglican/Episcopal Evangelicalism**

- What it is: Anglican Evangelicalism has its roots in 17th century England, and Episcopal Evangelicalism is the Americanized version of the Anglican approach. Both movements have a hierarchical form of church governance featuring bishops and priests. Bishops typically oversee several parishes in a city.
- View of the Bible: Many in these movements have a high view of Scripture and believe in the inspiration, inerrancy, and authority of Scripture.
- Interpretive approach:
  - o Uses a dual hermeneutic
  - o Is based on Covenant Theology
  - o Chooses to spiritualize or allegorize certain prophetic passages rather than taking them at face value
- Other beliefs:
  - o Holds to Replacement Theology
  - o Does not believe that Christ will one day return to reign over the earth
  - o Is typically the most liturgical brand of Evangelicalism

Point of Discernment: Different flavors of Evangelicalism exist apart from Biblical Christianity. With the exception of Lutheran Evangelicalism, all movements listed in this chapter are based on Covenant Theology and all use, to varying degrees, an inconsistently-applied, G-H-L hermeneutic. Apart from Covenant Premillennialism, none of these movements teach their flocks about Christ's glory during the Millennial Kingdom, nor the believer's role of returning with Christ at His Second Coming to reign with Him for a thousand years. In addition, few Covenant churches and no Lutheran churches make any attempt to teach the whole counsel of God, thus robbing their flocks of significant information about God's future dealings with His Bride, unbelievers, Israel, and the nations. Nevertheless, most of these movements do an excellent job of teaching the primacy of Christ and the particulars of the Christian life.

CHAPTER 36

Evangelical Movements that Differ from Biblical Christianity—Part II

The following Evangelical movements have moved still farther from Biblical Christianity. These movements represent, to a large extent, either the politicization or the very deconstruction of Evangelical Christianity, as will be discovered in the following survey of each.

III. The Politicization of Evangelical Christianity

7. Progressive Christianity

- What it is: Evangelical Progressive Christianity is an approach to Christianity which emphasizes and promotes social justice (including a more equitable distribution of income and wealth) through governmental lobbying efforts.
- View of the Bible: Most in the Evangelical Progressive Christianity movement believe in the inspiration and inerrancy of Scripture.
- Interpretive approach:
    - Uses a dual hermeneutic
    - Is based on Covenant Theology
- Other beliefs/characteristics:
    - Has no discernable eschatology
    - Has noticeably less interest in the Great Commission than other brands of Evangelicalism
    - Supports leftist political causes
    - Is the most utopian of all brands of Evangelicalism: believes fervently in social activism to create a better world
    - Is highly ecumenical in its approach; seemingly has little trepidation about God's prohibition of partnering with "tares"
    - Believes in ministry partnerships with non-Christian religions (in direct disobedience to II Cor. 6:14-15) in support of such causes, for example, as the elimination of poverty
- **Assessment**: Progressive Christianity's promotion of social justice implies victimhood—certain persons and groups are "victims" of some form of social injustice. Part of this "injustice" is economic in nature—some are rich; many are poor. To rectify this injustice, Progressive Christianity lobbies the government to pass laws supporting the redistribution of income or wealth in a more

equitable manner. Scripture teaches, however, that it is the *church* which is to take care of its poor (Acts 2:42-45; 4:32-35) and that Christians are also to be generous to non-believers in need (Matt. 5:42; 6:2-4). Furthermore, Scripture teaches that Christians are to be content with however much or little they have in terms of material goods (Phil 4:11-13). Paul says: *"If we have food and covering, with these we shall be content" (I Tim. 6:8)*. In contrast, the income-redistribution belief of Progressive Christianity tacitly promotes a love of mammon, which the Bible teaches can never satisfy. Finally, Jesus teaches that His kingdom is a spiritual kingdom (John 3:1-8) and is not of this world (John 18:36). Progressive Christianity, apparently ignoring or minimizing the nature of Christ's inter-advent *spiritual* kingdom, exerts most of its energy on improving an earthly kingdom that is passing away (I John 2:17)—and little energy on the Great Commission.

8. The New Apostolic Reformation

- What it is: Wikipedia and GotQuestions.org provide the following summary of the New Apostolic Reformation:

    The New Apostolic Reformation (NAR) is a movement which seeks to establish a fourth branch within Christendom, distinct from Catholicism, Protestantism (which includes Pentecostalism), and Eastern Orthodoxy. The movement largely consists of churches nominally or formally associated with the Pentecostal denominations and Charismatic movements but have diverged from traditional Pentecostal and Charismatic theology in that it advocates the restoration of the lost offices of church governance, namely the offices of prophet and apostle.[1]

    Growth in the New Apostolic Reformation is driven primarily through small groups and church planting, often completely independent of a parent congregation. The movement is not centrally controlled, and many of its followers will not self-identify as part of it or even recognize the name. All the same, thousands of churches and millions of believers adhere to the teachings of the New Apostolic Reformation.[2]

    Although the movement regards the church as the true body of saved believers, as most Evangelical Protestants do, it differs from the broader Protestant tradition in its view on the nature of church leadership, specifically the doctrine of Five-Fold Ministry, which is based upon a non-traditional interpretation of Ephesians 4:11 (the apostles, the prophets, the evangelists, the pastors, and the teachers). C. Peter Wagner writes that most of the churches in this movement have active ministries of spiritual warfare.[3]

    The term "New Apostolic Reformation" traces its historical roots to late twentieth-century American charismatic churches, and the earliest use of the moniker was by C. Peter Wagner. Though few organizations publicly espouse connection to the NAR, there are several notable individuals often associated with this movement, including:

    - Lou Engle – Founder of The Call
    - Mike Bickle – International House of Prayer

- o Chuck Pierce – Global Spheres, Inc.
- o Bill Johnson – Head Pastor of Bethel Church
- o Rick Joyner – Founder of Morning Star Ministries
- o Mike and Cindy Jacobs – Generals International
- o John P. Kelly – Founder of John P. Kelly Ministries and Convening Apostle
- o C. Peter Wagner – Founder of Global Harvest Ministries[4]

  According to Wagner, "The second apostolic age began in the year 2001" when the lost offices of prophet and apostle were restored.[5]

- View of the Bible: Many in the NAR believe in the divine inspiration of Scripture, and some also believe in its inerrancy and authority. However, others in the movement belittle the Scriptures as "moldy pages" and "old manna."[6] Says the NAR's Wendy Alec: "For the Word alone is yesterday's manna and even they [prophetic teachers] have seen deep in their hearts that it [the Bible] is no longer enough to feed my people."[7] Those who hold to such a belief have a patently low view of Scripture, and instead promote the efficacy of NAR prophecies and "new revelations."

- Interpretive approach:
  - o Some use a dual hermeneutic; others use eisegesis; still others have no hermeneutic at all.

- Key beliefs/teachings: Wagner has listed the differences between the NAR and traditional Protestantism as follows:
  - o Apostolic governance – According to the NAR, the Apostle Paul's assertion that Jesus appoints apostles within his church [Eph. 4:11] continues to this day.
  - o The office of the prophet – There is within the church a role and function for present-day prophets.
  - o Dominionism – "When Jesus came, He brought the kingdom of God and He expects His kingdom-minded people to take whatever action is needed to push back the long-standing kingdom of Satan and bring the peace and prosperity of His kingdom here on earth."
  - o Theocracy – Not to be confused with theocratic government, but rather the goal of the NAR to have "kingdom-minded people" in all areas of society. There are seven areas identified specifically: religion, family, education, government, media, arts & entertainment, and business.
  - o Extra-biblical revelation – There is available to all believers the ability to hear from God. The one major rule governing any new revelation from God is that it cannot contradict what has already been written in the Bible. It may supplement it, however.
  - o Supernatural signs and wonders – Signs and wonders such as healing, demonic deliverance and confirmed prophecies accompany the move of God.

- Relational structures – church governance has no formal structure but rather is by relational and voluntary alignment to apostles.[8]

Assessment: First, Scripture teaches that an apostle of Christ had to have been called by the Lord Himself; traveled with Jesus for at least part of His ministry; and been an eyewitness to the Resurrection (Acts 1:21-22). All of the NAR's modern-day "apostles" fail the latter two tests, and no modern-day "apostle" can prove he has been called to apostleship by Jesus Himself.

Second, the metaphor of "God's household" in Ephesians 2:19-22 clearly teaches that the apostles and prophets of Jesus existed during the first century only—during the foundation of the church. *All* believers today—including alleged modern-day "apostles" and "prophets"—are merely building blocks in the structure, most likely blocks near the top of the building (because the church is close to 2,000 years old).

Third, the NAR casts "secular humanism and pluralism as being in conflict with Christianity, thus conferring a duty on Christians to transform earthly institutions in order to combat non-Christian influence. As such, establishing the kingdom on earth to prepare for Christ's return requires Christians to transform the world, or to take 'dominion,' a view that has become an article of faith for the religious right."[9] In sharp contrast to the NAR mandate, however, are the words of Christ in John 18:36 (*"My kingdom is not of this world"*) and Matthew 28:19 (*"Go therefore and make disciples of all the nations, baptizing them in the name of the Father and the Son and the Holy Spirit"*). To be sure, Jesus teaches that the Christian's mandate is to go throughout the world and make disciples in His interadvent spiritual kingdom, not to take dominion over the world's institutions.

Fourth, no NAR "prophet" has prophesied with 100% accuracy, the standard set by God for His *divinely*-appointed prophets. In late 2020, the NAR received a substantial black eye in the aftermath of the U.S. election: the vast majority of NAR prophets had prophesied (some on Christian television) a Donald Trump victory in the November election.

Fifth, the movement is "introducing a flood of new doctrines and practices into the body of Christ that have never been a part of the church's teaching and which cannot be validated Biblically."[10] Such teachings include (1) unclaimed spiritual inheritances and assignments; (2) doors to heaven; (3) spiritual portals; (4) apostolic love covering a city from God's view; (5) the releasing of demonic activity via critical speech; (6) storehouse cities; (7) judicial intersession; (8) cleansing the land from demonic influence; (9) the establishment of "throne zones"; and (10) prophetic decrees.[11] Such questionable doctrines remind a discerning Christian of the Lord's admonition to the church at Thyatira: *"But I have this against you, that you tolerate the woman Jezebel, who calls herself a prophetess, and she teaches and leads My bond-servants astray. . . ."* (Rev. 2:20). Are not these non-biblical doctrines of NAR "prophets" leading their followers astray?

Sixth, a significant number—like Wendy Alec—have succumbed to Satan's ploy in Genesis 3:1-7, which (1) challenges the veracity of God's Word (Alec's "yesterday's manna") and (2) offers an alluring (but impotent) alternative to God's

Word (the extra-biblical revelation of supposed end-times super apostles and prophets).

Finally, NAR "prophets" routinely prophesy the coming of a final, massive, worldwide harvest of souls for Jesus Christ—indeed, "one to two billion souls over the next twenty to thirty years" according to one NAR prophet[12]. Such prophecies, however, cavalierly assume the world will continue "as is" for the next two-to-three decades and contradict Christ's teaching that His sheep should constantly be ready for His any-moment return for His bride (born-again Christians)—perhaps even tonight (Matt. 24:36-44). Indeed, many NAR leaders seem oblivious to the signs of the times (Matt. 24:32-34).

> **Points of discernment**: While its zeal for prayer and revival is *highly commendable* (and likely greater than most of Evangelicalism), the New Apostolic Reformation—in disobedience to Deuteronomy 4:3, Proverbs 30:5-6, and Revelation 22:18-19—adds to the Word of God (seemingly without reservation) through the "prophecies" of their self-proclaimed "apostles" and "prophets." In short, the NAR seems more interested in supposed words from God than in the Word of God itself. As well, let the following be stated categorically: because none of the NAR's apostles (1) can prove they have been called personally to apostleship by Christ, (2) traveled with Christ during His ministry, and (3) witnessed Christ's Resurrection, these "apostles" are self-appointed rather than divinely-appointed. Finally, the Word of the Lord (the Bible) will endure forever (Isaiah 40:8; I Peter 1:25), but the "prophecies" and new revelations of NAR apostles and prophets will quickly be forgotten.

IV. The Deconstruction of Evangelical Christianity

9. The Word of Faith (or Word-Faith) Movement

- What it is: According to Wikipedia…

    The Word of Faith Movement (also known as *Word-Faith* or simply *Faith*) essentially teaches that Christians can access the power of faith or fear through speech. Its distinctive teachings are found on the radio, Internet, television, and in many Christian churches. The basic doctrine preached is that of wealth and health through positive confession.

    The movement emphasizes choosing to speak the promises and provisions that the speaker wants—if they are in agreement with the Bible—as an act of faith and agreement with God's plans and purposes. The movement believes this is what Jesus meant in Mark 11:22–24, when he said believers shall have whatever they say, ask, and pray for with faith. The term *word of faith* itself is derived from Romans 10:8 which speaks of *the word of faith that we preach*.

    Evangelist E.W. Kenyon (1867–1948) is usually given credit as the originator of Word of Faith teaching. He began as a Methodist minister and evolved into a Pentecostal. Kenyon's principal disciple was Kenneth Hagin, Sr.—the recognized "father" of the Word of Faith movement. Hagin

(1917–2003) believed that it is God's will that believers would always be in good health, financially successful, and happy. Hagin's principal disciple was Kenneth Copeland, who is the unofficial leader of the Word of Faith movement.[13]

- View of the Bible: Most in the movement believe in or pay lip service to the divine inspiration of Scripture, and some adherents also believe in its inerrancy. However, others in the movement, through the substance of their teaching, demonstrate a limited or restricted view of the authority of Scripture.

- Interpretive approach:
  - Most in the movement use a loose hermeneutic or no hermeneutic at all. Both of these conditions lead to extensive eisegesis on the part of Word-Faith teachers.

- Key beliefs/teachings (verbatim from Wikipedia):
  - Healing: The Word of Faith teaches that complete healing (of spirit, soul, and body) is included in Christ's atonement and therefore is available here and now to all who believe. Frequently cited is Isaiah 53:5, "by his stripes we are healed," and Matthew 8:17, which says that Jesus healed the sick so that "it might be fulfilled which was spoken by Isaiah the Prophet, 'Himself took our infirmities, and bore our sicknesses'." Because Isaiah speaks in the present tense ("we *are* healed"), Word of Faith teaches that believers should accept the reality of a healing that is already theirs. Accepting this healing is done by confessing the verse or verses found in the Bible declaring they are healed (i.e. Word of Faith) and then believing them fully without doubt.[14]
  - Prosperity: Word of Faith teaching holds that God wants his people to be prosperous, which includes finances, good health, good marriages and relationships, i.e. to live generally prosperous lives in all areas. Word of Faith teaches that God empowers his people (blesses them) to achieve the promises that are contained in the Bible. Because of this, suffering does not come from God, but rather, from Satan. As Kenneth Copeland's ministry has stated, the idea that God uses suffering for our benefit is considered to be "a deception of Satan" and "absolutely against the Word of God." Additionally, if someone is not experiencing prosperity, it is because they have given Satan authority over their lives. God will not do anything at all unless the person invites him to.[15]
  - Faith and confession: Within Word of Faith teaching, a central element of receiving from God involves "confession". This doctrine is often referred to as "positive confession" or "faith confession" by practitioners. . . . Noted Word of Faith teachers, such as Kenneth E. Hagin and Charles Capps, have argued that God created the universe simply by speaking it into existence (Genesis 1), and that humans have been endowed with the ability (power) to speak things into existence. Thus, making a "positive confession" (by reciting a promise of scripture, for example), and believing that which God says, accesses the resurrection power that was released when Christ was raised from the dead (Ephesians 1:19-20), Ephesians 3:20, which causes those things to come into fruition. This teaching is interpreted from Mark 11:22-23. Word of Faith preachers have likened faith to a "force".[16]

Assessment: All three of these key beliefs contradict the teachings of the apostolic church—and represent a substantial deconstruction of God's Word. God heals some, but not all. God enables some to have material prosperity, but expects them to use it to care for those in need (Acts 2 and Acts 4). The word-faith "positive confession" doctrine which teaches that humans have the power to speak things into existence presumes on God and amounts to spiritual alchemy.

One Evangelical on-line commentary evaluates the Word of Faith movement as follows:

> At the heart of the movement is the belief in the "force of faith." It is believed that words can be used to manipulate the faith-force, and thus actually create what they believe Scripture promises (health and wealth). Laws supposedly governing the faith-force are said to operate independently of God's sovereign will and that God Himself is subject to these laws. This is nothing short of idolatry, turning our faith—and, by extension, ourselves—into god.
>
> From here, its theology strays farther and farther from Scripture: it claims that God created human beings in His literal, physical image as little gods. Before the fall, humans had the potential to call things into existence by using the faith-force. After the fall, humans took on Satan's nature and lost the ability to call things into existence. In order to correct this situation, Jesus Christ gave up His divinity and became a man, died spiritually, took Satan's nature upon Himself, went to hell, was born again, and rose from the dead with God's nature. After this, Jesus sent the Holy Spirit to replicate the incarnation in believers so they could become little gods as God had originally intended.
>
> Following the natural progression of these teachings, as little gods we again have the ability to manipulate the faith-force and become prosperous in all areas of life. Illness, sin, and failure are the result of a lack of faith, and are remedied by confession—claiming God's promises for oneself into existence. Simply put, the Word of Faith movement exalts man to god-status and reduces God to man-status. . . . Obviously, Word of Faith teaching does not take into account what is found in Scripture.
>
> Countering Word of Faith teaching is a simple matter of reading the Bible. God alone is the Sovereign Creator of the Universe (Genesis 1:3; I Timothy 6:15) and does not need faith—He is the object of faith (Mark 11:22; Hebrews 11:3). God is spirit and does not have a physical body (John 4:24). Man was created in the image of God (Genesis 1:26, 27; 9:6), but this does not make him a little god or divine. Only God has a divine nature (Galatians 4:8; Isaiah 1:6-11, 43:10, 44:6; Ezekiel 28:2); Psalms 8:6-8). Christ is eternal, the Only Begotten Son, and the only incarnation of God (John 1:1,2,14,15,18; 3:16; I John 4:1). In Him dwelled the fullness of the Godhead bodily (Colossians 2:9). By becoming a man, Jesus gave up the glory of heaven, but not His divinity (Philippians 2:6-7), though He did choose to withhold His power while walking the earth as a man.[17]

10. Emergent Christianity

- What it is: One Evangelical source describes the movement as follows:

  > The emerging, or emergent, church movement takes its name from the idea that as culture changes, a new church should emerge in response. In this

case, it is a response by various church leaders to the current era of post-modernism. Although post-modernism began in the 1950s, the church didn't really seek to conform to its tenets until the 1990s. Post-modernism can be thought of as a dissolution of "cold, hard fact" in favor of "warm, fuzzy subjectivity." The emerging/emergent church movement can be thought of the same way.[18]

This movement is still fairly new, so there is not yet a standard method of "doing" church amongst the groups choosing to take a post-modern mindset. In fact, the emerging church rejects any standard methodology for doing anything. Therefore, there is a huge range of how far groups take a post-modernist approach to Christianity. Some groups go only a little way in order to impact their community for Christ, and remain biblically sound. Most groups, however, embrace post-modernist thinking, which eventually leads to a very liberal, loose translation of the Bible. This, in turn, leads to liberal doctrine and theology.[19]

Notable individuals often associated with the Emergent movement include:
- Brian McLaren – author, speaker, and former pastor of Cedar Ridge Community Church
- Doug Pagitt – founder of Solomon's Porch (Minneapolis) and executive director of Vote Common Good
- Rob Bell – author, speaker, and former pastor of Mars Hill Bible Church (Michigan)
- Shane Claiborne – author and Christian activist
- Tony Jones – author and emergent theologian

- View of the Bible: Some in the movement believe in the divine inspiration of Scripture, and a few adherents believe in its inerrancy. Because of the movement's post-modernism, however, most in the Emergent church only pay lip service to the authority of Scripture.

- Interpretive approach:
  - Most in the movement use a flexible or "unfastened" hermeneutic (based on post-modernism): "the emerging/emergent church movement adheres to basic post-modernist thinking—it is about experience over reason; subjectivity over objectivity; spirituality over religion, images over words; outward over inward; feelings over truth."[20] Virtually all in the movement reject Biblical Christianity's consistently-applied Grammatical-Historical-Literal hermeneutic.

- **Assessment**:
  - It encourages the use of "conversations" about what the Bible teaches rather than a thoughtful examination of Scripture. These conversations invariably lead to assorted (and often erroneous) meanings of the text
  - It at times allows culture to inform its thinking rather than the Word of God
  - Many in the movement promote relativism—and have no use for "absolutes" or absolute truth (vs. John 14:6)

- Most in the movement have a disdain for the topic of eschatology, thus leaving their congregations ignorant of God's future purposes and the Christian's future destiny
- Most in the movement believe in Replacement Theology.
- A few in the movement question the reality of Hell
- Some in the movement are near-universalist—and promote a broad way of salvation (versus the narrow way taught by Jesus—Matt. 7:13-15)
- Many in the movement are theological liberals dressed in evangelical clothing

> **Point of discernment**: If Biblical Christianity is Evangelicalism's North Pole, Emergent Christianity is its South Pole. The latter makes little attempt to handle the Word of God accurately, and it eschews teaching the whole counsel of God. Worse, the leadership of Emergent Christianity—through its devotion to the quicksand of post-modernism—knowingly or unwittingly promotes a radical deconstruction of God's Word.

Wrap-up of Chapters 35 and 36:

All born-again Christians are brothers and sisters in Christ—and beloved children of Christ—regardless of doctrinal differences. We are to love one another (John 13:34) as a witness to the non-believing world (John 13:35), and each believer has been gifted uniquely by the Lord for the good of the body of Christ (I Corinthians 12). Nevertheless, the Word of God challenges all Christians with the following words: *"But to this one I will look, to him who is humble and contrite of spirit, and who trembles at My word" (Isaiah 66:2)*. Is this *your* heart, dear reader?

Satan wants no Christian to tremble at God's Word; instead, he wants believers to doubt the fidelity and veracity of the Word—be it the creation account, the fall of man, the universal flood, the universality of sin, the virgin birth, the sinless life of Christ, the deity of Christ, the substitutionary death of Christ, the resurrection of Christ, the necessity of the new birth, salvation by faith alone in Christ alone, the God-breathed nature of the Bible, Christ's Second Coming, the Millennial Kingdom, and so on. Satan's whisper is always the same: *"Indeed, has God said. . . .?"*

With this in mind, each Christian must decide how he views the Bible. Is it inspired, inerrant, authoritative, and sufficient—or something less? Each Christian must also decide the best way to interpret the Bible. Should it be the grammatical-historical-literal method, applied consistently throughout the Bible—or some other approach? Finally, each Christian must determine which brand of Evangelicalism (Chapters 31, 35, and 36) most accurately interprets, handles, and teaches the Word of God—and then align himself with it.

CHAPTER 37

Deceptive Practices in the Evangelical Church

But the Spirit explicitly says that in later times some will fall away from the faith, paying attention to deceitful spirits and doctrines of demons (I Tim. 4:1).

We are no longer to be children, tossed here and there by waves and carried about by every wind of doctrine, by the trickery of men, by craftiness in deceitful scheming (Eph. 4:14).

The Bible states that the true Church must stand firm against the trickery of men and be on guard against the infiltration of deceitful spirits and doctrines of demons. Evangelical churches that lack the desire or skills to discern such attacks run the risk of allowing deceptive or questionable practices to enter and take root.

Deceptive Practices

Two deceptive, demon-empowered practices now exist in certain parts of Evangelical Christianity: the practice of being "slain in the Spirit" and the practice of "holy laughter." Neither has the Holy Spirit as its source.

A. Slain in the Spirit

One Evangelical commentator describes the practice as follows: "Most commonly, being 'slain in the Spirit' happens when a minister lays hands on someone and that person collapses to the floor, supposedly overcome by the power of the Holy Spirit. Those who practice slaying in the Spirit use Bible passages that talk about becoming 'as dead' (Revelation 1:17) or of falling upon their face (Ezekiel 1:28; Daniel 8:17-18; 10:7-9)."[1]

Assessment: Being "slain in the spirit" is identical to the Hindu practice of "Shaktipat." In Hindu Shaktipat, a Hindu guru—knowingly or unknowingly being an instrument of demons—will touch a person and cause him to fall backwards. Other gurus simply blow on a person or touch him with a feather, thus causing the person to fall to the ground. The recipients of this activity indeed experience something supernatural, not realizing that that the force behind their push to the ground has come from a demon. The Christian practice of being "slain in the Spirit" closely parallels Hindu Shaktipat and likewise involves demons and demonic activity. Satan has thus brought into certain parts of the Evangelical church (principally the hyper-Charismatic and hyper-Pentecostal movements) a seductive counterfeit of the true work of the Holy Spirit—and gullible Christians, some hungering to experience the supernatural, mistakenly believe they have been touched by the power of the Holy Spirit.

B. Holy Laughter

According to one Evangelical source, "the term 'holy laughter' was coined to describe a phenomenon during which a person laughs uncontrollably, presumably as a result of being filled with the Holy Spirit's joy. It is characterized by peals of uncontrollable laughter, sometimes accompanied by swooning or falling down to the floor. Firsthand accounts from those who have had this experience vary somewhat, but all seem to believe it to be a sign of a 'blessing' or 'anointing' of the Holy Spirit."[2] Another source states:

> Holy laughter is a term used within charismatic Christianity to describe a religious behavior in which individuals spontaneously laugh during church meetings. It has occurred in many revivals throughout church history, but became normative in the early 1990s in Neo-charismatic churches and the Third Wave of the Holy Spirit. Many people claimed to experience this phenomenon at a large revival in Toronto, Ontario, Canada known as the Toronto Blessing. . . . It also occurred in Signs and Wonders meetings run by John Wimber in the 1980s. The practice came into prominence in meetings led by South African evangelist Rodney Howard-Brown in 1993 at the Carpenter's Home Church in Lakeland, Florida and was often accompanied by the "slain in the Spirit" phenomenon. The laughter ranges from very quiet to loud convulsive hysterics, which are said to be accompanied by temporary dissociation.[3]

Assessment: When placed next to the sure truths of the Word of God, it is hard not to conclude that "holy laughter" is a demon-inspired, demon-driven activity which entices the flesh and produces a counterfeit of the actual activity of the Holy Spirit. Its demonic end is to divide the church, diminish the importance of God's Word, and counterfeit the true working of the Holy Spirit in a believer's life—which is to convict of sin, righteousness, and judgment (John 16:8) and to guide the believer into all truth (John 16:13).

A critic of the practice expresses the following: "The most convincing scriptural argument against what is called 'holy laughter' is found in Galatians 5:22-23. It says, 'but the fruit of the Spirit is love, joy, peace, patience, kindness, goodness, faithfulness, gentleness, self-control; against such things there is no law.' If self-control is a fruit of the Spirit of God, then how can uncontrollable laughter also be a fruit of the Holy Spirit? Revival leaders claim that being filled with the Spirit means that we are sort of 'tossed about' by His whims. But the idea that God would make people act drunk or act uncontrollably or make animal noises as a result of the Spirit's anointing is directly opposed to the way the Spirit acts according to Galatians 5:22-23. The Spirit described in Galatians 5 is one who promotes self-control within us, not the opposite."[4]

[Note: None of the first century Apostles were ever recorded as having been "slain in the Spirit" or as having exhibited "holy laughter."]

Questionable Practices

Questionable practices are not necessarily frontally demonic, but none of them were practiced by the Apostolic church—and their roots can often be found in either pagan worship or more mystical traditions. Four such practices in Evangelical circles are listed below.

A. Labyrinths

Noted one source on the subject:

> Ancient labyrinths may have served as traps for malevolent spirits or as paths for ritual dances. Many Roman and Christian labyrinths appear at the entrance of buildings, suggesting that they may have served a similar apotropaic [magical powers to turn away harm or evil] purpose. In their cross-cultural study of signs and symbols, *Patterns that Connect*, Carl Shuster and Edmund Carpenter present various forms of the labyrinth and suggest various possible meanings, including not only a sacred path to the home of a sacred ancestor, but also perhaps a representation of the ancestor himself/herself. . . . One can think of labyrinths as symbolic of pilgrimage; people can walk a path, ascending toward salvation or enlightenment. Author Ben Radford conducted an investigation into some of the claims of spiritual and healing effects of labyrinths, reporting his findings in his book Mysterious New Mexico.[5]

Assessment: Numerous labyrinths predate the Christian era, thus alerting a discerning observer—in view of the spiritual darkness of the pre-Christian world—to the likelihood of fleshly or demonic origin. Moreover, several of the pagan religions use labyrinths as symbolic pathways toward "enlightenment." The term "enlightenment" stands in sharp contrast to the Bible's prescription of regeneration and sanctification—i.e., spiritual birth and spiritual growth toward maturity. The appearance of labyrinths in Christian cathedrals and worship during medieval times coincides with the spiritual "winter" of the Church Age (see Chapter 26), when the Roman Catholic church, then preeminent in Christendom, was filled with error and apostasy. Because of her deadness, the medieval Roman church can be seen as an easy target for satanic deception. In the case of labyrinths, the deception involved syncretism with the pagan world and their labyrinths—using them as symbolic of the journey toward "salvation." The Apostle Paul, however, warns against syncretism in II Corinthians 6:14-15,17: *"Do not be bound together with unbelievers, for what partnership have righteousness and lawlessness, or what fellowship has light with darkness? Or what harmony has Christ with Belial, or what has a believer in common with an unbeliever? . . . 'Therefore, come out from their midst and be separate,' says the Lord. 'And do not touch what is unclean.'"*

B. Drumming / Drumming circles

Christian Blogger Susan Brinkmann notes the following about the practice of drumming:

> Drumming circles are founded in shamanism and were not designed to be used for praising God. They have a distinct spiritual component to them in that they are all meant to create some kind of trance or altered state of consciousness—a state which leaves us open to the direct influence of evil spirits. None of us needs to enter an altered state of consciousness to have a dialogue with Christ—which is the point of Christian prayer. And no matter where the drumming circle is being hosted, in or outside of a Church, a Christian should be very wary of participating in them.[6]

Assessment: Christians who place a "Christian" veneer on the practice of drumming or drumming circles—and who participate in such practices run the risk of opening themselves to demonic deception or influence. Such a practice, even though perhaps sanctioned by well-meaning Christians, is hardly a "whatsoever things are pure, whatsoever things are lovely" activity, on which we are to let our minds dwell (Phil. 4:8-9).

C. Centering Prayer

Wikipedia writes the following about Centering Prayer:

> Cistercian monk Father Thomas Keating, a founder of Centering Prayer, was abbot throughout the 1960s and 1970s at St. Joseph's Abbey in Spencer, Massachusetts. This area is thick with religious retreat centers, including the well-known Theravada Buddhist center, Insight Meditation Society. Fr. Keating tells of meeting many young people, some who stumbled on St. Joseph's by accident, many of them born Catholic, who had turned to Eastern practices for contemplative work. He found many of them had no knowledge of the contemplative traditions within Christianity and set out to present those practices in a more accessible way. The result was the practice now called Centering Prayer.[7]

Fr. M. Basil Pennington in turn suggests these steps for practicing Centering Prayer:

1. Sit comfortably with your eyes closed, relax, and quiet yourself. Be in love and faith to God.
2. Choose a sacred word that best supports your sincere intention to be in the Lord's presence and open to His divine action within you.
3. Let that word be gently present as your symbol of your sincere intention to be in the Lord's presence and open to His divine action within you.
4. Whenever you become aware of anything (thoughts, feelings, perceptions, images, associations, etc.), simply return to your sacred word, your anchor.[8]

In addition, Fr. Keating writes, the method consists in letting go of every kind of thought during prayer, even the most devout thoughts. In centering prayer, the participant seeks the presence of God directly (aided by the Jesus Prayer, perhaps) and explicitly rejects discursive thoughts and imagined scenes. The participant's aim is to be present with the Lord, to "consent to God's presence and action during the time of prayer." Centering Prayer advocates link the practice to traditional forms of Christian meditation, such as on the rosary, or Lectio Divina.[9]

Assessment: Scripture warns against the empty repetition of words (Matthew 6:7); and the "clearing of our minds" is not a biblical command. Indeed, Scripture exhorts the Christian to let the Word of God dwell richly on his heart (Col. 3:16). Furthermore, the Christian is not to empty his mind, but instead to meditate on God's Word (Psalm 1:2; 63:6; 77:12; 119:15; 143:5; et.al.), God's attributes (Psalm 145:5), Christ's character (Psalm 34:8), and Christ's promises (Psalm 34:8).

With regard to prayer, should not the Christian be instructed by the examples of Hannah, King David, and the Lord Himself? Hannah knew nothing of repeating a "sacred" word to the Lord, but instead earnestly poured out her heart to the Lord (I Sam. 1:1-20). She shared with the Lord her deepest desire. The Lord honored her deep, intimate relationship with Him and answered her prayer affirmatively.

King David likewise often poured out his heart to the Lord. Hear his words in the well-known verse 1 of Psalm 42: *"As the deer pants for the water brooks, so my soul pants for You, O God."* In Psalm 3:1-2 David cries out to the Lord: *"O Lord, how my adversaries have increased! Many are rising against me. Heed the sound of my cry for help, my King and my God; for to You I pray."* Surely, just as David cried out for help in his time of need, God invites you and me to cry out for help in our time of need. In Psalm 6:1-4 David again speaks his heart to the living God: *"O Lord, do not rebuke me in Your anger, nor chasten me in Your wrath. Be gracious to me, O Lord, for I am pining away. Heal me, O Lord, for my bones are dismayed. And my soul is greatly dismayed. But You, O Lord, how long? Return, O Lord, rescue my soul; save me because of Your lovingkindness."* Nowhere do we see David in the Psalms repeating a "sacred" word over and over. Everywhere, however, we see him pouring out his heart to the Lord in confession, thanksgiving, and petition. Should not you and I do the same thing?

When the disciples asked Jesus how to pray (Matt. 6:5-15), the Lord instructed them to pray with *intention*, specifically (1) that the Father's name would be hallowed on this earth, (2) that the Father's kingdom would come to this earth, (3) that the Father's will would be done on this earth as it presently is being done in heaven, (4) that the Father would provide our daily needs, (5) that the Father would forgive us our trespasses as we forgive those who trespass against us, and (6) that the Father would not allow us to be tempted by the devil, but that we would be delivered from all such demonic efforts. Nowhere in this prayer and nowhere in the gospels does Jesus encourage us to focus on, and repeat, a sacred word when praying. Indeed, in Matthew 6:7-8 Jesus appears to be criticizing something akin to centering prayer when he says, *"And when you are praying, do not use **meaningless repetition** [emphasis added] as the Gentiles do, for they suppose that they will be heard for their many words. So do not be like them, for your Father knows what you need before you ask Him."*

D. Christian Yoga

GotQuestions.org summarizes and evaluates the Eastern practice of yoga as follows:

> In the Eastern world, yoga is an overtly spiritual practice connected to the worship of the Hindu gods. In the West, yoga is usually presented as a physical exercise or means to manage stress. The goal of yoga in Hinduism is to acquire deep knowledge of the Self and to unite the Self with the impersonal, all-pervading Brahman. Holy yoga or Christian yoga tweaks that goal so that it sounds more "Christian"; the goal of holy yoga is to acquire deep knowledge of the Self *in Christ*. During holy yoga sessions, Christian music is played in the background, and the chanting of names of Hindu deities is changed to the chanting of Bible verses. All of this is an attempt to use yoga as a Christian worship experience to deepen one's faith in God. Yoga has been practiced for decades in some Catholic, Episcopal, and mainline Protestant churches; in more recent years, "holy yoga" has made inroads into some Evangelical churches.[10]

> The origins of yoga are pagan. The question thus becomes, can yoga be transformed into something of spiritual value to Christians? Can secular (or pagan) yoga be turned into holy (Christian) yoga? Here are some considerations: Yoga's

focus on Self is inherently unbiblical. The Bible never tells us to focus on ourselves; rather, we are to die to self and follow Christ (Matthew 16:24). Our focus is to be on our Savior, "the pioneer and perfecter of faith" (Hebrews 12:2). We concentrate on the Creator of heaven and earth, not on His creation.[11]

The intrinsic philosophy of yoga is that we have everything we need within ourselves—and that we ourselves are god. This is also unbiblical. Such a philosophy cannot really be "Christianized." God is transcendent; He exists outside of ourselves, and we are told to seek Him (Zephaniah 2:3). Connection with God does not come through yogic meditation, concentration, or the disassociation of one's senses from one's Self. Scripture tells us that Jesus is the only way to "connect" with God (John 14:6), and the Word of God itself is sufficient to guide us through life (2 Timothy 3:16–17). Reading the Bible and praying may sound mundane to some, but those are the means God has given us to know Him better. Holy yoga comes close to being a form of Christian mysticism that exalts experience over traditional Bible study and prayer.[12]

Assessment: Are there inherent dangers in the practice of "Christian" yoga? For many Christians, the answer is no. For others, potential hazards exist. First, it could subtly invite some Christians to believe that all religions are valid. Second, it could deceive some Christians into believing that Hinduism itself is a valid path to God. As well, it could cause still others to study the origins and beliefs which underpin Yoga, which in turn could cause at least a few Christians to embrace some of the demonic deceptions contained in Yoga. Finally, though most born-again Christians involved in yoga will not be lured away from Christianity, it can nevertheless be argued that Satan gets some measure of victory through Christian yoga: he has deceived large numbers of born-again Christians to utilize the same Yoga positions used by countless nonbelieving Hindus to awaken the "serpent" energy within them. To this degree at least, the forces of darkness have achieved a victory among the less-than-discerning Christians involved in Christian yoga.

CHAPTER 38

Testing the Spirits

*Beloved, do not believe every spirit, but test the spirits to see whether they are from God, because many false prophets have gone out into the world. By this you know the **Spirit of God**: every spirit that confesses that Jesus Christ has come in the flesh is from God; and every spirit that does not confess Jesus is not from God; this is the **spirit of the antichrist**, of which you have heard that it is coming, and now it is already in the world (I John 4:1-3). [emphasis added]*

Woe to those who call evil good, and good evil; *who substitute darkness for light and light for darkness; who substitute bitter for sweet and sweet for bitter (Isa. 5:20). [emphasis added]*

*We are from God; he who knows God listens to us; he who is not from God does not listen to us. By this we know the **spirit of truth** and the **spirit of error** (I John 4:6). [emphasis added]*

But there were false prophets also among the people, even as there shall be false teachers among you, who shall secretly bring in damnable heresies, even denying the Lord who bought them, and bring upon themselves swift destruction (II Pet. 2:1). [KJV]

The Apostle John exhorts believers not to believe every spirit, but instead to "test the spirits." Why? Because false prophets, false teachers, and deceptive spirits have gone out into the world. Thus, is the source of a message from the Spirit of God or the spirit of the antichrist (I John 4:1-3)? Does the substance of the message proclaim that evil is good or good is evil (Isa. 5:20)? Does the substance of a message come with the spirit of truth or the spirit of error (I John 4:6)? Notice, too, that John states the scope of the deception: it is throughout the world (I John 4:1-3).

Not only have false prophets gone out into the world, but the Apostle Peter informs his readers that false teachers will infiltrate the church and introduce destructive heresies in the process. Chapter 25 gave examples of this infiltration and traced the systematic falling away of the church into various error and heresy during its first 1200 years. Chapter 26 in turn highlighted a number of those errors and heresies. Today, Christian cults reject the deity of Jesus Christ and, in doing so, are *"denying the Lord who bought them [with His blood] (II Pet. 2:1b)."* In short, because of the threats spelled out above by Isaiah, John and Peter, born-again Christians are exhorted to "test the spirits."

Introduction to the Term "Spirit"

The term "spirit" in Scripture typically has one of five usages: (1) the Holy Spirit; (2) an unclean, evil, demonic spirit; (3) a person's general character, nature, tendencies, or disposition (e.g., a "spirit of grace" vs. a "lying spirit"); (4) a prevailing tone or tendency (e.g., the "spirit of the age"); or (5) a general intent (e.g., the "spirit of truth" vs. the "spirit of error").

In a prophecy about the coming Messiah (Jesus Christ), the prophet Isaiah states: *"The Spirit of the LORD will rest on Him, the spirit of **wisdom** and **understanding**, the spirit of **counsel** and **strength**, the spirit of **knowledge** and the **fear of the LORD**" (Isa. 11:2)*. Notice the descriptions:

- The spirit of wisdom
- The spirit of understanding
- The spirit of counsel
- The spirit of strength
- The spirit of knowledge
- The fear of the LORD

The reader/hearer of Isaiah 11:2 is thus introduced to six positive manifestations of the Spirit of God: the spirit of wisdom, understanding, counsel, strength, knowledge, and fear of the Lord.

What are the opposites?

- The spirit of foolishness
- The spirit of confusion
- The spirit of misguidance
- The spirit of weakness
- The spirit of ignorance
- No fear of the LORD

From I John 4:6 we see the notion of contrasting spirits—e.g., the spirit of truth or the spirit of error. To be sure, Scripture offers numerous contrasting spirits. The Apostle Paul talks about the "spirit of the world" versus "the Spirit who is from God" (I Cor. 2:12). Positive and negative spirits are likewise given. Several verses of Scripture mention the "spirit of jealousy." Isaiah talks about the "spirit of justice" (Isa. 28:6). Zechariah mentions the "spirit of grace" and the "spirit of supplication" (Zech. 12:10). Other positive (or Christ-like) spirits mentioned in the New Testament include:

- the spirit of gentleness
- the spirit of faith
- the spirit of love

Other negative spirits mentioned in the New Testament include:

- the spirit of divination
- the spirit of slavery/bondage
- the spirit of fear

- the spirit of the world
- the spirit of partiality

Each of these spirits provides the believer a window into the *source* and *substance* of a message or teaching: is it from the Spirit of God or another spirit? Is it truth or error?

Testing the Spirits

How does a Christian "test the spirits" both inside and outside the church? He does so by assessing both the *message* and the *messenger*—the substance of a message and the source of a message.

With regard to the **substance** of a message, he develops an "ear" for (1) the spirit of the world (i.e. fallen human wisdom rather than the wisdom of the Word), (2) the spirit of the flesh (i.e., the lust of the flesh, the lust of the eyes, and the boastful pride of life), (3) the spirit of the devil (which deceives and wants to turn people away from God's Word, grace, will and ways), and (4) the spirit of antichrist (which does not confess that Jesus is from God—I John 4:3). Does a message contain a spirit of wisdom or a spirit of foolishness? Understanding or confusion? Counsel or misguidance? Holiness or wickedness? Love or hate? Good or evil? Grace or bondage? Compassion or indifference? Gentleness or harshness?

The devil is a liar, deceiver, divider, and destroyer. Thus, any message—be it from a politician, educator, businessman, broadcaster, entertainer, celebrity, or religious devotee—which carries the tone of untruth, deception, division, or destruction is from the world, the flesh, or the devil. In contrast, a Spirit-enabled message will come across as true, honorable, right, pure, lovely, and upstanding (Phil. 4:8). Indeed, Jesus tells His disciples: *"Sanctify them in truth; Your [God's] word is truth"* (John 17:17).

With regard to the **source** of a message, the Christian endeavors to ascertain the world view or belief system of a person, speaker, or writer. For example, is he an atheist, an agnostic, a deist, a humanist, a nihilist, a hedonist, a spiritualist, a proponent of an Eastern religion, a Muslim, a New Ager, a professing Christian, or a born-again Christian? If not the latter, then the discerning Christian knows that all or parts of the messenger's message will be suspect.

When the messenger is not a born-again believer, the Christian should ask himself rhetorical questions similar to these:

Does the writer/speaker/teacher . . .

- promote worldly wisdom?
- promote the "spirit of the age"?
- pander to the flesh (e.g., by promoting the lust of the eyes, the lust of the flesh, or the boastful pride of life)?
- convey that evil is good or good is evil?
- promote a New Age/New Spirituality message?
- Promote a syncretistic "Monomyth" message?
- promote the syncretism of Eastern religions with Christianity?
- promote mysticism and the mystical?
- elevate the Eastern religions?

- exalt Eastern thought?
- contend that all religions to be from God?
- consider all religions to have merit?
- believe there are many ways to God?
- consider the Bible to be just one of many sacred or divine books?
- promote a subtle message of esotericism ("secret knowledge")
- promote the occult?
- promote belief in a benevolent spirit world?
- advocate getting in touch with the spirit world?
- encourage the use of spirit guides?
- teach that God is a cosmic energy force?
- teach that God is in everything and everyone?
- disparage the notion of personal sin?
- teach the Jesus was merely a prophet?
- teach that Jesus didn't come in the flesh?
- teach reincarnation?
- teach that man is on a path toward self-realization or enlightenment?
- believe in the inherent divinity of man?

If a writer, speaker, or teacher promotes any of the above, then he is knowingly or unknowingly being used by the enemy to blind and deceive.

Essentials for Biblical Discernment

If, however, it is determined that a writer, speaker, or teacher is a born-again Christian, then the issue becomes: **How does his message or teaching line up with Scripture?** The Christian in I Thessalonians 5:21 is exhorted to "examine everything carefully" and to "hold fast to that which is good." In Acts 17:10-11, the Christian is exhorted to measure a person's teaching with the Scriptures. Thus, does a person's teaching harmonize with or contradict Scripture? Is it an accurate handling of God's Word?

Deviations from reliable Biblical teaching typically arise as a result of the following factors: (1) allowing the historical beliefs of a denomination or theological system to trump the straightforward teaching of Scripture; (2) failing to use sound principles of Biblical interpretation (thus leading to a lax or poor handling of God's Word); (3) allegorizing or spiritualizing a passage of Scripture when it is not called for; (4) resorting to "eisegesis" (reading one's viewpoint into a passage of Scripture) instead of carefully extracting the meaning from a passage and any related passages (exegesis) ; (5) taking a verse or passage of Scripture out of context; or (6) failing to take into account or ignoring other passages of Scripture which relate to the topic at hand.

Accordingly, the Christian (even before analyzing a person's teaching) is well-served to ask himself the following rhetorical questions about the background of a born-again writer, speaker, or teacher.

Is he . . .

- a Calvinist, Arminian, or neither?
- Covenantal or Dispensational?
- Premillennial, Amillennial, or Postmillennial?
- a Preterist, Historicist, or Futurist?
- a denominational or non-denominational Christian?
- a Progressive, NAR, Word-Faith, or Emergent Christian?

Does he . . .

- Adhere to Biblical Christianity (Chapter 31) or a different form of Evangelicalism (Chapters 35 and 36)?
- Believe that the Bible is the inspired, inerrant, and authoritative Word of God? [If not, then he is more liberal theologically]
- Believe in the sole authority of the Bible?
- Believe in the sufficiency of the Bible?
- Add to, or subtract from, the Word of God? [Deut. 4:2 and Rev. 22:18-19]
- Allegorize or spiritualize some or much of Bible prophecy?
- Minimize or marginalize the role or importance of Bible prophecy?
- Believe in Replacement Theology?
- Insist that all Christians should speak in tongues?
- Exalt the entire Bible or question certain parts of the Bible?
- Offer Biblical wisdom or worldly wisdom?
- Question or deny the existence of absolute truth?
- Minimize or marginalize Christ's atoning work on the Cross?
- Deny the existence of Hell?
- Promote Christian mysticism?
- Claim to have new revelation from God?
- Consider himself to be a present-day apostle or prophet?
- Promote unbiblical or occultic practices (e.g., being "slain in the spirit" or "holy laughter")
- Promote Christian ecumenism? [i.e., evangelicals working together with liberal Protestants, Catholics and Orthodoxes (vs. II Cor. 6:14-15)]
- Promote inter-faith ecumenism? [i.e., evangelicals working together with other religions—Hindus, Buddhists, Taoists, Shintos, Muslims—in opposition to II Cor. 6:14-15]

Answers to questions such as these will provide insight into the speaker or teacher's approach to a topic or passage of Scripture—and his likely interpretive bents. For example, if a speaker/teacher adheres to Biblical Christianity, he will not hesitate to teach eschatology from a literal viewpoint. He will not hesitate to teach a pre-Tribulation Rapture and seven-year Tribulation period. He will not hesitate to talk about Jesus Christ's second coming to the earth and Christ's subsequent 1,000-

year reign over the earth. On the other hand, if a speaker/teacher comes from an Evangelical Lutheran background or an Emergent Christianity background, then he will likely allegorize verses which describe a literal Millennial Kingdom or ignore the topic of eschatology altogether.

The Berean Approach to Biblical Discernment

Says one commentator: "Christians are to test the message that people and spirits proclaim. . . . The test is to compare what it being taught with the clear teaching of Scripture. The Bible alone is the Word of God; it alone is inspired and inerrant. Therefore, the way to test the spirits is to see if what is being taught is in line with the clear teaching of Scripture."[1]

The New Testament example of the Bereans informs Evangelicals how to practice Biblical discernment: *"The brethren immediately sent Paul and Silas away by night to Berea; and when they arrived, they went into the synagogue of the Jews. Now these were more noble-minded than those in Thessalonica, for they received the word with great eagerness, examining the Scriptures daily to see whether these things were so" (Acts 17:11).* In short, the Bereans used the Scriptures to assess the accuracy of Paul's teaching—"to see whether these things were so."

Christians should likewise use the Berean approach to assess the accuracy of a teaching. Bereans today, for example, would examine Reformed Theology's doctrine of Limited Atonement to see whether it lines up with Scripture—and would readily determine that such a doctrine contradicts at least fifteen passages of Scripture. Accordingly, the Bereans would conclude that such a teaching must be rejected. Similarly, the doctrine of amillennialism is widely held in Evangelical circles, though the doctrine contradicts dozens of Old and New Testament verses which teach that Christ will one day return to the earth and reign over it from Jerusalem. When examining the doctrine of amillennialism, Bereans would readily conclude that amillennialism, because it contradicts numerous Scriptures, also must be rejected.

To sum up, Biblical discernment involves the ability to assess how a particular teaching or doctrine lines up with Scripture. Using Scripture as the plumbline, it is the capacity to distinguish truth from error (I John 4:6). Scripture cannot contradict itself, and church doctrine should not contradict Scripture.

Testing the Spirits with Regard to Practices in the Church

Beloved, do not believe every spirit, but test the spirits to see whether they are from God, because many false prophets have gone out into the world (I John 4:1).

Because false prophets have gone out into the world and, logically, can infiltrate the church, believers are not only to discern the source behind the messages given to the church, but also the practices within the church: Are they from the Spirit of God—or from the world, the flesh, or the devil?

As discussed in Chapter 37, the failure to test the spirits by certain Evangelical movements has allowed contemporary Evangelicalism to see the infiltration of two blatantly demonic practices into these movements: the practice of being "slain in the spirit" and the practice of "holy laughter." While its proponents believe that they are experiencing a manifestation of the Holy Spirit, in reality they are experiencing demonic activity widely seen in Hinduism. In addition, certain other practices within parts of Evangelicalism are problematic: Labyrinths and drumming circles have pagan roots. Clearing one's mind for "centering prayer" is not a biblical command—and contradicts the Bible's exhortation to let the Word of God dwell richly on one's heart. It also contradicts the Bible's warning against using meaningless repetition (Matt. 6:6-7). Because Hindu yoga is a key component of Eastern meditation and its so-called path to "enlightenment," "Christian" yoga strikes some (including this writer) as a not-so-subtle syncretic intrusion of the enemy into Evangelicalism. Still other current-day practices are likewise problematic. For example, does a church countenance:

- Being "drunk with the Spirit"?
- Crawling on one's hands and knees while barking and howling?
- Shaking uncontrollably in ecstasy?
- "Fire tunnels" through which participants walk to receive the laying on of hands, prayer, prophecy, and an "impartation of the spirit"?
- "Glory clouds"?
- "Blasting"—an ear-piercing verbal onslaught meant to cast out demons?
- Tongues-speaking without interpretation in a worship service?
- Tongues interpretations that contradict Scripture?
- The selection of elders and deacons who do not have Biblical qualifications?

For sure, Evangelicals must be vigilant to discern and avoid practices which do not come from the Spirit of God

Testing the Unseen or the Unknown—and Calling on the Name of Jesus Christ (Psalms 50:15)

Put on the full armor of God, so that you will be able to stand firm against the schemes of the devil. For our struggle is not against flesh and blood, but against the rulers, against the powers, against the world forces of this darkness, against the spiritual forces of wickedness in the heavenly places (Eph. 6:11-12).

Call upon Me in the day of trouble, and I shall rescue you, and you will honor Me (Ps. 50:15)

Satan will also look for ways to derail the hearts of truth-seeking non-believers. The following real-life example is instructive. It involves a seeking non-believing couple whom God eventually called out of the New Age movement—and how God enabled them to overcome pre-conversion demonic buffeting.

Warren B. Smith, in his 1992 book, *The Light that Was Dark*, describes his journey out of the New Age Movement to repentance and faith in Jesus Christ. A few months before his conversion, Smith and his wife were both heavily influenced by the false Christ presented in the New Age book, *A Course in Miracles*. (Several years earlier, Warren unwittingly had invited deception into his life after seeing a psychic.)

Fortuitously, the couple had been challenged to read the New Testament, then the entire Bible. One night, as the truth of Scripture had begun to transform their thinking, Warren and his wife (Joy) were both attacked by a demonic force—Warren first, then Joy. Writes Warren:

> I was startled out of my sleep by an awful evil presence pressing in on me. I bolted upright and in a horrified, broken voice called out, 'Help me God!' Joy sprang out of bed in a flash and was immediately by my side. She knew exactly what was going on. Looking directly at me, she addressed the unseen presence, 'In the name of Jesus Christ, leave Warren alone!'
>
> And "woosh"! It was as if a huge weight had been removed from my throat. Whatever the presence was, it left as soon as Joy called on the name of Jesus.
>
> I sat on the edge of the bed still stunned by the suddenness and severity of the spiritual attack and by the fact that the presence had been forced to leave so quickly. 'That's amazing,' I said. 'Something was literally going down my throat, but it left as soon as you addressed in the name of Jesus!'. . . .
>
> Joy and I were both unnerved. . . . After about a half an hour, we finally went back to sleep.
>
> Almost immediately, Joy was awakened by a spiritual presence. She could hardly speak as it now attacked her throat area. This time I commanded, 'In the name of Jesus Christ, I command you to leave.'
>
> When Joy told me the presence had left, we both looked at each other in bewilderment. What in the world was going on?[2]

Ultimately, Warren and Joy both invited Jesus Christ into their lives as their personal Savior and Lord. What are the takeaways from the Smith's involvement in the New Age and their eventual brush with demonic oppression? They are (1) the truth of the Word of God, (2) the power of Jesus Christ, and (3) the efficacy of calling on the name of Jesus Christ in the event of direct demonic oppression. As of this writing, Warren and Joy have honored the Lord with thirty-seven years of faithful service.

Summary: ***spiritual discernment*** enables a born-again Christian to identify the *source* and *substance* of a teaching: is it from the Holy Spirit or another spirit? Does it contain the spirit of truth or the spirit of error? If the writer-teacher-messenger indeed is a believer, then ***Biblical discernment*** enables the born-again Christian to assess *how a teaching lines up with Scripture.* Is it an accurate handling of God's word? To be sure, Biblical discernment develops increasingly as the believer grows in his knowledge of the Word and unreservedly chooses to take Scripture at face value. It is a heart which agrees with God's words in Isaiah 66:2: *"But to this one I will look, to him who is humble and contrite of spirit, and who trembles at My word."*

Assorted Discernment Verses

*Now the serpent was more crafty than any beast of the field which the LORD God had made. And he said to the woman, **"Indeed, has God said**, 'You shall not eat from any tree of the garden'?" The woman said to the serpent, "From the fruit of the trees of the garden we may eat; but from the fruit of the tree which is in the middle of the garden, God has said, 'You shall not eat from it or touch it, or you will die.'" The serpent said to the woman, "You surely will not die! For God knows that in the day you eat from it your eyes will be opened, and you will be like God, knowing good and evil." When the woman saw that the tree was good for food, and that it was a delight to the eyes, and that the tree was desirable to make one wise, she took from its fruit and ate; and she gave also to her husband with her, and he ate. Then the eyes of both of them were opened, and they knew that they were naked; and they sewed fig leaves together and made themselves loin coverings (Gen. 3:1-7).*

By this you know the Spirit of God: every spirit that confesses that Jesus Christ has come in the flesh is from God; and every spirit that does not confess Jesus is not from God; this is the spirit of the antichrist, of which you have heard that it is coming, and now it is already in the world (I John 4:2-3).

We are from God; he who knows God listens to us; he who is not from God does not listen to us. By this we know the spirit of truth and the spirit of error (I John 4:6).

"You will know them by their fruits. Grapes are not gathered from thorn bushes nor figs from thistles, are they? So every good tree bears good fruit, but the bad tree bears bad fruit. A good tree cannot produce bad fruit, nor can a bad tree produce good fruit. Every tree that does not bear good fruit is cut down and thrown into the fire. So then, you will know them by their fruits" (Matt. 7:16-20).

As He was sitting on the Mount of Olives, the disciples came to Him privately, saying, "Tell us, when will these things happen, and what will be the sign of Your coming, and of the end of the age?" And Jesus answered and said to them, "See to it that no one misleads you. For many will come in My name, saying, 'I am the Christ,' and will mislead many" (Matt.24:3-5).

"You shall not add to the word which I am commanding you, nor take away from it, that you may keep the commandments of the LORD your God which I command you" (Deut.4:2).

". . . so that no advantage would be taken of us by Satan, for we are not ignorant of his schemes" (II Cor. 2:11). [the discerning Christian is to be aware of how Satan and false teachers work]

Do not participate in the unfruitful deeds of darkness, but instead even expose them; for it is disgraceful even to speak of the things which are done by them in secret. But all things become visible when they are exposed by the light, for everything that becomes visible is light (Eph. 5:11-13). [Therefore, expose false teaching and false doctrine with the truth of God's Word and the light of sound doctrine.]

Finally, be strong in the Lord and in the strength of His might. Put on the full armor of God, so that you will be able to stand firm against the schemes of the devil. For our struggle is not against flesh and blood, but against the rulers, against the powers, against the world forces of this darkness, against the spiritual forces of wickedness in the heavenly places (Eph. 6:10-12).

Do not be bound together with unbelievers; for what partnership have righteousness and lawlessness, or what fellowship has light with darkness? Or what harmony has Christ with Belial, or what has a believer in common with an unbeliever? (II Cor. 6:14-15).

"You [the Pharisees] are of your father the devil, and you want to do the desires of your father. He was a murderer from the beginning, and does not stand in the truth because there is no truth in him. Whenever he speaks a lie, he speaks from his own nature, for he is a liar and the father of lies" (John 8:44).

I testify to everyone who hears the words of the prophecy of this book: if anyone adds to them, God will add to him the plagues which are written in this book; and if anyone takes away from the words of the book of this prophecy, God will take away his part from the tree of life and from the holy city, which are written in this book (Rev. 22:18-19). [The Christian is not to add to or take away from the prophecies in the book of Revelation. Sadly, both practices exist in much of Evangelicalism today.]

For I did not shrink from declaring to you the whole purpose of God (Acts 20:27).

Be diligent to present yourself approved to God as a workman who does not need to be ashamed, accurately handling the word of truth (II Tim.2:15).

But if some of the branches were broken off, and you [i.e., the Gentiles], being a wild olive, were grafted in among them and became partaker with them of the rich root of the olive tree, do not be arrogant toward the branches; but if you are arrogant, remember that it is not you who supports the root, but the root supports you (Rom. 11:17-18). [Regrettably, those Gentiles who embrace Replacement Theology fail to recognize that they are merely "wild olive branches" whom God has graciously been grafted in to the natural olive tree—including God's New Covenant promise (Jer. 31:31-33; Luke 22:24; I Cor. 11:25).]

For I do not want you, brethren, to be uninformed of this mystery—so that you will not be wise in your own estimation—that a partial hardening has happened to Israel until the fullness of the Gentiles has come in (Rom. 11:25). [This verse clearly teaches that God, at some point in the future, will once again take up for Israel.]

Part VII

Discerning the Times

The Pharisees and Sadducees came up, and testing Jesus, they asked Him to show them a sign from heaven. But He replied to them, "When it is evening, you say, 'It will be fair weather, for the sky is red.' And in the morning, 'There will be a storm today, for the sky is red and threatening.' Do you know how to discern the appearance of the sky, but cannot discern the signs of the times?" (Matt. 16:1-3).

Part VII sharpens the reader's sense that "summer is near" on God's prophetic calendar (Matt. 24:32-34).

CHAPTER 39

Harbingers of the End-Times Deluding Influence

For the mystery of lawlessness is already at work; only he who now restrains will do so until he is taken out of the way. Then that lawless one will be revealed whom the Lord will slay with the breath of His mouth and bring to an end by the appearance of His coming; that is, the one whose coming is in accord with the activity of Satan, with all power and signs and false wonders, and with all the deception of wickedness for those who perish, because they did not receive the love of the truth so as to be saved. For this reason, God will send upon them a deluding influence so that they will believe what is false, in order that they all may be judged who did not believe the truth, but took pleasure in wickedness (II Thess. 2:7-12).

Over the past 2,000 years, the gospel of Jesus Christ and the offer of His kingdom have been proclaimed to an increasingly large percentage of the world's population. As noted in Chapter 20, however, the Good News of salvation through faith in Jesus Christ always generates a continuum of response on the part of those who hear the message. Some believe; most do not, because *"men loved the darkness rather than the Light"* (John 3:19).

Due to His hatred of sin, our long-suffering God has ordained an end-times Tribulation period of seven years. Though the Tribulation will produce a massive harvest of souls (Rev. 7:9-10,13-14), it will also bring horrific judgment upon those who reject this final offer of salvation. Soberingly, God has made it clear that, as part of the judgment, He will send a deluding influence upon the stiff-necked and hard-hearted (II Thess. 2:7-12), causing them to embrace the foolishness of men and the lies of the devil. Harbingers of this Tribulation-period deluding influence exist today—many having come to the forefront over the past twenty to thirty years. Most assuredly, all of these harbingers will grow into a full-fledged, God-sent delusion after the Rapture. Some of them are as follows:

- **The call for a one-world government**

Unregenerate intellectual and political leaders throughout the Western world routinely assert that the only way for mankind to solve its myriad of problems is through a one-world government. This dream of a united, "global village" mirrors the same dream of the rebellious post-Flood human family approximately 4,400 years ago: *Now the whole earth used the same language and the same words. It came about as they journeyed east, that they found a plain in the land of Shinar and settled there. They then said to one another, "Come, let us make bricks and burn them thoroughly." And they used brick for stone, and they used tar for mortar. They said,* ***"Come, let us build for ourselves a city, and a tower whose top will reach into heaven, and let us make for ourselves a name, otherwise we will be scattered abroad over the face*** *of the whole earth [emphasis added]." The LORD came down to see the city and the tower which the sons of men had built. And the LORD said, "Behold, they are one people, and they all have the same language. And this is what they began to do, and now nothing which they purpose to do will be impossible for them. Come, let Us go down there and confuse their language, so that they will not understand one another's speech." So the LORD scattered them abroad from there over the face of the whole earth; and they stopped building the city. Therefore, its name was called Babel, because there the LORD confused the language of the whole earth; and from there the LORD scattered them abroad over the face of the whole earth (Gen. 11:1-9).* The same mindset that caused the post-Flood human family to remain in one location (in disobedience to God's explicit command to spread out over the earth) today causes unregenerate man to long for a one-world "global village" and a global government unfettered by a transcendent God.

Because one-world government dreamers refuse to acknowledge (let alone bow to) the God of the Bible, God has allowed this delusion to enter the minds and hearts of the unregenerate today.

- **The call for open borders (and global citizenship)**

The call for "open borders" by unregenerate Western elites is likewise a delusion sent by God because of their willful ignorance of the source of the nations (God) and the boundaries of each nation (set by God after His judgment of man at Babel): *The God who made the world and all things in it, since He is Lord of heaven and earth, does not dwell in temples made with hands; nor is He served by human hands, as though He needed anything, since He Himself gives to all people life and breath and all things; and* **He made from one man every nation of mankind to live on all the face of the earth, having determined their appointed times and the boundaries of their habitation** *[emphasis added], that they would seek God, if perhaps they might grope for Him and find Him, though He is not far from each one of us (Acts 17:24-27).* Today, unregenerate man dreams of a one-world, humanist utopia (just as it did at Babel) run by a superman. God's will for man after Babel, however, involved separate nations and a desire for persons within those nations to worship Him. Ultimately, after the arrival of Jesus Christ, God's will for man included a different citizenship (Phil. 3:20), one attained through faith in Jesus Christ. This universal kingdom provides true riches (spiritual and eternal in nature), riches which man's open-borders dream can never provide.

- **Moral relativism**

In most academic circles today, it is no longer acceptable to hold to or proclaim the existence of moral absolutes. Instead, it is taught that each person should be free to have his own set of morals—his own set of "truths." Moreover, each person is now expected to respect someone else's truths. Thus, the saying goes: "My truth may not necessarily be your truth, but I respect your right to have your own truth."

This delusion, of course, stands in direct opposition to God's Word, which reveals that each human being is born with a conscience (and therefore a knowledge of good and evil)—a conscience which spells out God's eternal laws (Exodus 20-23 and elsewhere). Hence, the human conscience as well as God's written law in the

Bible are designed to make each human aware of his sin and to hold in check (at least to some degree) man's inhumanity to man. Though Jesus Himself—God in the flesh and the living Word—tells mankind, *"I am the way, the truth, and the life" (John 14:6)*, today's humanist snickers at such a proclamation.

Because of the invasion of moral relativism and its lie of no moral absolutes, the world is once again coming perilously close to the situation that once existed in Israel when *"everyone did what was right in his own eyes" (Judges 21:25)*. During the end-times Tribulation, this moral relativism will lead not only to a moral free-for-all (during the first half of the Tribulation), but also a radical increase in man's inhumanity to man (during the second half of the Tribulation).

- **Political correctness**

To the Western humanist mind, a certain set of acceptable principles, values and beliefs must be promulgated throughout the world in order to have unity and peace. Today, humanists and academics tell us, for example, that one must embrace the Big Bang theory, evolution, global climate change, open borders, abortion on demand, income redistribution, social justice, the co-exist movement, moral relativism, the sanctity of the environment, the equality movement, same-sex marriage, multiple genders, LBGQT rights, and a one-world government.

All of these politically-correct beliefs elevate man, and none of them acknowledge or honor God. The ultimate manifestation of the political correctness movement will occur during the future Tribulation period when the charismatic leader of a multi-national one-world government will demand that all earthlings place a loyalty mark on their right hand or forehead: *"And he [the False Prophet] causes all, the small and the great, and the rich and the poor, and the free men and the slaves, to be given a mark on their right hand or on their forehead; and he provides that no one will be able to buy or to sell, except the one who has the mark, either the name of the beast [the Antichrist] or the number of his name" (Rev. 13:16-17)*. Like sheep being led to slaughter, the use of political correctness by humanist elites is setting the stage for a world-wide decree to accept the Antichrist's mark. Sadly, none of the unregenerate have any idea of the ultimate outcome of today's emphasis of universal, "politically correct" positions.

- **The "coexist" movement**

To the Western humanist mind, world peace can only be achieved when man's various religions agree to coexist. This mantra, of course, suggests that the practitioners of each religion must tolerate and respect the views of the practitioners of other religions. "Coexist" bumper stickers currently abound throughout the Western world.

Problems, however, face with the "coexist" concept. First, the more radical elements of Islam have no desire to coexist with the other religions, but instead want to bring them into subjugation or eradicate them. In addition, the Shiite and Sunai camps of Islam have been fighting each other for a thousand years—and the more radical elements of each camp have no desire to coexist. What's more, Hinduism's belief in each person's "god-within" and Christianity's belief in a transcendent God who provided a savior for the "whosoever believes" are diametrically opposed to one another. Finally, the intransigence of radical Islam toward the Western world—the core of the Antichrist's future empire—allows the discerning Christian to see the likelihood of an end-times conflict between Islam and the West. The bottom line? The coexist movement is a delusion sent by God upon the unregenerate of the Western world.

- **Global warming / global climate change**

The Western humanist mind foolishly believes that man can control the climate. From Scripture, however, we know that God controls the climate: *"But the Lord is the true God; He is the living God and the everlasting King. At His wrath the earth quakes, and the nations cannot endure His indignation. . . . It is He who make the earth by His power, Who established the world by His wisdom; and by His understanding He has stretched out the heavens. When He utters His voice, there is a tumult of waters in the heavens, and He causes the clouds to ascend from the end of the earth" (Jer. 10:10-13). "Whatever the Lord pleases, He does, in heaven and in earth, in the seas and in all deeps. He causes the vapors to ascend from the ends of the earth, Who makes lightnings for the rain, Who brings forth the wind from His treasuries" (Ps. 135:6-7).*

Two thousand years ago Jesus Christ (God the Son) demonstrated His power over the climate during the following episode on the sea of Galilee: *"Now on one of those days Jesus and His disciples got into a boat, and He said to them, 'Let us go over to the other side of the lake.' So they launched out. But as they were sailing He fell asleep; and a fierce gale of wind descended on the lake, and the began to be swamped and to be in danger. They came to Jesus and awakened Him, saying 'Master, Master, we are perishing!' And he got up and rebuked the wind and the surging waves, and they stopped, and it became calm" (Luke 8:22-24).*

The consternation over global climate change—and its alleged disastrous consequences—is a delusion sent from God upon Christ-rejecting intellectual and political elites. This delusion will likely be one of the catalysts for a future uniting together of ten powerful nations under the leadership of the Antichrist. This Satan-empowered world leader will subsequently gather peacefully (during the first half of the Tribulation) all of the "Christian" West into a massive collection of nations, "Babylon the Great." From there, during the second half of the Tribulation, he will attempt to bring the entire world under his rule.

- **Global sustainability**

For the past two decades, humanists have become increasingly concerned about the viability and sustainability of an "overcrowded" earth, which has "limited" natural resources. An illustrative synopsis of this concern comes from a Cambridge University journal entitled *Global Sustainability*:

"Global sustainability defines the conditions under which humans and nature, societies and the biosphere, the world and the Earth can co-exist in ways that enable productive harmony, stability and resilience to support present and future generations. Global sustainability science explores interactions between social and natural systems, from local to global scales, with a particular focus on sustainability as an avenue for human development in the context of global environmental change and Earth resilience."[1]

Unregenerate man—tragically oblivious to the truths of God's Word (and God's future disposition of the planet)—focuses on issues like "global environmental change" and "Earth resilience." The Bible, in contrast, deals with, and offers, reconciliation of sinful man with a holy God—and prophesies a future return of Jesus Christ in great glory to evaluate the hearts of all men: *"For what will it profit a man if he gains the whole world and forfeits his soul? Or what will a man give in exchange for his soul? For the Son of Man is going to come in the glory of His Father with His angels, and will then repay every man according to his deeds"* (Matt. 16:26-27).

In the beginning, God created the earth ex-nihilo and subsequently prepared it for human habitation. God then created man in His own image for the purpose of fellowshipping with man. However, when man, the crown of God's creation, disobeyed God's one command, it threw all of creation into the slavery of corruption: *For the creation was subjected to futility, not willingly, but because of Him who subjected it, in hope that the creation itself also will be set free from its slavery to corruption into the freedom of the children of God. For we know that that whole creation groans and suffers the pains of childbirth together until now"* (Romans 8:20-22). Why does the whole of creation groan? *For the anxious longing of the creation waits eagerly for the revealing of the sons of God (Romans 8:19).* In the meantime, unregenerate man, who in his spiritual blindness concerns himself with the "sustainability" of the globe, knows nothing of God's larger *eternal* drama of the salvation of souls through Jesus Christ, which is quietly playing out behind the scenes throughout the world.

What is the future of planet earth? *Then I saw a new heaven and a new earth,* **for the first heaven and the first earth passed away** *[emphasis added], and there is no longer any sea. And I saw the holy city, new Jerusalem, coming down out of heaven from God, made ready as a bride adorned for her husband. And I heard a loud voice from the throne, saying, 'Behold, the tabernacle of God is among men, and He will dwell among them, and they shall be His people, and God Himself will be among them, and He will wipe away every tear from their eyes; and there will no longer be any death; there will no longer be any mourning, or crying, or pain; the first things have passed away.' . . . He who overcomes will inherit these things, and I will be his God and he will be My son. But for the cowardly and unbelieving and abominable and murderers and immoral persons and sorcerers and idolaters and liars, their part will be in the lake that burns with fire and brimstone, which is the second death (Revelation 21:1-8).*

To be sure, mankind bears significant responsibility to care for the earth (Gen. 1:26; 2:5; 2:15). Nevertheless, planet earth—the temporal location of God's far greater purpose (the invitation of eternal life with Him through faith in Jesus Christ)—will one day be destroyed by God Himself. Thus, while perhaps noble on the surface, man's global sustainability endeavor amounts to a delusion which keeps him from seeing his true need: reconciliation with a holy God and a personal relationship with his Savior, Jesus Christ.

- **The equality movement**

Western-world political correctness now calls for universal "equality"—including more equitable pay throughout economies and more equitable status for all: no one must be exalted above another.

God, however, offers a completely different view. It is clear from Scripture that God, in His design for the common good of mankind, bestows different gifts to men: *"Adah gave birth to Jabal; he was the father of those who dwell in tents and have livestock. His brother's name was Jubal; he was the father of all those who play the lyre and pipe. As for Zillah, she also gave birth to Tubal-cain, the forger of all implements of bronze and iron; and the sister of Tubal-cain was Naamah" (Genesis 4:20-22).* Furthermore, it is clear that God's plan for the common good of man includes some who have more strategic gifts and some have more ordinary gifts: *"On the contrary, who are you, O man, who answers back to God? The thing molded will not say to the molder, 'Why did you make me like this,' will it? Or does not the potter have a right over the clay, to make from the same lump one vessel for honorable use and another for common use?" (Romans 9:20-21).*

Is this apparent "inequality" on the part of God's design fair you say? Christ gives us the answer in Mark 9:35: *Sitting down, He called the twelve and said to them,* ***"If anyone wants to be first, he shall be last of all and servant of all** [emphasis added]."* Jesus Christ, the creator of man, explains that, in His reckoning, the greatest is not the President or the CEO or the brightest scholar or the celebrity, but the least and the servant. In addition, Christ dismisses the notion of "equality," by teaching that each person has different capacities—some with greater abilities, some with less: *"For it is just like a man about to go on a journey, who called his own slaves and entrusted his possessions to them. To one he gave five talents, to another, two, and to another, one, each according to his own ability; and he went on his journey" (Matt. 25:14-15).* Notice that Jesus does not talk about equality of ability, but the faithful utilization and application of however much or little He has given each person.

Finally, God's Word explains that all persons, regardless of position or ability, are designed for the common good of the whole: *But now there are many members, but one body. And the eye cannot say to the hand, "I have no need of you"; or again the head to the feet, "I have no need of you." On the contrary, it is much truer that the members of the body which seem to be weaker are necessary; and those members of the body which we deem less honorable, on these we bestow more abundant honor, and our less presentable members become much more presentable, whereas our more presentable members have no need of it. But God has so composed the body, giving more abundant honor to that member which lacked, so that there may be no division in the body, but that the members may have the same care for one another (I Cor. 12:20-25).*

In short, unregenerate man's attempt to mandate equality of status and equality of outcome amounts to a humanist delusion which opposes God's better design for mankind.

- **The social justice movement**

Over the past two decades, the term "social justice" has emerged from obscurity to become etched in political, academic and popular discourse. One dictionary defines social justice as "justice in terms of *wealth*, opportunities, and privileges within society [emphasis added]."[2] Hence, those who support the notion of social justice typically promote public dialogue which encourages "Caesar" (Western governments and their leaders) to adopt policies of income and wealth redistribution so that the poor get their "just" share. But is such a notion biblical? The answer is no.

So, the question must be asked: what are some of the dangers in an "social justice" message? Specifically, the income and wealth redistribution component of the social justice message . . .

- tacitly promotes a mindset of economic "victimhood" rather than servanthood and contentment in the midst of an unjust, fallen world
- unknowingly, subconsciously, or tacitly—nurtures a love of money and mammon
- nurtures a belief that the mammon of this world can satisfy the soul
- tacitly promotes a love of this world and a focus on earthly things
- subconsciously nurtures a mindset of entitlement and discontent
- runs the risk of fostering the sins of envy and covetousness

- **Wokeness and cancel culture**

Two of the more recent offspring of the political correctness movement are "wokeness" and the proliferation of a "cancel culture."

Says one website: "Woke is typically defined as 'an awareness of social-justice and racial-justice issues.' But that deliberately hides the most important part. Here's a more realistic definition: 'Having certain far-left views regarding social and racial justice and believing that any who disagree are under the thought control of the oppressive capitalist system.' The idea that all who don't believe the woke ideology are subject to capitalist mind control ('asleep') is central."[3]

According to another source: "Cancel Culture is a way of behaving in a society or group, especially on social media, in which it is common to completely reject and stop someone because he has said or done something that offends you."[4] Wikipedia notes that "Cancel culture is a modern form of ostracism in which someone is thrust out of social or professional circles—whether it be online, on social media, or in person. Those subject to this ostracism are said to have been 'cancelled'. . . . Former U.S. President Barack Obama warned against the social media call-out culture, saying that 'people who do really good things have flaws.' Former U.S. President Donald Trump also criticized cancel culture in a July, 2020 speech, comparing it to totalitarianism and claiming that it is a political weapon used to punish and shame dissenters by driving them from their jobs and demanding submission."

Both of these phenomena—wokeness and the cancel culture—are products of humanism, envy, and self-interest. Because both phenomena either pit one group against another or a "preferred" view against a different view, wokeness and the cancel culture promote divisiveness and societal turmoil. Because the devil is liar, deceiver, divider, and destroyer, it should be clear to the discerning believer that the wokeness and the cancel culture movements are products of the devil. Both in turn are setting the stage for the godless group-think of the Tribulation period.

- **Same-sex marriage**

God's Word defines marriage as the union of one man and one woman: *Out of the ground the Lord God formed every beast of the field and every bird of the sky, and brought them to the man to see what he would call them; and whatever the man called a living creature, that was its name. The man gave names to all the cattle, and to the birds of the sky, and to every beast of the field, but for Adam there was not found a helper suitable for him. So the Lord God caused a deep sleep to fall upon the man, and he slept; then He took one of his ribs and closed up the flesh at that place. The Lord God fashioned into a woman the rib which He had taken from the man, and brought her to the man. The man said, "This is now bone of my bones, and flesh of my flesh; She shall be called woman, because she was taken out of man." For this reason, a man shall leave his father and his mother, and be joined to his wife; and they shall become one flesh (Gen 2:19-24)*. Because God has specified marriage to be a man and a woman, same-sex marriage represents a blatant rebellion against God's expressed will for His creature man.

In Leviticus 18, where God catalogues a number of sexual sins, He has this to say about homosexuality and lesbianism: *You shall not lie with a male as one lies with a female; it is an abomination (Lev. 18:22)*. Leviticus 20:13 calls homosexual activity detestable. Romans 1:18 states that the those engaged in ungodliness and unrighteousness (including homosexuals and lesbians) are suppressing the truth. As a result of Adam and Eve's original sin, all men are born with a conscience—a knowledge of good and evil. Because of the human conscience—and its check on all manner of sin (including sexual sin)—it is clear that those who practice homosexuality and those in a same sex marriage are suppressing the truth of their sin in order to justify their lifestyle.

- **Multiple genders / transgenderism / gender-identity issues**

One of the most obvious harbingers of the prophesied end-times deluding influence has emerged recently in the now politically-correct dogmas of multiple genders and transgenderism. Such beliefs discard the human conscience and truth of God's Word (and are a delusion sent by God upon the minds of those who accept such folly). God's Word unequivocally reveals two genders—male and female—not three or four or many: *Then God said, 'Let Us make man in Our image, according to Our likeness. And let them rule over the fish of the sea and over the birds of the sky and over the cattle and over all the earth, and over every creeping thing that creeps on the earth.' God created man in His own image, in the image of God He created them;* ***male and female He created them*** *[emphasis added] (Genesis 1:26-27)*

- **Behavioral psychology**

Virtually all brands of behavioral psychology present man as a victim—a victim of his environment, his upbringing, poor parenting, lack of opportunity, sibling rivalry, and so on. God's Word, in contrast, declares man to be self-centered, self-preoccupied, and egocentric. Furthermore, God's Word states that a man can be transformed by the renewing of his mind (Rom. 12:2). In order to accomplish this, the born-again Christian is to let the living and active Word of God dwell richly on his heart (Col. 3:16).

Jesus says, *"Apart from Me, you can do nothing"* (John 15:5). To those who are troubled, Jesus says, *"Come unto Me all who are weary and heavy-laden, and I will give you rest"* (Matt. 11:28). The Psalmist says, *"Cast your burden on the Lord, and He will sustain you."* (Ps. 55:22). In order to become others-centered, Paul says, *"Do nothing from selfish ambition or empty conceit, but with humility of mind regard others as more important than yourself; do not merely look out for your own personal interests, but also for the interests of others"* (Phil. 2:3). He then adds, *"Have this attitude in yourselves which was in Christ Jesus who, although He existed in the form of God, did not regard equality with God a thing to be grasped, but emptied Himself, taking the form of a bond-servant and being made in the likeness of men. And being found in appearance as a man, He humbled Himself by becoming obedient to the point of death, even death on a cross"* (Phil. 2:5-8).

Paul also offers this prescription: *"More than that, I count all things to be loss in view of the surpassing value of knowing Christ Jesus my Lord, for whom I have suffered the loss of all things, and count them but rubbish so that I may gain Christ, and may be found in Him, not having a righteousness of my own derived from the Law, but that which is through faith in Christ, a righteousness which comes from God on the basis of faith, that I may know Him and the power of His resurrection and the fellowship of His sufferings, being conformed to His death"* (Phil. 3:8-10).

In short, God's Word—not the behavioral theories of secular and unregenerate men—provides the way to deliverance, wholeness, and emotional maturity. When a person can get past his "victimhood" and recognize his true problem (that of self-centeredness and self-focus rather than others-centeredness and God-focus), then true deliverance from his emotional challenges can take place. Until then, he will remain in bondage to impotent, humanistic solutions.

[Note: Though it will vehemently deny it, the Christian psychology movement rejects the sufficiency of Scripture. Instead, most in the movement routinely integrate assorted behavioral psychology models into their counseling. Thus, Christian psychology has chosen to syncretize the Word of God with the wisdom of the age. It makes little difference to Christian psychologist that many of the leading lights of behavioral psychology (Sigmund Freud, Carl Rogers, and Carl Jung, for example) were atheists or agnostics. To be sure, the admonition of Paul in II Cor. 6:15—*"Or what harmony has Christ with Belial, or what has a believer in common with an unbeliever?"*—is ignored in the world of Christian psychology. Yet, is not the "wisdom" of atheists like Freud, Rogers, and Jung foolishness to God (I Cor. 1:19-20)]?

- **The feminist movement**

The feminist movement variously dislikes or rejects the roles God has ordained for men and women. Indeed, most feminists chafe at the concept of male headship. God's hierarchy of submission is explained in Ephesians 5:22-30: *"Wives, be subject to your own husbands, as to the Lord. For the husband is the head of the wife, as Christ also is the head of the church, He Himself being the Savior of the body. But as the church is subject to Christ, so also the wives ought to be to their husbands in everything. Husbands, love your wives, just as Christ also loved the church and gave*

Himself up for her, so that He might sanctify her, having cleansed her by the washing of water with the word, that He might present to Himself the church in all her glory, having no spot or wrinkle or any such thing; but that she would be holy and blameless. So husbands ought also to love their own wives as their own bodies. He who loves his own wife loves himself; for no one ever hated his own flesh, but nourishes and cherishes it, just as Christ also does the church, because we are members of His body."

In God's economy, the husband is to love His wife in the same way Christ loves us (John 13:34), and the wife is to honor her husband by submitting herself to his leadership (just as all Christians are to submit themselves to Christ's headship and leadership). The feminist movement, however, rejects God's prescription for marital harmony and often attempts to hijack the man's role altogether.

- **The effort to wipe out global poverty**

Globalists need causes to "unite" mankind. One of these causes is the call—in political and ecumenical religious circles alike—to wipe out global poverty. While a noble cause in the minds of most, Jesus Himself informs us that the elimination of poverty will never happen through the efforts of man: *"But Jesus, aware of this, said to them, 'Why do you bother the woman? For she has done a good deed to Me. For **you always have the poor with you** [emphasis added]; but you do not always have Me.'" (Matt. 26:10-11).* Indeed, it can be postulated that poverty will not be eradicated from planet earth until Jesus Himself returns and reigns for a thousand years.

- **Panentheism: The belief that God is "in everything and *everyone*"**

Unregenerate New Age thinkers currently promote the heresy that God is *in* everything—including humans. This belief came to the forefront on Western New Age thinking in 1980 through Marilyn Ferguson's book, *The Aquarian Conspiracy*.[5] Says one Evangelical critic of the book:

> Marilyn Ferguson was suggesting that what the Bible described as a great heresy—"God within *everyone*"—is actually a great "truth" which could save the world. People would no longer look to Jesus Christ as their Savior. They would save themselves by "awakening" to the "God within." "God within" would be the "yeast"—the leaven—the foundational centerpiece of a New Age/New Spirituality/New World Religion. Thus, the coming New World Religion would result from a "great awakening" of the world to the "great heretical idea" that God is in everyone and everything. And make no mistake about it, Ferguson is taking dead aim at the Bible's explicit warning about destructive heresies (II Peter 2:1) with her "great heretical idea" of the "God within."[6]

This same critic also points to another 1980 New Age book by Benjamin Crème, *Messages from Maitreya the Christ*. In this channeled book, "Maitreya presented the 'great heretical idea' of the 'God within' as follows: 'My friends, God is nearer to you than you can imagine. God is yourself. God is within you and all around you.'"[7]

Finally, our critic reveals how Maitreya's "God within" teaching will be at the heart of the New Age one-world religion of the Tribulation period. He notes that New-Ager Crème states:

Eventually a new world religion will be inaugurated which will be a fusion and synthesis of the approach of the East and the approach of the West. The [Maitreya] Christ will bring together, not simply Christianity and Buddhism, but the concept of God transcendent—outside of His creation—and the concept of God immanent in all creation—in man and all creation.[8]

Tragically, many of today's professing "Christians"—not born-again, biblically illiterate, and left behind on earth after the Rapture—will likely buy into the "God within" deception during the Tribulation period and will join with Hindus, Buddhists, Confucianists, Sihks, humanists and others to embrace this New Age lie.

Point of discernment: Many foreshadows of the prophesied end-times deluding influence dot the current landscape. Each of these foreshadows stands in opposition to God's Word, and most of them have been spawned in the Western world through the utopian impulses of unregenerate academic and political elites.

CHAPTER 40

Is "Summer" Near?

Because He hates sin, our long-suffering God has ordained the horrors of an end-times Tribulation period to bring judgment upon the earth's unrepentant, who refuse to believe the truth so as to be saved (II Thess. 2:7-10). These judgments have been impending for the past nineteen hundred years. But are they now *imminent*?

"Leaves Bursting Forth"

Does evidence exist today which indicates the Lord's return is imminent? The answer is yes. Jesus Himself gives the Church today a sign that will point to the nearness of His return. Specifically, in Matthew 24:3 the disciples ask the Lord about His return: *"Tell us, what will be the sign of the end of the age?"* Jesus answers their question in Matthew 24:32-36:

> *Now learn the parable from the fig tree: when its branch has already become tender and puts forth its leaves, you know that summer is near; even so you, too, when you see all these things, recognize that He is near—right at the door. Truly I say to you, this generation [i.e., the generation that sees the 'leaves' burst forth] will not pass away until all these things take place. Heaven and earth will pass away, but My words shall not pass away. But of that day and hour no one knows, not even the angels of heaven, nor the Son, but the Father alone (Matt. 24:32-36).*

Jesus thus informs His disciples that, even though no one but the Father knows the day or hour of the Rapture, His unannounced return for His Bride (born-again believers) will be preceded by "leaves bursting forth"—by world events which have such end-times significance that they serve to "announce" (just as the leaves of the spring announce the coming of summer) the nearness of the end of the age.

Are such events taking place? The answer is yes. The rebirth of Israel in 1948 represents the largest and most obvious "leaf" of all. But dozens of other "leaves" have been bursting forth as well—including the staggering and sobering nuclear weapons capabilities of the United States and Russia—and, over the past decade, the growing nuclear arsenal of China. The following charts highlight some of these "leaves" and shows us that "summer" is right at the door.

"LEAVES" BURSTING FORTH (1940s - 50s - 60s)

the birth of the atomic bomb

the rebirth of Israel as a nation

the birth of the hydrogen bomb

the strategic air forces of the U.S. & the U.S.S.R.

the "multinational corporation" phenomenon in the West

<u>Playboy</u> magazine and the acceptability of the playboy mentality

the ease of intercontinental travel via commercial jets

the deployment of land-based ICBM's by the U.S. & U.S.S.R.

the deployment of submarine-based ICBM's by the U.S. & U.S.S.R.

the drug culture of the 60s

the sexual revolution in the West (facilitated by the "pill")

the recapture and possession of Jerusalem by the Jews in 1967

Apollo 8's "earthrise" photograph: the visual birth of "globalism"

"LEAVES" BURSTING FORTH (70s)

spy satellites

legalized abortion

widespread fornication

the removal of prayer from the schools

the breakdown of the family unit

the declining influence of the Judeo-Christian ethic in the West

the feminist movement (chafing under man's headship)

the "self" movement ("look out for #1")

"LEAVES" BURSTING FORTH (80s)

widespread pornography

homosexuality and lesbianism: out of the closet

the out-of-control drug problem

the increasing litigiousness of society

the AIDS epidemic

global communications

the global economy

the New Age movement

the increase in the acceptability of psychics and the occult

the increasing belief in UFO's and ET's

the decline in respect for elected officials

the increase in television worldliness

the increase in motion picture violence, nudity, and vulgarity

the increasing acceptability and spread of legalized gambling

heavy metal rock's dark lyrics

gangster rap's insurrection lyrics

"LEAVES" BURSTING FORTH (90s)

the "politically correct" phenomenon

the ever-growing momentum of the "save the planet" movement

cruise missiles

laser-guided weapons

stealth technology

the spread of gang violence throughout the U.S.

the "safe sex" campaign

microchip technology implanted into animals

Islamic terrorism

the threat of Islamic nuclear proliferation

the concern over weapons of mass destruction

the reemergence of the peace movement

global satellite television

the "victim" mentality of society (vs. personal responsibility)

the Internet (and its facilitation of instant global communication)

"LEAVES" BURSTING FORTH (00s)

the revelation that China has eleven nuclear missiles aimed at the U.S.

the proliferation of New Age teaching throughout the West

the drive in the West to legalize same-sex marriage

the efforts of Iran to develop weapons-grade plutonium

the efforts of North Korea to build ICBMs that can reach the U.S.

the embracing of Eastern mystical practices in public education

the infiltration of Eastern mysticism into parts of Christendom

the sobering reality of radical Islam—and its call to destroy Israel

"LEAVES" BURSTING FORTH (10s)

the reality of virtually world-wide cell phone coverage

the reality of instant global communication through smart phones

the legalization of same-sex marriage

the LBGTQ movement

the cry for a world without borders

the rise of gender-identity confusion

the divisiveness of identity politics

the birth of "cancel" culture

the emergence of big tech censorship

the ascent of the "great reset" movement

"LEAVES" BURSTING FORTH (20s)

the increased authoritarianism in the Western World (facilitated by the Covid-19 pandemic)

CHAPTER 41

The Church is Sound Asleep

"The kingdom of heaven will be comparable to ten virgins, who took their lamps and went out to meet the bridegroom. Five of them were foolish, and five were prudent. For when the foolish took their lamps, they took no oil with the; but the prudent took oil in flasks along with their lamps. **Now while the bridegroom was delaying, they all got drowsy and began to sleep** *[emphasis added]. But at midnight there was a shout, 'Behold, the bridegroom! Come out to meet him.' Then all those virgins rose and trimmed their lamps. The foolish said to the prudent, 'Give us some of your oil, for our lamps are going out.' But the prudent answered, 'No, there will not be enough for us and you too; go instead to the dealers and buy some for yourselves.' And while they were going away to make the purchase, the bridegroom came, and those who were ready went in with him to the wedding feast; and the door was shut. Later the other virgins also came, saying, 'Lord, lord, open up for us.' But he answered, 'Truly I say to you, I do not know you.' Be on the alert then, for you do not know the day nor the hour (Matt. 25:1-13)."*

In His Parable of the Ten Virgins, Jesus provides additional information about the Rapture. Previously, in Matthew 24:40-42 (a parenthetical passage, not a chronological one), He has given His disciples a description of *what happens* at the Rapture: some will be taken and some will be left behind. Here in Matthew 25:1-13, our Lord explains *who* will be taken at the Rapture and *who* will be left behind. [Note: the context of the parable is the (now long) Church Age: *"now while the bridegroom was delaying...."* (v. 5).]

Jesus uses the metaphor of a typical Jewish betrothal, marriage, and marriage supper to augment His earlier teaching on the Rapture. The first century Jewish betrothal was unlike a typical Gentile engagement of today. In the Jewish betrothal, the bridegroom, after proposing to his loved one, would "go away" to his "father's house" to "make a place" for them to live on the father's land. He would often be away for a year while he completed their home. Then, when the home was ready and all the arrangements had been made for the wedding feast, the bridegroom, in a touch of Jewish romance, would come for his bride *unexpectedly*, usually in the middle of the night. The bride, of course, was to be alert and ready for his return, eager to have their marriage consummated. To be fully prepared (after all, her groom might come for her in the middle of the night), she would have to have her lamp trimmed with oil so that she would have sufficient light to go out to greet him.[1]

And so it is today with the living Church, the Bride of Christ (Eph. 5:22-32; Rev. 19:7). All persons indwelled with the Holy Spirit are to be alert and ready for an *any-moment* coming of the Bridegroom (Christ) to take them to the Father's home for the consummation of their marriage (the completion and perfection of their salvation). Those having the "oil" (the indwelling Holy Spirit)—the "wheat" of Matthew 13:36-39, or born-again Christians—are taken by the Groom to heaven for their wedding and wedding feast (Rev. 19:7-9). Those not having the "oil"—the "tares" of Matthew 13:36-39—are left behind on the earth. It is now too late for the tares (counterfeit Christians): the door to the "ark" (heaven in this case) has been closed, even though some of them will apparently finally embrace salvation by grace through faith and will want to be with the Lord: *"And later the other virgins also came, saying, 'Lord, lord, open up for us.' But he answered and said, 'Truly I say to you, I do not know you'" (vv. 11-12)*. It is also too late for all other unbelievers on earth; they will have to face the travail of the Tribulation judgments, just as all unbelievers in Noah's day had to face the Flood after the door to the ark was closed. At this juncture in the parable, Jesus (for a fourth time in the Olivet Discourse) exhorts those hearing Him to be ready for an any-moment coming: *"Be on the alert, then, for you do not know the day or the hour" (v. 13)*.

Unfortunately, despite Jesus Himself imploring His Bride to be alert and ready for His return, most believers (Chapters 35 and 36) are not. Why is the Evangelical church sound asleep? This writer would suggest two reasons: first, the widespread use of a non-literal interpretation of eschatology and, second, an overall distaste for the topic of eschatology. Covenant Theology and Lutheran Theology both utilize a dual hermeneutic, which allows them to spiritualize or allegorize much of Bible prophecy. Accordingly, most dual-hermeneutic pastors teach that the book of Revelation is either unknowable or simply a metaphor of "good vanquishing evil." Covenant Premillennialists teach a post-Tribulation Rapture, a belief which contradicts Christ's exhortations to be alert for an any-moment Rapture. The founding pastor of the Purpose Driven church believes that Christ told the disciples that the details of His return were "none of your business".[2] The founding church of the Seeker Sensitive movement eschews the topic of eschatology. Evangelical Lutheranism, a champion of Replacement Theology and a believer that Israel has no future blessings from God, knows nothing of an any-moment return of Jesus for His bride. Progressive Christianity has no discernable eschatology and apparently believes it is irrelevant. The New Apostolic Reformation's "prophets" are so busy prophesying "a great final end-times harvest of souls" they've lost sight of an any-moment return of Christ. Emergent Christianity universally ridicules Biblical Christianity's pre-tribulation, pre-millennial eschatology—and likewise pays no attention to Christ's exhortations to be alert for His any-moment return.[3]

To be sure, Jesus has already told His Bride what will happen on earth during the end times. The book of Revelation and other scriptures describe such events as the Rapture of the Church; the rise and reign of a world leader known as the Antichrist; a seven-year Tribulation period in which one-half of the earth's post-Rapture population will be killed during the first two series of judgments; the Second Coming of Jesus Christ to the earth with His holy angels and resurrected saints; Christ's defeat of all His enemies upon His return; Christ's judgment of the earth's remaining inhabitants; Christ's subsequent reign over the earth for a thousand years;

Christ's binding of Satan during His reign; God's exaltation of Israel during the Millennial Kingdom; and so on. Unfortunately (and tragically), perhaps ninety percent of Evangelicals have had little or no teaching on these and other future events.

Unlike the 1970s and 1980s, most of today's Evangelical churches (with the exception of the Calvary Chapels, dispensational Bible churches, and a sprinkling of independent churches) don't touch the topic of eschatology. Instead, the standard Sunday-morning fare in most of Evangelicalism consists of "how to" sermons on living the Christian life. As a result, though the "leaves" of world events are currently bursting forth, born-again Christians who attend churches that shun Biblical eschatology remain in a deep slumber with regard to Christ's any-moment return—just as Jesus prophesied two thousand years ago (Matt. 25:1-13).

A Final Word

It is sincerely hoped that the forty-one topics covered in this book have helped each reader understand the importance, necessity, nature, and scope of spiritual and biblical discernment. Both types of discernment can and must be cultivated by born-again Christians—particularly those called to lead and teach the flock of Jesus Christ (pastors, elders, teachers, and disciplers). It is also hoped that, almost by osmosis, your own level of discernment has grown appreciably after taking in the material.

From our survey of the "Summer-Fall-Winter-Spring" pattern of church history, it was easy to observe how, over time, the deceptions of Satan and the flesh of men brought substantial error into Christ's inter-advent kingdom. Furthermore, though the Protestant Reformation brought new life and a measure of correction into the church, we saw that significant error remained. Fortunately, as Spring became "warmer," a hermeneutics reformation began to take place and additional correction ensued: increasing numbers of Evangelicals began to use the grammatical-historical-literal method of Bible interpretation, consistently applied. Among other results, this reformation restored the apostolic belief in premillennialism to parts of the Evangelical church. Yet, despite this progress, unfortunate error has remained in certain segments of Evangelicalism.

Today, Satan is buffeting the world as never before: indeed, evil is being declared good and good is being declared evil. Over the past thirty years, Evangelicalism has not been immune from Satan's whispers. During this time, new forms of error and deception have entered the church because top-level Christian leaders, seminaries, pastors, and vast numbers of Christians have either made light of sound doctrine, left poor teaching unchallenged, or failed to test the spirits. As a result, the need for spiritual and biblical discernment is crucially important—perhaps as never before—in this buffeted environment.

In conclusion, isn't it time for Evangelicals to become truly adept at testing the spirits and then, like the Bereans, become skilled at assessing Christian teaching? Isn't it time for all evangelical denominations and independent churches to examine their doctrine and practices with tender, teachable hearts—with a desire to root out error? Isn't it time for pastors and teachers to take seriously Paul's exhortations to handle God's Word accurately and to teach the whole counsel of God's Word? Isn't it time for Isaiah's closing exhortation to become a reality in *every* Evangelical heart? *"But to this one I will look, to him who is humble and contrite of spirit, and who trembles at My word" (Isa. 66:2).*

Appendix A

Assorted Verses Which Attest to a Millennial Kingdom

The following are some of the verses which attest to a future literal reign of Jesus Christ over the present earth:

And the Lord will be king over all the earth; in that day the Lord will be the only one, and His name the only one. All the land will be changed into a plain from Geba to Rimmon south of Jerusalem; but Jerusalem will rise and remain on its site from Benjamin's Gate as far as the place of the First Gate to the Corner Gate, and from the Tower of Hananel to the king's wine presses. And people will live in it, and there will be no more curse, for Jerusalem will dwell in security (Zech. 14:9-11).

And it will come about in the last days that the mountain of the house of the Lord will be established as the chief of the mountains. It will be raised above the hills, and the peoples will stream to it. And many nations will come and say, "Come and let us go up to the mountain of the Lord and to the house of the God of Jacob, that He may teach us about His ways and that we may walk in His paths." For from Zion will go forth the law, even the word of the Lord from Jerusalem.

Then it will come about that any who are left of all the nations that went against Jerusalem will go up from year to year to worship the King, the Lord of hosts, and to celebrate the Feast of Booths. And it will be that whichever of the families of the earth does not go up to Jerusalem to worship the King, the Lord of hosts, there will be no rain on them (Zech. 14:16-17).

In that day there will be inscribed on the bells of the horses, "HOLY TO THE LORD." And the cooking pots in the Lord's house will be like the bowls before the altar. And every cooking pot in Jerusalem and in Judah will be holy to the Lord of hosts; and all who sacrifice will come and take of them and boil in them. And there will no longer be a Canaanite in the house of the Lord of hosts in that day (Zech. 14:20-21).

And the wolf will dwell with the lamb, and the leopard will lie down with the kid, and the calf and the young lion and the fatling together; and a little boy will lead them. Also the cow and the bear will graze; their young will lie down together; and the lion will eat straw like the ox. And the nursing child will play by the hole of the cobra, and the weaned child will put his hand on the viper's den. They will not hurt or destroy in all My holy mountain, for the earth will be full of the knowledge of the Lord as the waters cover the sea. Then it will come about in that day that the nations will resort to the root of Jesse, who will stand as a signal for the peoples; and His resting place will be glorious (Isa. 11:6-10).

And they will no longer defile themselves with their idols, or with their detestable things, or with any of their transgressions; but I will deliver them from all their dwelling places in which they have sinned, and will cleanse them. And they will be My people, and I will be their God. And My servant David will be king over them, and they will all have one shepherd; and they will walk in My ordinances, and keep My statutes, and observe them. And they shall live on the land that I gave to Jacob My servant, in which your fathers lived; and they will live on it, they, and their sons, and their sons' sons, forever; and David My servant shall be their prince forever.

Therefore, I will deliver My flock, and they will no longer be a prey; and I will judge between one sheep and another. Then I will set over them one shepherd, My servant David, and he will feed them; he will feed them himself and be their shepherd. And I, the Lord, will be their God, and My servant David will be prince among them; I, the Lord, have spoken.

And I will make a covenant of peace with them and eliminate harmful beasts from the land, so that they may live securely in the wilderness and sleep in the woods. And I will make them and the places around My hill a blessing. And I will cause showers to come down in their season; they will be showers of blessing. Also the tree of the field will yield its fruit, and the earth will yield its increase, and they will be secure on their land. Then they will know that I am the Lord, when I have broken the bars of their yoke and have delivered them from the hand of those who enslaved them. And they will no longer be a prey to the nations, and the beasts of the earth will not devour them; but they will live securely, and no one will make them afraid (Eze. 34:23-28).

"Therefore, wait for Me," declares the Lord, "For the day when I rise up to the prey. Indeed, My decision is to gather nations, to assemble kingdoms, to pour out on them My indignation, all My burning anger; for all the earth will be devoured by the fire of My zeal. For then I will give to the peoples purified lips, that all of them may call on the name of the Lord, to serve Him shoulder to shoulder.

"From beyond the rivers of Ethiopia My worshipers, My dispersed ones, will bring My offerings. In that day you will feel no shame because of all your deeds by which you have rebelled against Me; for then I will remove from your midst your proud, exulting ones, and you will never again be haughty on My holy mountain. But I will leave among you a humble and lowly people, and they will take refuge in the name of the Lord. The remnant of Israel will do no wrong and tell no lies, nor will a deceitful tongue be found in their mouths; for they shall feed and lie down with no one to make them tremble."

Shout for joy, O daughter of Zion! Shout in triumph, O Israel! Rejoice and exult with all your heart, O daughter of Jerusalem! The Lord has taken away His judgments against you, He has cleared away your enemies. The King of Israel, the Lord, is in your midst; you will fear disaster no more. In that day it will be said to Jerusalem: "Do not be afraid, O Zion; do not let your hands fall limp. The Lord your God is in your midst, a victorious warrior. He will exult over you with joy, He will be quiet in His love, He will rejoice over you with shouts of joy" *(Zeph. 3:8-17).*

So many peoples and mighty nations will come to seek the Lord of hosts in Jerusalem and to entreat the favor of the Lord. Thus says the Lord of hosts, "In those days ten men from all the nations will grasp the garment of a Jew saying, 'Let us go with you, for we have heard that God is with you' " (Zech. 8:22-23).

"The wolf and the lamb shall graze together, and the lion shall eat straw like the ox; and dust shall be the serpent's food. They shall do no evil or harm in all My holy mountain," says the Lord (Isa. 65:25).

When the Lord will have compassion on Jacob, and again choose Israel, and settle them in their own land, then strangers will join them and attach themselves to the house of Jacob. And the peoples will take them along and bring them to their place, and the house of Israel will possess them as an inheritance in the land of the Lord as male servants and female servants; and they will take their captors captive, and will rule over their oppressors (Isa. 14:1-2).

Thus says the Lord God, "Behold, I will lift up My hand to the nations, and set up My standard to the peoples; and they will bring your sons in their bosom, And your daughters will be carried on their shoulders. And kings will be your guardians, and their princesses your nurses. They will bow down to you with their faces to the earth, and lick the dust of your feet; and you will know that I am the Lord; those who hopefully wait for Me will not be put to shame" (Isa. 49:22-23).

And the sons of those who afflicted you will come bowing to you, and all those who despised you will bow themselves at the soles of your feet; and they will call you the city of the Lord, The Zion of the Holy One of Israel. Whereas you have been forsaken and hated with no one passing through, I will make you an everlasting pride, a joy from generation to generation (Isa. 60:13-15).

But you will be called the priests of the Lord; you will be spoken of as ministers of our God. You will eat the wealth of nations, and in their riches you will boast. Instead of your shame you will have a double portion, and instead of humiliation they will shout for joy over their portion. Therefore, they will possess a double portion in their land, everlasting joy will be theirs. Then their offspring will be known among the nations, and their descendants in the midst of the peoples. All who see them will recognize them because they are the offspring whom the Lord has blessed (Isa. 61:6-7,9).

And He will judge between many peoples and render decisions for mighty, distant nations. Then they will hammer their swords into plowshares and their spears into pruning hooks; nation will not lift up sword against nation, and never again will they train for war (Micah 4:1-3).

Then the nations that are left round about you will know that I, the Lord, have rebuilt the ruined places and planted that which was desolate; I, the Lord, have spoken and will do it (Ezek. 36:36).

"At that time I will bring you in, even at the time when I gather you together; Indeed, I will give you renown and praise among all the peoples of the earth, when I restore your fortunes before your eyes," says the Lord (Zeph. 3:20).

For Zion's sake I will not keep silent, and for Jerusalem's sake I will not keep quiet, until her righteousness goes forth like brightness, and her salvation like a torch that is burning. And the nations will see your righteousness, and all kings your glory; and you will be called by a new name, which the mouth of the Lord will designate.
You will also be a crown of beauty in the hand of the Lord, and a royal diadem in the hand of your God. It will no longer be said to you, "Forsaken," nor to your land will it any longer be said, "Desolate"; but you will be called, "My delight is in her," and your land,"

Married "; for the Lord delights in you, and to Him your land will be married. For as a young man marries a virgin, so your sons will marry you; and as the bridegroom rejoices over the bride, so your God will rejoice over you.

On your walls, O Jerusalem, I have appointed watchmen; all day and all night they will never keep silent. You who remind the Lord, take no rest for yourselves; and give Him no rest until He establishes and makes Jerusalem a praise in the earth.

The Lord has sworn by His right hand and by His strong arm, "I will never again give your grain as food for your enemies; nor will foreigners drink your new wine, for which you have labored." But those who garner it will eat it, and praise the Lord; and those who gather it will drink it in the courts of My sanctuary (Isa. 62:1-9).

Then I saw an angel coming down from heaven, holding the key of the abyss and a great chain in his hand. And he laid hold of the dragon, the serpent of old, who is the devil and Satan, and bound him for a thousand years; and he threw him into the abyss, and shut it and sealed it over him, so that he would not deceive the nations any longer, until the thousand years were completed; after these things he must be released for a short time.

Then I saw thrones, and they sat on them, and judgment was given to them. And I saw the souls of those who had been beheaded because of their testimony of Jesus and because of the word of God, and those who had not worshiped the beast or his image, and had not received the mark on their forehead and on their hand; and they came to life and reigned with Christ for a thousand years. The rest of the dead did not come to life until the thousand years were completed. This is the first resurrection. Blessed and holy is the one who has a part in the first resurrection; over these the second death has no power, but they will be priests of God and of Christ and will reign with Him for a thousand years (Rev. 20:1-6).

Appendix B

Christ's Revelation of a Pre-Tribulation Rapture

Except for the book of Revelation, Jesus teaches more about the end-times events in Matthew 24-25—the Olivet Discourse—than in any other part of the New Testament. Christians from different theological perspectives use the Olivet Discourse to argue their respective positions on the end times, particularly their position on the Rapture of the Church. For example, some Christians contend that the Olivet Discourse teaches a post-tribulation Rapture. Other Christians suggest that the Discourse teaches a pre-tribulation Rapture. Still others contend that the Rapture isn't even pictured in the Olivet Discourse. It is this writer's contention, however, that Christians from all theological persuasions have overlooked one of the nuances of the Discourse's narrative. *Specifically, most Christians assume that Christ's teaching in the Olivet Discourse is entirely chronological in nature. It is not.*

The Literary Structure of the Olivet Discourse (Matthew 24 – 25):

Christ presents four clearly-defined *chronological* vignettes in the Discourse and seven clearly-defined *parenthetical* vignettes. Accordingly, the Olivet Discourse is a mixture of (1) the future sequence of human events and (2) parenthetical exhortations, descriptions, promises, and warnings which relate in some way to these events—but which do not advance the sequence of events. This "chronological vs. parenthetical" pattern in the Olivet Discourse is similar to the one found in the book of Revelation. Both C.I. Scofield[1] and John Walvoord[2] recognized a chronological-parenthetical pattern in the book of Revelation and used it as the basis of their Revelation outlines and commentaries. Likewise, J. Dwight Pentecost acknowledges that certain parts of the Olivet Discourse are parenthetical.[3]

Unfortunately, many proponents of the pre-tribulation Rapture fail to understand the chronological-parenthetical literary structure of the Olivet Discourse and simultaneously insist that Christ does not teach on the Rapture in Matthew 24 & 25. In doing so, however, these proponents miss the New Testament's most powerful evidence in support of a pre-tribulation Rapture.

This Writer's Outline of the Olivet Discourse (Matt. 24 – 25):

I. CHRIST'S PROPHECY ABOUT THE JERUSALEM TEMPLE (24:1-2)

II. THE DISCIPLES' QUESTIONS ABOUT THIS PROPHECY (24:3)

III. CHRIST'S ANSWERS TO THE DISCIPLES' QUESTIONS AND CHRIST'S EXPLANATION OF THE END-TIMES EVENTS (24:4 - 25:46)

    A. **THE CHURCH AGE (24:4-8)**

    B. **THE TRIBULATION PERIOD (24:9-14)**

    Parenthetical: Christ's Exhortation to Flee the Abomination of Desolation and His Pronouncement of the Severity of the 2nd Half of the Tribulation (24:15-22)

    Parenthetical: Christ's Exhortation to Avoid False Christs While He is Away (24:23-28)

    C. **THE SECOND COMING OF CHRIST TO THE EARTH (24:29-31)**

    Parenthetical: The Parable of the Fig Tree—and the Sign of the End of the Age (24:32-35)

    Parenthetical: Christ's First Teaching on the Rapture and His Exhortation to Be Alert for It at All Times (24:36-44)

    Parenthetical: Christ's Promise of Blessing and Reward for Faithful, Sensible Servanthood While He is Away (24:45-51)

    Parenthetical: The Parable of the Ten Virgins—the Picture of Christ's Coming for His Own at the Rapture (25:1-13)

    Parenthetical: The Parable of the Talents (25:14-30)

    D. **THE JUDGMENT OF THE REMAINING NATIONS BY CHRIST (25:31-46)**

Summary of Christ's Olivet Discourse teaching:

- Christ presents a four-fold chronology of future events in the Olivet:
  (1) the Church Age (Matt. 24:4-8)
  (2) the Tribulation period (Matt. 24:9-14)
  (3) the Second Coming of Christ to the earth (Matt. 24:29-31)
  (4) the Judgment of the earth's remaining nations by Christ before He begins His Millennial reign over the earth (Matt. 25:31-46)

- Christ teaches that the Church Age will be characterized by the following phenomena (Matt. 24:4-8):
  (1) many will come in Christ's name, claiming to be Christ
  (2) many will be misled by these claims
  (3) there will be wars and rumors of wars
  (4) nation will rise against nation, and kingdom will rise against kingdom
  (5) there will be earthquakes in various places
  (6) there will be famines in various places

- Christ teaches that the Church Age will last for a long time and that His return will not take place for a long time (Matt. 24:48; 25:5; 25:19)

- Christ confirms, by referring the disciples to Daniel 9:24-27, that the Tribulation period will last for seven years

- Christ teaches that the seven-year Tribulation period will be characterized by the following phenomena (Matt. 24:9-14):
  (1) Many Tribulation Christians (i.e., post-Rapture Christians) will be killed
  (2) Tribulation Christians will be hated by all nations because of Christ
  (3) many so-called "Christians" will fall away, will hate Tribulation Christians, and will deliver up Tribulation Christians to be killed
  (4) false prophets will arise—and will mislead many
  (5) lawlessness will increase
  (6) most people's love will grow cold
  (7) those Tribulation Christians who manage to survive the Tribulation judgments will enter the Millennial Kingdom
  (8) the gospel of the kingdom will be preached in the whole world as a witness to all nations

- Christ teaches that the second half of the Tribulation will be a time of unimaginable horror on earth—and that "unless those days be cut short no life would survive" (Matt. 24:19-22)

- Christ teaches that His bodily return to the earth will be "announced" by four signs in the sky—the sun will be darkened; the moon will not give off its light; the stars will move out of their customary positions in the sky; and the celestial laws which govern the solar systems and galaxies will be altered—and then by *the* sign of His return (Matt. 24:29-30)

- Christ introduces the disciples to the doctrine of the pre-tribulation Rapture of the Church in two parenthetical passages: Matthew 24:36-44 and 25:1-11. Unlike the Second Coming of Christ to the earth, which will be announced by signs in the sky, the Rapture will be *unannounced* and will occur *unexpectedly*

- Christ teaches, in four separate verses, that the born-again Christian is to be ever-expectant and always ready for this any-moment Rapture (Matt. 24:42; 24:43-44; 24:50; 25:13)

- Christ teaches that those within Christendom who are born-again believers will be taken from the earth at the time of the Rapture—and that the Rapture will occur *before* the Tribulation judgments (Matt. 24:36-44; 25:1-11)

- Christ teaches that those within Christendom who are not born-again believers will be left behind on earth at the time of the Rapture—and will not be able to escape the Tribulation judgments even if some of them want to turn to Christ after the Rapture (Matt. 24:36-44; 25:1-11)

- Christ teaches that the born-again Christian, even though he/she cannot know the day or the hour of the Rapture, can nevertheless discern when the Lord's return is near: Just as a person knows that summer is near when the leaves begin to burst forth in the spring, so too a person can know that Christ's return is near when the "leaves" of world events begin to burst forth in ways which could allow for a literal fulfillment of the end-times prophecies (Matt. 24:32-35)

- Christ teaches that all persons who survive the horrors of the Tribulation will be judged by Jesus Himself after His return. Those who have put their faith in Him will be allowed to enter the Millennial Kingdom. Those who have not put their faith in Him will be slain (Matt. 25:31-46)

- Christ points out that most persons during the Church Age—including persons today—will pay no attention to God's pronouncement of impending judgment, just as humans paid no attention to God's pronouncement of impending judgment in Noah's day (Matt. 24:36-39)

- Christ teaches that virtually all of Christendom—including His own children (those indwelled with the Holy Spirit)—will be drowsy and asleep (i.e., not alert) when He comes unexpectedly at the Rapture (Matt. 25:1-11)

- Christ exhorts today's believer to set his heart on doing the Lord's work and to be a faithful, sensible servant of the Lord while He is away (Matt. 24:45-51)

- Christ teaches that all who claim to be Christians (i.e., both the "wheat" and the "tares) will one day give an accounting of their lives to Christ. Those who are born again will enter into the joy of their Master; those who are not born again will be cast into Hell (Matt. 25:14-30)

- Christ teaches that faithfulness with however much or little the Lord gifts each born-again believer is all that Christ asks of His children and that equal faithfulness will be rewarded equally (Matt. 25:14-29)

- Christ teaches that Hell will be a place of utter separation from God (and from God's people) and will be a place of weeping and gnashing of teeth (Matt. 25:30)

Conclusion

Jesus describes *two* very different comings of the Son of Man in the Olivet Discourse. These comings not only are two separate events, but they are *mutually exclusive* events (i.e., an event cannot be both unannounced and announced at the same time; an event cannot simultaneously be unexpected and expected). In addition, these two events are separated in time, thus allowing the human condition to disintegrate from the one described parenthetically in Matthew 24:37-38 to the one described in Matthew 24:15-22. The chart on the next page shows the contrasts and the mutual exclusivity of these two comings of the Son of Man.

One coming is *unannounced* (like a thief in the night), unexpected, and occurs when the human condition is one of "eating, drinking, and marrying." Scoffers in fact will ask during this timeframe: *"Where is the sign of His coming? For ever since the fathers fell asleep, all continues just as it was from the beginning of creation"* (II Pet. 3:4). This previously undisclosed coming of the Son of Man (introduced and explained parenthetically in Matthew 24:36-44 and Matthew 25:1-13) is the **pre-tribulation Rapture of the Church**—Christ's sudden, unannounced, unexpected, instantaneous coming in the air for His own. To be sure, Jesus provides significant information about the Rapture in the Olivet Discourse. First, He describes the *human condition* prior to the Rapture—people will be eating and drinking, and marrying and giving in marriage. It will be "business as usual" on earth at the time of this unexpected coming. Second, He describes *what happens* at the Rapture—some will be taken and others will be left behind. Third, He teaches *who* will be taken into heaven at the Rapture—born again believers in Jesus Christ (those having indwelling Holy Spirit)—and *who* will be left behind on earth to face judgment—counterfeit Christians (those not having the indwelling Holy Spirit) and all other unbelievers. Fourth, He explains that the Rapture will occur *before* the Tribulation judgments.

The other coming is *announced* (by signs in the sky), expected (thirty days after the end of the Tribulation period—Dan. 12:11-12), and takes place immediately after the final three-and-a-half years of the Tribulation period—a period filled with death, horror, terror, panic, and fright. It will *not* be "business as usual" on earth prior to the Lord's bodily return. Instead, it is a time when "unless those days had been cut short, no life would have been saved" (Matt. 24:22). This particular coming of the Son of Man (presented chronologically in Matthew 24:29-31) is the **Second Coming of Jesus Christ**—the bodily return of Christ to the earth with His own (including resurrected Old Testament saints, resurrected and raptured Church Age saints, and resurrected Tribulation saints). Upon His return, Christ will save Israel from annihilation, judge the earth's remaining nations, and set up His long-awaited Millennial Kingdom (inhabited by Christ, His resurrected saints, and those post-Rapture believers who survive the Tribulation).

Finally, Christ's revelation of two very different, mutually-exclusive comings of the Son of Man—separated in time by two entirely different human conditions—renders the post-tribulation Rapture position Biblically impossible.

TWO COMINGS OF THE SON OF MAN IN THE OLIVET DISCOURSE

THE RAPTURE:

BEFORE THE TRIBULATION
"just like the days of Noah . ."
(Matt. 24:37-39)

RETURNS FOR HIS SAINTS
(Matt. 24:36-41; 25:1-10)

UNANNOUNCED (LIKE THIEF . .)
(Matt. 24:43-44)

UNEXPECTED
(Matt. 24:43-44; 24:50; 25:5-6)

UNKNOWN DAY OR HOUR
(Matt. 24:36; 24:42; 24:50; 25:13)

CONDITION ON EARTH PRIOR:
"business as usual"
eating & drinking
marrying & giving in marriage
(Matt. 24:37-39)

INVISIBLE RETURN [2]

A CATCHING UP [3]

UP INTO HEAVEN
(Matt. 25:6-12)

FOR DELIVERANCE
(Matt. 24:37-42)

THE SECOND COMING:

AFTER THE TRIBULATION
"immediately after the tribul. . "
(Matt. 24:29-30)

RETURNS WITH HIS SAINTS
(Matt. 24:31)

ANNOUNCED (BY SIGNS IN SKY)
(Matt. 24:29-30)

EXPECTED
(Matt. 24:29-30)

KNOWN DAY [1]

CONDITION ON EARTH PRIOR:
not "business as usual"
woe to those with child . .
unless those days be cut short . .
(Matt. 24:19-22)

VISIBLE (THEY WILL SEE . .)
(Matt. 24:30)

A COMING DOWN
(Matt. 24:29-30)

DOWN TO THE EARTH
(Matt. 25:31-32a)

FOR JUDGMENT
(Matt. 25:14-19, 24-30; 25:31-46)

---

[1] Dan. 12:11-12
[2] I Cor. 15:50-52; I Thess. 4:15-18
[3] I Thess. 4:15-18; I Cor. 15:50-52

Appendix C

The Question of Evil in the World

Because evil has been so pervasive throughout human history, unregenerate men over the millennia have had difficulty believing that God is a caring or loving God. Yet for those who choose to embrace the Bible, the source and problem of evil is clearly explained.

To be sure, the Bible portrays God as an all-loving (indeed perfectly loving) God, who is also holy and just. According to the Bible, God created his two highest forms of creation—angels and humans—with a free will. God did not, in the case of angels, and does not, in the case of humans, *coerce* these two groups to want Him, love Him, or worship Him. Instead, He gives them freedom of choice.

Sometime after his creation, Lucifer (the highest-ranking angel) chose to rebel against God—and sin entered the universe for the first time. Because Lucifer (now called Satan) and one-third of heaven's angels (now called fallen angels or demons) throughout human history have stood in opposition to God and God's purposes for man, it is apparent from Scripture that *Satan*—whose goal is to deceive, devour, and destroy as much of mankind as possible—*is the primary architect and cause of evil on earth today.* God, in His permissive will for creation, has allowed Satan wide latitude on earth and in heaven, including his spiritual battle with mankind (Eph. 6:10-17).

In addition, Eve, because she succumbed to the deception of Satan, rather than adhering to God's will, suffered the consequences of her disobedience—including spiritual separation from God and *a new propensity toward self-centeredness, sin, and evil.* Adam, because he listened to his wife, rather than obeying God's instruction, likewise suffered the same consequences. As previously discussed, Scripture teaches that each of Adam and Eve's progeny (i.e., every human ever conceived or born) inherits a sin nature (Ps. 51:5), including the inevitable commission of sins. As well, Satan and his demons work both frontally and subtly to tempt every man and woman to sin.

Scripture indicates that God has allowed Satan to be the "god of this world" for a season of time. Eventually, however, Satan will be prohibited from deceiving or destroying mankind—being bound in a place called the Abyss—when Jesus Christ returns to the earth to reign over His creation for a thousand years (Rev. 20:1-6). In the meantime, all of mankind is confronted head-on with "the world, the flesh, and the devil"—and evil is a natural consequence of this Age.

Thus, evil exists in the world today, not because of God, but because of (1) *man's inherent sin nature* which breeds all manner of sin and (2) *Satan's efforts to deceive, devour, and destroy* as many persons as possible. **In reality, the evil which man sees and experiences on earth today should be a *perpetual reminder* of both the fall of Satan and the fall of man**. Unfortunately, because most of mankind has never read the Bible (and many would not believe it or accept it if they did), unregenerate man continues to stumble over the question of evil in the world.

Appendix D

Perpetual Reminders of Man's Rebellions Against God

God has left mankind with perpetual reminders of his early rebellions and God's judgment of these rebellions. These reminders are wholly evident and are intended to cause man to see both the consequences of sin and his need for reconciliation with God.

- **Perpetual Reminders of Adam and Eve's Fall (Gen. 1-19)**
    - **The human conscience**—knowing the difference between good and evil (Gen. 3:5,7)
    - **Clothes** [man is ashamed/embarrassed to be naked in public] (Gen. 3:7)
    - **Enmity between Christ and non-believers** (Gen. 3:15b)
    - **Multiplied pain in childbirth** (Gen. 3:16a)
    - **A woman's desire to rule over her husband** (Gen. 3:16:b)
    - **The toil of labor** (particularly in the non-Western world) (Gen. 3:17)
    - **Physical death** (Gen. 3:17,19a)
    - **The decomposition of a corpse** back to dust (Gen. 3:19b)

The human conscience gives each person a moral compass from God—one designed to keep a person from harm. Unfortunately, most humans eventually suppress their conscience in order to indulge their favorite sins. Virtually no one understands that humans wear clothes today because of Adam and Eve's original sin against God; instead, man exalts the newest fashions in clothes. Pain in childbirth is meant to be a perpetual reminder to women of Eve's disobedience toward God. Toil in labor is meant to be a reminder to men of Adam's disobedience toward God. Physical death in turn is the most obvious reminder of Adam and Eve's rebellion against God. The Bible teaches that the "wages" of sin is death. Many people, however, don't even bother to consider what happens after death, let alone any eventual accountability before a Holy God.

- **Perpetual Reminder of the Genesis Flood (Gen. 9:8-16)**
    - **Rainbows** (Gen. 9:13-16)

When a person sees a rainbow during a rainstorm or its aftermath, it is designed to remind him of man's universal rebellion against God before the Genesis Flood as well as God's gracious promise never again to destroy the earth with a world-wide flood. God's epitaph of man's pre-Flood corruption is found in Genesis 6:5-6 and 6:11-12: *"Then the Lord saw that the wickedness of man was great on the earth, and that every intent of the thoughts of his heart was only evil continually. And the Lord was sorry that He had made man on the earth, and He was grieved in His heart." "Now the earth was corrupt in the sight of God, and was filled with violence. And God looked at the earth, and behold, it was corrupt; for all flesh had corrupted their way upon the earth."* Unfortunately, because most of the world pays no attention to the Bible, such persons have no concept of a rainbow's significance.

- **Perpetual Reminder of Man's Rebellion at Babel (Gen. 11:1-9)**
  - **The different languages on earth** (Gen. 11:7,9)
  - **The different nations on earth** (Gen. 11:8-9)
  - **The different races on earth** (Gen. 11:6-9)

Because post-Flood mankind refused to heed God's command to begin to spread out over the earth, God intervened supernaturally to execute His will. Specifically, God took approximately seventy families (the number of separate family units living at the time), placed them in seventy separate locations ("lands") on earth, gave each of the seventy families a separate language (and, over time, the subsequent dialects evident today), and then began to bring forth the different racial distinctions seen on earth today (Gen. 10:1 - 11:9).* Out of each of these seventy family-land-language units (and their offspring) came the nations of the world today: e.g., the Greeks, the Italians, the Spanish, the French, the Germans, the Russians, the Turks, the Egyptians, the Libyans, the Ethiopians, the Iranians, the Chinese, the Japanese, and so on.

Hence, when a person hears someone speaking a different language, or meets someone from a different country, or interacts with someone of a different "race," God intends for this interaction to remind the person of man's rebellion against God at Babel. Nearly all persons on earth today, however, including leading sociologists and intellectuals, are oblivious to this truth.

What was the ultimate purpose of the three judgments at Babel? God orchestrated them so that it would be difficult for mankind ever again to unite *en masse* against Him for the purpose of exalting man and Satan instead. During the end-times Tribulation period, mankind nevertheless will attempt once again to do just that. The seeds of this future rebellion exist everywhere today in the humanist mantras of globalism and a one-world government.

Note: All of these "perpetual reminders" are designed to show man his root problem—that of sin and rebellion against God and his fellow man. Because this problem begins in man's heart, it is clear that he needs a new heart (Ezek. 36:26)—one that can only come supernaturally from above through a personal relationship with Jesus Christ (John 3:1-8; II Cor. 5:17).

---

* Through the genetic makeup existing in humans, it can be concluded that God at this point not only separates the human family into nations and languages, but He also brings forth the different "races" (i.e., the different human tribes or "people groups") and the "racial distinctions" (i.e., lighter skin vs. darker skin, etc.) now seen on earth. [Note: in truth there is but *one* race: the human race.] Heretofore, man had been one family/tribe/race (Gen 11:6)—all speaking the same language.

Appendix E

Assorted Occult Symbols

Just as Christians have symbols that remind us of and represent our faith in Jesus Christ—for example, a cross, an Icthus fish, or a dove—Satan has symbols (indeed, myriads of symbols) that either point to or promote allegiance to him. Says one noted expert on occultism and the New Age:

> A strategic part of Satan's Plan . . . includes a worldwide initiation into his service through the imposition of a mark on the forehead or right hand. . . . What will the mark be? Nobody knows for sure. But it will almost certainly be one of the marks occultists and New Age enthusiasts are beginning to use. These mysterious marks—pentagrams, triangles, twisted crosses, and others . . . are being used to break down resistance to the coming great Luciferic Initiation. The past few years have seen a dramatic increase in the spread of these unholy symbols—on CD's, posters, t-shirts, in magazines and other media, and even as corporate logos.[1]

This same expert listed the following types of symbols used by the occultists and the New Age movement:

- pentagrams (a five-pointed star)
- triangles
- circles
- the Egyptian ankh
- rainbows
- the hexagram
- the sun
- swastikas
- the all-seeing eye
- wheels
- the lotus
- crystals
- diamonds
- yin/yang
- unicorn, Pegasus, centaur

Today, these occult/New Age symbols are seemingly ubiquitous in the Western world. What do these widely-used symbols look like? Here are a few examples:

The pentagram:

 A five-pointed star commonly associated with Wicca, Ritual magick, Satanism, and Masonry

 The Eastern Star, the emblem of the female Masonic organization

Circles:

 A Pentacle, a pentagram in a circle—the most recognized symbol in Wicca

 A more disguised Pentacle, also used in Wicca

 Ouroboros (tail swallower), a widely used serpent-snake occultic symbol.

 The emblem of a Satanic secret society, the Order of the Nine Angles

The Egyptian ankh:

The ankh appears in the hand or in proximity of almost every deity in the Egyptian pantheon. Thus, it is widely understood as a symbol of early religious pluralism: all sects believed in a common story of eternal life, and this is the literal meaning of the symbol. This rationale contributed to the adoption of the ankh by New Age mysticism in the 1960s, to mean essentially the same tolerance of diversity of belief and common ethics as in Ancient Egypt.[2]

Swastikas / Neo-Nazi:

The **swastika**—an archetypal, universal human religious symbol. It appears on every continent and is perhaps as old as humankind. Long before the symbol was co-opted as an emblem of Hitler's Nazi party, the Swastika was a sacred symbol to Hindu, Jain, and Buddhist religions, as well as in Norse, Basque, Baltic, and Celtic Paganism.

The Black Sun, a Nazi emblem consisting of three swastikas arrayed in a circle to form a sun design.

A neo-Nazi symbol

Wheels:

An Astrological wheel

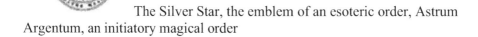
The Silver Star, the emblem of an esoteric order, Astrum Argentum, an initiatory magical order

The Labyrinth, a winding maze-like path found in many ancient cultures. Ancient Minoan labyrinths were associated with the cult of the mother Goddess—and were possibly used in initiatory rituals.

Yin/Yang:

The **Yin Yang**, a Taoist symbol of the interplay of forces in the universe. In Chinese philosophy, yin and yang represent the two primal cosmic forces in the universe. Yin (moon) is the receptive, passive, cold female force. Yang (sun) is masculine-force, movement, heat. The Yin Yang symbol represents the idealized harmony of these forces; equilibrium in the universe.

Unicorns/Pegasus:

Still other common occult/New Age symbols:

The Chaos star, a spoked device with eight equidistant arrows. It is currently a symbol of Chaos Magick

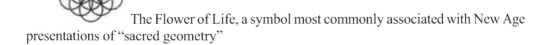 The Flower of Life, a symbol most commonly associated with New Age presentations of "sacred geometry"

 A solar disk—wrapped in a cobra snake. Depictions of snakes permeate occult and New Age symbols. The snake is a universal picture of Satan

 The Triple Crescent or Triple Goddess symbol, representing the three aspects of the moon (waxing, waning, and full) as well as the Lady, or Goddess, the feminine polarity of the universe

A Horned Goat, an archetypical horned shaman

Goat of Mendes (a Satanic goat)

Dot in a circle. According to one New Age writer: "The **circle** represents The Infinite; Eternity. It also represents the flow of time—and the ever repeating Cycles of Eternity, which have no beginning and no end, Cycles which, when complete, flow back into themselves and repeat anew. The **dot** represents the Seed, the Spark, the Focused Thought which gives birth to creation in the physical and mental realms. As Divinity resides within us as our Atman—our God Within—we too possess the Divine

Seed, the Divine Spark of creation. All of the latent skills, talents and ideas necessary for us to create whatever it is that we choose to create already exists with us. We can become anyone we Choose to become. We can accomplish anything we Choose to accomplish. We can create anything we Choose to create. We can experience anything we Choose to experience. We are the Dot with the Circle!"[1] [Author's Note: Such New Age rhetoric is sparked by the enemy of our souls, Satan. In contrast to "we can accomplish anything we choose to accomplish," Jesus says: *"Apart from Me, you can do nothing"* (John 15:5).]

Many of these symbols have appeared throughout the world since man's rebellion at Babel—and still appear today. Moreover, in addition to their use in Occult/New Age circles, some of these symbols also appear in other worldviews such as Atheism, Humanism, Gnosticism, and Paganism. Let look briefly at a collage of other symbols:

Why should born-again Christians be cognizant of these symbols? First, the beliefs behind these symbols come from the enemy of our souls, Satan himself. None of these beliefs are true, edifying, or holy. All of them lead to some form of bondage, deception, or death. Second, the Word of God exhorts Christ's children to seek truth, goodness, and purity: *"Finally, brethren, whatever is true, whatever is honorable, whatever is right, whatever is pure, whatever is lovely, whatever is of good repute, if there is any excellence and if anything worthy of praise, dwell on these things"* (Phil. 4:8).

Appendix F

Other Occult Practices

In addition to the nine occult practices mentioned in Deuteronomy passage earlier, a number of other occult **practices** exist today as well. Definitions are taken verbatim from Wikipedia.

Chanting – A chant is the rhythmic speaking or singing of words or sounds, often primarily on one or two main pitches called reciting tones. . . . Chanting (e.g., mantra, sacred text, the name of God/Spirit, etc.) is a commonly used spiritual practice. Like prayer, chant may be a component of either personal or group practice. Diverse spiritual traditions consider chant a route to spiritual development. Some examples include chant in African, Hawaiian, Native American, and Australian Aboriginal cultures; a Gregorian chant, Vedic chant, Qur'an reading, Islamic Dhikr, Baha'i chants, various Buddhist chants, various mantras, Jewish cantillation, and the chanting of psalms and prayers especially in Roman Catholic, Eastern Orthodox, Lutheran, and Anglican churches. Chant practices vary.

Soothsaying – (per dictionary.com) Soothsaying is the practice or art of foretelling events.

Clairvoyance – clairvoyance (from French *clair* meaning "clear" and *voyance* meaning "vision") is the purported ability to gain information about an object, person, location, or physical event through extrasensory perception. A person who has this ability is called a clairvoyant ("one who sees clearly").

Crystal gazing – a Crystal-gazing (also known as crystallism, crystal-seeing, crystallomancy, gastromancy, and spheromancy) is a method for seeing visions achieved through trance induction by means of gazing at a crystal. Traditionally it has been seen as a form of divination or scrying, with visions of the future, something divine etc., though research into the content of crystal-visions suggest the visions are related to the expectations and thoughts of the seer.

Fortune telling – Fortune-telling is the practice of predicting information about a person's life. The scope of fortune-telling is in principle identical with the practice of divination. The difference is that divination is the term used for predictions considered part of a religious ritual, invoking deities or spirits, while the term fortune-telling implies a less serious or less formal setting, even one of popular culture, where belief in occult workings behind the prediction is less prominent than the concept of suggestion, spiritual or practical advisory or affirmation.

Incantation – An incantation (or enchantment) is a charm or spell created using words. An incantation may take place during a ritual, either a hymn or prayer, and may invoke or praise a deity. In magic, occultism, shamanism, and witchcraft it is used with the intention of casting a spell on an object or a person. The term derives from Latin "incantare" (tr.), meaning "to chant (a magical spell) upon."

Invocation – In some religious traditions including Paganism, Shamanism and Wicca, "invocation" means to draw a spirit or spirit force into one's own body and is differentiated from "evocation", which involves asking a spirit or force to become present at a given location. Some have performed invocation for the purpose of controlling or extracting favors from certain spirits or deities. These invocations usually involve a commandment or threat against the entity invoked.

Séances – A séance is an attempt to communicate with spirits. The word "*séance*" comes from the French word for "seat," "session," or "sitting," from the Old French *seoir*, "to sit." In French, the word's meaning is quite general: one may, for example, speak of "*une séance de cinéma*" ("a movie session"). In English, however, the word came to be used specifically for a meeting of people who are gathered to receive messages from ghosts or to listen to a spirit medium discourse with or relay messages from spirits.

Channeling – Channeling can be seen as the modern form of the old mediumship, where the "channel" (or channeler) receives messages from "teaching-spirit," an "Ascended Master," from God, or from an angelic entity, but essentially through the filter of his own waking consciousness (or "Higher Self").

Reliance on spirit guides – "Spirit guide" is a term used by the Western tradition of Spiritualist Churches, mediums, and psychics to describe an entity which remains a disincarnate spirit in order to act as a guide or protector to a living incarnated human being.

Magic circle – A magic circle is circle (or sphere, field) of space marked out by practitioners of many branches of ritual magic, which they generally believe will contain energy and form a sacred space, or will provide them a form of magical protection, or both. It may be marked physically, drawn in salt or chalk, for example, or merely visualized. Its spiritual significance is similar to that of mandala and in some Eastern religions.

Automatic writing – Automatic writing, or psychography, is a psychic ability allowing a person to produce written words without consciously writing. The words are claimed to arise from a subconscious, spiritual or supernatural source. . . . More recent cases of reported automatic writing have included Jane Roberts, Helen Schucman, and Neale Donald Walsch.

Black magic – a Black magic or dark magic has traditionally referred to the use of supernatural powers or magic for evil and selfish purposes. With respect to the left-hand path and right-hand path dichotomy, black magic is the malicious, left-hand counterpart of benevolent white magic. In modern times, some find that the definition of "black magic" has been convoluted by people who define magic or ritualistic practices that they disapprove of as "black magic".

White magic – a White magic or light magic has traditionally referred to the use of supernatural powers or magic for good and selfless purposes. With respect to the phi left-hand path and right-hand path, white magic is the benevolent counterpart of malicious black magic. Because of its ties to traditional pagan nature worship, white magic is often also referred to as "natural magic.

Reiki – Reiki is a form of alternative medicine developed in 1922 by Japanese Buddhist Mikao Usui. Since its beginning in Japan, Reiki has been adapted across varying cultural traditions. It uses a technique commonly called *palm healing* or *hands-on-healing*. Through the use of this technique, practitioners believe that they are transferring "universal energy" through the palms of the practitioner, which they believe encourages healing.

Worship of totems/totem poles – (per legendsofamerica.com) A totem is a spirit being, sacred object, or symbol of a tribe, clan, family or individual. Native American tradition provides that each individual is connected with nine different animals that will accompany each person through life, acting as guides. Different animal guides come in and out of one's life depending on the direction one is headed and the tasks that need to be completed along one's journey.

Alchemy – Alchemy is a philosophical and protoscientific tradition practiced throughout Egypt and Eurasia which aimed to purify, mature, and perfect certain objects. Common aims were chrysopoeia, the transmutation of "base metals" (e.g., lead) into "noble" ones (particularly gold); the creation of an elixir of immortality; the creation of panaceas able to cure any disease; and the development of an alkahest, a universal solvent. The perfection of the human body and soul was thought to permit or result from the alchemical magnum opus and, in the Hellenistic and western tradition, the achievement of gnosis. In Europe, the creation of a philosopher's stone was variously connected with all of these projects.

Ouija – The ouija, also known as a spirit board or talking board, is a flat board marked with the letters of the alphabet, the numbers 0–9, the words "yes", "no", "hello" (occasionally), and "goodbye", along with various symbols and graphics. It uses a planchette (small heart-shaped piece of wood or plastic) as a movable indicator to indicate a spirit's message by spelling it out on the board during a séance. Participants place their fingers on the planchette, and it is moved about the board to spell out words. Spiritualists believed that the dead were able to contact the living and reportedly used a talking board very similar to a modern Ouija board at their camps in Ohio in 1886 to ostensibly enable faster communication with spirits.

Tarot reading – Tarot reading is the belief in using cards to gain insight into the past, current and future situations by posing a question to the cards, i.e. cartomancy. Variations on the reasons for such belief range from believing in guidance by a spiritual force, to belief that the cards are but instruments used to tap either into a collective unconscious or into their own creative, brainstorming subconscious. . . . The belief in the divinatory meaning of the cards is closely associated with a belief in their occult, divine, and mystical properties.

Astrology – Astrology is the study of the movements and relative positions of celestial objects as a means for divining information about human affairs and terrestrial events.

Horoscopes – A horoscope is an astrological chart or diagram representing the positions of the Sun, Moon, planets, astrological aspects, and sensitive angles at the time of an event, such as the moment of a person's birth. . . . Other commonly used names for the horoscope in English include "Natal Chart" astrological chart, astro-chart, celestial map, sky-map, star-chart, cosmogram, vitasphere, radical chart, radix, chart wheel, or simply chart. It is used as a method of divination regarding events relating to the point in time it represents, and it forms the basis of the horoscopic traditions of astrology.

Yoga – Yoga is a physical, mental, and spiritual practice or discipline which originated in India. There is a broad variety of schools, practices, and goals in Hinduism, Buddhism (particularly Vajrayana Buddhism), and Jainism. The most well-known types of yoga are Hatha yoga and Rāja yoga. The origins of yoga have been speculated to date back to pre-Vedic Indian traditions, but most likely developed around the sixth and fifth centuries B.C., in ancient India's ascetic and śramaṇa movements. . . . According to David Gordon White, from the 5th century A.D. onward, the core principles of "yoga" were more or less in place, and variations of these principles developed in various forms over time:

1. Yoga as an analysis of perception and cognition; illustration of this principle is found in Hindu texts such as the *Bhagavad Gita* and *Yogasutras*, as well as a number of Buddhist Mahāyāna works;[31]
2. Yoga as the rising and expansion of consciousness;[32]
3. Yoga as a path to omniscience; examples are found in Hinduism Nyaya and Vaisesika school texts as well as Buddhism Mādhyamaka texts, but in different ways;[33]
4. Yoga as a technique for entering into other bodies, generating multiple bodies, and the attainment of other supernatural accomplishments; these are described in Tantric literature of Hinduism and Buddhism, as well as the Buddhist Sāmaññaphalasutta.

Shaktipat – a Shaktipat refers in Hinduism to the conferring of spiritual "energy" upon one person by another. Shaktipat can be transmitted with a sacred word or mantra, or by a look, thought or touch—the last usually to the ajna chakra or third eye of the recipient. Shaktipat is considered an act of grace (*anugraha*) on the part of the guru or the divine. It cannot be imposed by force, nor can a receiver make it happen. The very consciousness of the god or guru is held to enter into the Self of the disciple, constituting an initiation into the school or the spiritual family (kula) of the guru. It is held that Shaktipat can be transmitted in person or at a distance, through an object such as a flower or fruit or else by telephone or letter.

Firewalking – Firewalking is the act of walking barefoot over a bed of hot embers or stones. Firewalking has been practiced by many people and cultures in all parts of the world, with the earliest known reference dating back to Iron Age India – c. 1200 B.C. It is often used as a rite of passage, as a test of an individual's strength and courage, or in religion as a test of one's faith.

In addition to the above, the practice of **hypnosis** has long been associated with the occult and "has been used by witch doctors, spirit mediums, shamans, Hindus, Buddhists, and yogis. The hypnotic trance being done through medical doctors [today] is not significantly different from occultic hypnosis."[1]

Appendix G

Discernment Websites

The Berean Call
thebereancall.org

> . . . a nonprofit, tax-exempt corporation which exists to alert believers in Christ to unbiblical teachings and practices impacting the church

> Offers numerous books, booklets, DVDs, CDs, a newsletter, and a YouTube Channel

Lighthouse Trails
lighthousetrails.com

> . . . a discernment ministry designed to alert believers in Christ to unbiblical teachings and practices in the church

> Offers numerous books, booklets, pamphlets, DVDs, and CDs.

New Age to Amazing Grace
newagetoamazinggrace.com

> . . . a discernment ministry which deals with how the deceptions of the New Age / New Spirituality movements have subtly infiltrated parts of Evangelicalism

> Offers books and booklets, audio and video presentations, and a YouTube channel

Biblical Discipleship Ministries
biblicaldiscipleship.org

> . . . a discernment and discipleship ministry with an emphasis on creation vs. evolution, the New Age movement, eschatology, and the Christian life

> Offers books, DVDs, articles, Power Point presentations, and Creation cards

Olive Tree Ministries
olivetreeviews.org

> . . . a discernment ministry designed to help people understand the times according to the Bible, contend for the faith in Jesus Christ, and help the Church stand against deception as watchmen on the wall in these last days.

> Offers books, booklets, DVDs, CDs, newsletters, and prophecy conferences.

Appendix H

Additional Discernment Resources

Books

General

Smith, Paul. *New Evangelicalism: The New World Order*. Costa Mesa: Calvary Chapel Publishing, 2011. 215 pp.

Yungen, Ray. *A Time of Departing*. Silverton, OR: Lighthouse Trails Publishing Company, 2002, 2006 (Second Edition). 245 pp.

McMahon, T.A. *Temporal Delusion*. Bend, OR: The Berean Call. 157 pp.

Smith, Warren B. *The Titanic and Today's Church: A Tale of Two Shipwrecks*. Fortine, MT: Mountain Streams Press, 2020. 262 pp.

New Age / New Spirituality

Smith, Warren B. *False Christ Coming: Does Anybody Care?* Magalia, CA: Mountain Streams Press, 2011. 159 pp.

Emergent Church

Oakland, Roger. *Faith Undone: The Emerging Church . . . A New Reformation or An End-Time Deception*. Eurika, Montana: Lighthouse Trails Publishing, 2007. 261 pp.

DeWaay, Bob. *The Emergent Church: Undefining Christianity*. self-published, 2009. 205 pp.

New Apostolic Reformation

Gibson, Keith. *Wandering Stars*. Birmingham (USA): Solid Ground Christian Books, 2011. 306 pp.

Purpose Driven Movement

Hartzell, Tamara. *In the Name of Purpose: Sacrificing Truth on the Altar of Unity*. USA: Xlibris, 2007. 399 pp.

Smith, Warren B. *Deceived on Purpose: The New Age Implications of the Purpose-Driven Church*. Magalia, CA: Mountain Streams Press, 2004. 211 pp.

Smith, Warren B. *A "Wonderful" Deception: The Further New Age Implications of the Emerging Purpose-Driven Movement*. Magalia, CA: Mountain Streams Press, 2011. 243 pp.

5-Point Calvinism

Vance, Laurence M. *The Other Side of Calvinism*. Pensacola: Vance Publications, 1991, 1999. 788 pp.

Hunt, Dave. *What Love is This? Calvinism's Misrepresentation of God.* Sisters, OR: Loyal Publishing, Inc., 2004. 436 pp.

Olson, C. Gordon. *Beyond Calvinism & Arminianism.* Lynchburg. VA: Global Gospel Publishers, 2012. 467 pp.

Replacement Theology

Fruchtenbaum, Arnold G.. *Israelology: The Missing Link in Systematic Theology.* Ariel Ministries, 1989, revised 1992, 1994, 1996, 2001. 1052 pp.

Wilkinson, Paul Richard. *For Zion's Sake.* Eugene, OR: Wipf and Stock Publishers, 2007. 308 pp.

Evolution

Martin, Jobe. *The Evolution of a Creationist.* Rockwall, TX: Biblical Discipleship Publishers, 1994, 2002. 287 pp.

Matrisciana, Caryl & Oakland, Roger. *The Evolution Conspiracy: The Impact of Darwinism on the World and the Church.* Eurika, Montana: Lighthouse Trails Publishing, 2016 (Updated Expanded Edition). 245 pp.

Ham, Ken. *The Lie: Evolution/Millions of Years.* Green Forest, AR: Master Books, 1987, 2012. 236 pp.

Christian Psychology

Hunt, Dave & McMahon, T.A. *Psychology and the Church: Critical Questions & Crucial Answers.* Bend, OR: The Berean Call, 2008. 415 pp.

Political Correctness

Lutzer, Erwin W. *We Will Not Be Silenced.* Eugene, OR: Harvest House Publishers, 2020. 280 pp.

Footnotes

Chapter 1:

1. Elwell, Walter A., editor. *Evangelical Dictionary of Theology*. Grand Rapids: Baker Book House. pp. 1190-1191.
2. Sykes, Len. Ministry newsletter, 2015.

Chapter 2:

1. Ryrie, Charles C. *Basic Theology*. Wheaton: Victor Books. p. 122
2. *Ibid.* pp. 129-130.
3. *Ibid.* pp. 129-130.
4. *Ibid.* pp. 138-140.

Chapter 5:

1. [source of citation lost]
2. [source of citation lost]

Chapter 7:

1. spiritualray.com. Is Hinduism Really a Religion?

Chapter 8:

1. Wikipedia – Occult
2. Wikipedia – Occult
3. Wikipedia – Spiritism
4. Wikipedia – Necromancy

Chapter 9:

1. Wikipedia – New Age.
2. [source of citation lost]

Chapter 10:

1. Ryrie, Charles C. *Basic Theology*. Wheaton: Victor Books. p. 69.
2. *Ibid.* p. 70.
3. Smith, Paul. *New Evangelicalism: The New World Order*. Costa Mesa: Calvary Chapel Publishing. p. 37.
4. *Ibid.* p. 38.
5. *Ibid.* p. 39.
6. Chafer, Lewis Sperry. *Systematic Theology, Vol.1, Abridged Edition*. Wheaton: Victor Books. p. 89.
7. Chafer, Lewis Sperry. *Systematic Theology, Vol.1, Abridged Edition*. Wheaton: Victor Books. p. 90.
8. *Ibid.* p. 93.

9. 2002 Grace Community Church. Adapted from John MacArthur. *Our Sufficiency in Christ* (Wheaton: Crossway Books, 1998).
10. 2002 Grace Community Church. Adapted from John MacArthur. *Our Sufficiency in Christ* (Wheaton: Crossway Books, 1998).
11. GotQuestions.org. What does it mean the Bible is infallible? p.1.
12. GotQuestions.org. What does it mean the Bible is infallible? p.1.
13. GotQuestions.org. What does it mean the Bible is infallible? pp.1-2.
14. GotQuestions.org. What is the doctrine of the perspicuity of Scripture?

Chapter 11:

1. GotQuestions.org. What does it mean that the Word of God is living and active (Hebrews 4:12)? pp.1-2.
2. H.L. Wilmington. *Wilmington's Book of Lists*. 1987. Wheaton, Illinois: Tyndale House Publishers, Inc. pp. 260-263.

Chapter 13:

1. Sproul, R.C. *Grace Unknown*. Grand Rapids: Baker Books. pp. 56-57.
2. Stott, John. *The Incomparable Christ*. Downers Grove: InterVarsity Press. pp. 234-235.

Chapter 16:

1. Alcorn, Randy. *Heaven*. Wheaton: Tyndale House Publishers, Inc.

Chapter 18:

1. Couch, Mal, general editor. *An Introduction to Classical Evangelical Hermeneutics*. Grand Rapids: Kregel Publications. "Matthew 13: The Church or the Kingdom?" pp. 210-220.

Chapter 21:

1. [source of citation lost]

Chapter 25:

1. Shelley, Bruce L. *Church History in Plain Language*. 1982. Dallas: Word Publishing.
2. *Ibid*. pp. 85-85.
3. Ibid. p. 86.
4. Ibid. pp. 98-100.
5. Ibid. p. 90.
6. Ibid. pp. 149-158.
7. Ibid. pp. 187-190.
8. Ibid. pp. 191-196.
9. Ibid. p. 199.

10. *Ibid.* p. 203.

Chapter 26:
1. Ankerberg, John & Weldon, John. *Protestants & Catholics: Do They Now Agree?* Eugene, Oregon: Harvest House Publishers. pp. 258-260.
2. *Ibid.* pp. 258-260.

Chapter 27:
1. Shelley, Bruce L. *Church History in Plain Language.* 1982. Dallas: Word Publishing. pp. 233-241.
2. *Ibid.* pp. 242-251.
3. *Ibid.* pp. 255-264.
4. *Ibid.* pp. 265-270.
5. *Ibid.* pp. 274-281.
6. *Ibid.* pp. 319-326.

Chapter 28:
1. Wikipedia – Covenant Theology. Covenant of works.
2. Wikipedia – Covenant Theology. Covenant of grace.
3. Ryrie, Charles C. *Dispensationalism* (revised and expanded). Chicago: Moody Press, 1995. p. 17
4. *Ibid.* p. 18
5. *Ibid.* pp. 51-56
6. *Ibid.* pp. 51-52
7. *Ibid.* pp. 52-53
8. *Ibid.* p. 53
9. *Ibid.* pp. 53-54
10. *Ibid.* p. 55
11. *Ibid.* p. 56
12. *Ibid.* p.56

Chapter 29:
1. Wikipedia – City of God

Chapter 32:
1. C. Gordon Olson. *Beyond Calvinism & Arminianism.* Global Gospel Publishers. pp. 379-382
2. Ken Keathly. Journal of the Grace Evangelical Society – Spring 2006. p. 8
3. Norman L. Geisler. *Systematic Theology, Volume Three.* Bethany House Publishers. p. 476
4. R.C. Sproul. *Grace Unknown: The Heart of Reformed Theology.* Baker Books. pp. 130-134

5. In his early writings, Augustine had taught the predestination of individuals based on God's foreknowledge. The idea was that God merely chose those human beings whom He foreknew would freely choose to believe in Him. However, the later writings of Augustine promoted a predestination of individuals based on God's autonomous and inscrutable choice. "This position holds that God chooses to extend his saving grace to some (the elect), but not to all (bypassing the reprobate). Thus, God predestines some to eternal life via irresistible though not coercive grace, but leaves others in their sin to be justly condemned through their own choice and deeds. Augustine's great and terrible doctrine of so-called 'double predestination' was rejected by many in his time as it is by some today." [Reasons.org. Augustine's view of Predestination: St. Augustine, Part 9]
6. C. Gordon Olson. *Beyond Calvinism & Arminianism*. Global Gospel Publishers. pp. 17, 23
7. www.crivoice.org/The Canons of the Second Council of Orange (529)
8. Norman L. Geisler. *Chosen But Free*. Bethany House Publishers. pp. 57-58
9. Norman L. Geisler. *Systematic Theology, Volume Three*. Bethany House Publishers. pp. 477-478
10. Norman L. Geisler. *Chosen But Free*. Bethany House Publishers. p. 94
11. Wikipedia – Norman Geisler
12. Wikipedia – Norman Geisler
13. Norman L. Geisler. *Chosen But Free*. Bethany House Publishers. p. 54
14. *Ibid.* pp. 46-52
15. *Ibid.* p. 85
16. *Ibid.* pp.101-102
17. Grace Online Library / "Calvinism vs. Arminianism – Comparison Chart
18. Wikipedia – Arminianism. p. 6, "Corporate view of election"
19. Wikipedia – Arminianism. p. 6, "Corporate view of election"
20. Wikipedia – Arminianism. p. 6, "Corporate view of election"
21. Wikipedia – Arminianism. p. 4, "Classical Arminianism"
22. Laurence M. Vance. *The Other Side of Calvinism*. Vance Publications. p. ix.
23. C. Gordon Olson. *Beyond Calvinism & Arminianism*. Global Gospel Publishers. p. 13
24. *Ibid.* p. 1
25. *Ibid.* pp. 17-23
26. *Ibid.* p. 99
27. *Ibid.* pp. 23-24
28. *Ibid.* pp. 330-345
29. *Ibid.* pp. 378-380
30. *Ibid.* pp. 23, 385-394
31. *Ibid.* p. 39

Chapter 33:

1. Benware, Paul N. *Understanding End Times Prophecy*. 1995. Chicago: Moody Press. p.103.
2. *Ibid.* p. 104
3. *Ibid.* p. 106
4. *Ibid.* p. 106
5. *Ibid.* pp. 107-109
6. *Ibid.* p. 105
7. *Ibid.* p. 121-122
8. *Ibid.* p. 122
9. *Ibid.* p. 123
10. *Ibid.* p. 123
11. *Ibid.* p. 124
12. *Ibid.* p. 122-128
13. GotQuestions.org. What is replacement theology/supercessionism?
14. Ice, Thomas & Demy, Timothy J., General Editors. *The Return*. 1999. Grand Rapids: Kregel Publications. p.14.
15. Wikipedia – Preterism. pp. 1-2.
16. Theopedia – Preterism. pp. 1-2
17. *Ibid.* p. 2

Chapter 34:

1. Ham, Ken. *The Lie: Evolution/Millions of Years.* Revised edition, sixth printing: November 2017. Master Books, pp. 207-214.
2. Snelling, Andrew A. answersingenesis.org/geology/radiometric-dating/dating-problems-with-the-assumptions, October 1, 2009. pp. 1-2.
3. *Ibid.* pp. 3-5
4. *Ibid.* pp. 5-6
5. *Ibid.* pp. 6-7
6. *Ibid.* p. 7
7. Martin, Jobe. *The Evolution of a Creationist*. Rockwall, Texas: Biblical Discipleship Publishers

Chapter 35:

1. Fruchtenbaum, Arnold G. *Israelolgy: The Missing Link in Systematic Theology*. Ariel Ministries, 1989, revised 1992, 1994, 1996, 2001. p. 315
2. *Ibid.* pp. 313-314
3. *Ibid.* pp. 316-317
4. Twelve Characteristics of a Purpose Driven Church, http:/pd.church/12 characteristics-purpose-driven-church/ p.1

5. Twelve Characteristics of a Purpose Driven Church, http:/pd.church/12 characteristics-purpose-driven-church/ p.3

Chapter 36:

1. Wikipedia – New Apostolic Reformation. p. 1
2. GotQuestions.org. What is New Apostolic Reformation? p. 1
3. Wikipedia – New Apostolic Reformation. p. 2
4. Wikipedia – New Apostolic Reformation. p. 2
5. Wikipedia – New Apostolic Reformation. p. 2
6. Gibson, Keith. *Wandering Stars*. Solid Ground Christian Books, 2011. pp. 83-86
7. *Ibid*. p.86
8. Wikipedia – New Apostolic Reformation (2018 version, no longer available)
9. religiondispatches.org/dominion-theology-christian-reconstructionism-and-the-new-apostolic-reformation
10. Gibson, Keith. *Wandering Stars*. Solid Ground Christian Books, 2011. p. 225
11. *Ibid*. pp. 36-36; 227-238
12. Dutch Sheets, YouTube video, May, 2021
13. Wikipedia – Word of Faith (2018 version, no longer available). p. 1
14. Wikipedia – Word of Faith. p. 1
15. Wikipedia – Word of Faith. pp. 1-2
16. Wikipedia – Word of Faith. p. 2
17. GotQuestions.org. Is the Word of Faith movement biblical? pp. 2-3
18. GotQuestions.org. What is the emerging/emergent church movement? p. 1
19. *Ibid*. pp. 1-2
20. *Ibid*. p. 1

Chapter 37:

1. GotQuestions.org. Is being slain in the Spirit biblical? p. 1
2. GotQuestions.org. What is holy laughter? p. 1
3. Wikipedia – Holy laughter. p. 1
4. GotQuestions.org. What is holy laughter? p. 2
5. Wikipedia – Labyrinth. p. 9.
6. Susan Brinkman, Women of Grace blog. September 7, 2011. Womenofgrace.com
7. Wikipedia – Centering prayer. p. 1.
8. Wikipedia – Centering prayer. pp. 1-2.
9. Wikipedia – Centering prayer. p. 2.
10. GotQuestions.org. What is holy yoga? p.1.
11. GotQuestions.org. What is holy yoga? pp.1-2.
12. GotQuestions.org. What is holy yoga? p.2.

Chapter 38:

1. GotQuestions.org. What does it mean to test the spirits? p.1.
2. Smith, Warren B. *The Light That Was Dark*. 1992. Magalia, CA: Mountain Stream Press. pp. 129-130.

Chapter 39:

1. *Global Sustainability* journal, Cambridge University Press.
2. Oxford English Dictionary
3. zfacts.com. What is Woke Cancel Culture?
4. Cambridge English Dictionary
5. Smith, Warren B. *The Titanic and Today's Church*. Mountain Streams Press, 2020. pp. 38-41
6. *Ibid.* p. 40.
7. *Ibid.* p. 45.
8. *Ibid.* p. 45.

Chapter 41:

1. Levitt, Zola. *A Christian Love Story* (booklet). Self-published, 1978.
2. Warren, Rick. *The Purpose Driven Life*. Grand Rapids, MI: Zondervan, p. 285
3. Oakland, Roger. *Faith Undone*. Eureka, MT: Lighthouse Trails Publishing, pp. 202-204.

Appendix B:

1. Scofield, C.I., editor. The New Scofield Reference Bible. New York: Oxford University Press, 1967. p. 1351.
2. Walvoord, John F. *The Revelation of Jesus Christ*. Chicago: Moody Press, 1966. pp. 169, 187, and others.
3. Pentecost, J. Dwight. Thy *Kingdom Come*. Grand Rapids: Kregel Publications, 1995. p. 255.

Appendix F:

1. talkjesus.com/threads/hypnotism-christian-or-occult-please-read. 26587

About the Author

Steve Griffith was born again in the late 1970s when a series of personal setbacks caused him to turn to the Lord. After college, Steve enjoyed a twenty-year banking and management career. Before leaving the private sector, he served in a senior management position with a major U.S. transportation company.

Having read the Old Testament several times and the New Testament numerous times, Steve taught a citywide men's Bible study for six years and is a veteran of teaching an assortment of classes and electives at his home church and other churches. He also has served as an elder, elder chairman, and interim executive pastor at his church.

Steve's major theological influences are Charles Ryrie and John Walvoord. Christian Life influences, among others, include Phillip Keller, Ian Thomas, Elisabeth Elliot, Miles J. Stanford, A.W. Tozer, Andrew Murray, Mark Martin, and Leslie Martin. Influences in helping to understand God's use of trials and testing in the life of a believer include Sandy Edmonson, Charles Stanley, Ron Dunn, R.T. Kendall, and Blaine Allen. Discernment influences include Jobe Martin, Warren B. Smith, Caryl Matrisciana, Dave Hunt, Roger Oakland, Keith Gibson, and T.A. McMahon.